7 LEADERSHIP LESSONS OF THE AMERICAN REVOLUTION

7
LEADERSHIP
LESSONS
OF THE
AMERICAN
REVOLUTION

*The Founding Fathers,
Liberty, and the Struggle
for Independence*

JOHN ANTAL

CASEMATE
Philadelphia & Oxford

Special thanks to Mrs. Carolyn Petracca for help in editing the manuscript.
As a good friend, and gatekeeper for good grammar, you are the best!—JFA

First published in the United States of America and Great Britain in 2013.
Reprinted in 2018 by
CASEMATE PUBLISHERS
1950 Lawrence Road, Havertown, PA 19083, USA
and
The Old Music Hall, 106–108 Cowley Road, Oxford OX4 1JE, UK

Copyright 2013 © John Antal

ISBN 978-1-61200-202-6
Digital Edition: ISBN 978-1-61200-203-3

Cataloging-in-publication data is available from the Library of
Congress and from the British Library

For a complete list of Casemate titles, please contact:

CASEMATE PUBLISHERS (US)
Telephone (610) 853-9131
Fax (610) 853-9146
Email: casemate@casematepublishers.com
www.casematepublishers.com

CASEMATE PUBLISHERS (UK)
Telephone (01865) 241249
Email: casemate-uk@casematepublishers.co.uk
www.casematepublishers.co.uk

Contents

OTHER BOOKS BY JOHN ANTAL

Attack the Enemy's Strategy, Lessons in Counterinsurgency Warfare, Historical Explorations, February 6, 2009.

Hell's Highway: The True Story of the 101st Airborne Division During Operation Market Garden, September 17–25, 1944, Presidio Press, Random House, July 29, 2008.

Brothers in Arms Hells Highway [a Random House novel]; 2008, Presidio Press, Random House.

Forests of Steel: Modern City Combat From the War in Vietnam to the Battle for Iraq, Historical Explorations, Feb 15, 2007.

City Fights: Selected Histories of Urban Combat from World War II to Vietnam, Presidio Press, Random House, August 26, 2003.

Talon Force: Thunderbolt, (Pen name: Cliff Garnett) Signet Publishing, February 1, 2000.

Proud Legions, A Novel of America's Next War, Random House, 1999.

Combat Team; The Captain's War, An Interactive Exercise in Company-Level Command in Battle, Presidio Press, 1998.

Infantry Combat; The Rifle Platoon, An Interactive Exercise in Small-Unit Tactics and Leadership, Presidio Press, 1995.

Armor Attacks; The Tank Platoon, An Interactive Exercise in Small-Unit Tactics and Leadership, Presidio Press, 1991.

John Antal has also contributed to several anthologies:

Wrath of Achilles: Essays of Command in Battle, CSI Press, 2008.

Digital War, A View from the Front Lines, I Books, 2003.

By Their Deeds Alone, Presidio Press, 2003.

Maneuver Warfare, Presidio Press, 1993.

On June 14, 1777, the Second Continental Congress passed the Flag Resolution which stated: "Resolved, That the flag of the United States be thirteen stripes, alternate red and white; that the union be thirteen stars, white in a blue field, representing a new Constellation."

The important political cartoon, Join, or Die, *was created by Benjamin Franklin and used by patriots to fire up the former colonies to oppose rule by Great Britain.*

PREFACE: *Leadership, Liberty, and the American Revolution*

Freedom is a fragile thing and is never more than one generation away from extinction.—RONALD REAGAN, 40th President of the United States of America

LEADERSHIP IS THE ART OF *INFLUENCE*.

Moments define us. Moments of adversity reveal character. Moments of challenge disclose courage or cowardice. Moments of action uncover decision or irresolution. Defining moments reveal leadership.

This book is about *seven defining leadership moments* from the American Revolution. This book is not a complete study of the American Revolution; readers will have to go elsewhere for such a chronicle, but it is the story of seven leadership moments that helped to win Liberty during the struggle for Independence. On these pages you will learn about real people facing real challenges and overcoming what reasonable people believed were insurmountable odds. These leaders, thankfully, were *unreasonable* for the cause of Liberty.

7 Leadership Lessons of the American Revolution is your guide to learning about the leadership that created a revolution, opposed the greatest power of its age, and created the most free society on earth. It is a compact collection of dramatic stories that tell a part of how the United States of America was created. These stories—for leadership is best learned by storytelling, rather than by lectures on process, style or technique—offer you insights into the meaning of leadership that are as relevant today as they were essential at the birth of the United States. These stories are about the leadership that forged Americans into a nation. They define the leadership that hammered out the standard for how Americans are expected to lead. In 1775 this leadership created the flame of Liberty that lit the world, and offered a beacon of freedom and human progress to all men.

WHAT IS LEADERSHIP?

Leadership is not just management. Understanding how to manage—the process of directing and controlling—is a vital part of effective leadership. Peter Drucker, the influential author of a number of essential management and leadership books, said: "Management is doing things right; leadership is doing the right things."

Leadership is not just about making decisions. Decision-making is a key aspect of effective leadership, but if making decisions were all there was to leadership, decision-making could be turned into an algorithm with the calculations made by your smartphone.

No. Leading human beings requires much more. "Leadership is not about titles positions or flowcharts," leadership expert and author John C. Maxwell writes, "it is about one life influencing another." In his book, *The Little BIG Things: 163 ways to Pursue Excellence* (2010), leadership guru Tom Peters added a vital insight to the definition of leadership: "Leadership is a sacred trust. The decision to lead is the decision to be responsible for the growth and development of your fellow human beings." Whether you are leading a business team to win the next contract or a company of soldiers in defense of the nation, *leadership is a sacred trust.*

Here then, is your definition of leadership: *Leadership is a sacred trust and the art of influence. It is the ability to motivate, inspire and impel people to accomplish a mission.*

All of us have a leadership quotient. In every aspect of life, your level of leadership determines your level of success, defining who you are and who you will become. John C. Maxwell described this as "the Law of the Lid" in his book *The 21 Irrefutable Laws of Leadership.* The level of your leadership is the level you will rise to in life and the level at which you will be able to do the most good for yourself, family, community, state, nation, and the world. The higher your leadership quotient, the more effective you become.

You will see in the seven leadership stories in this book that each leader acted differently, according to his own experiences, intelligence, and talents, yet there is a set of leadership elements that most of them shared. These elements include the courage to lead, the ability to influence others to act with them; the passion to motivate people to accomplish goals; the resolute determination do whatever it takes to win and never give up; the competence to plan and organize; the skill to communicate clearly a shared vision; the capacity to develop creative solutions to problems; and the self-confidence and essential brilliance to decide and act *in time.*

They also shared the attribute of selflessness, which is the first require-ment of good leadership. Although leaders can be powerful, effective leader-ship is an act of selflessness. Aristotle once said, "You must learn to obey before you can command," or put another way, "You must learn to follow be-fore you can lead." He meant that to be an effective leader you must first learn to be an effective follower. To be an effective follower you must willingly sur-render some of yourself for the good of the team. This selflessness is what makes a team work. Effective leaders are good followers first, learning and understanding selflessness in order to be a leader who puts team and goal (mission) before self. By learning to follow a person can grow into an effective leader who inspires and influences others to perform selflessly for the good of the team and the cause.

The art of leadership should be a life-long effort, because knowing how to lead demands knowledge of self, knowledge of those you lead, and know-ing how to get things done. To learn leadership directly, from personal ex-perience alone, is impractical. To learn leadership indirectly takes study. Good leaders are life-long learners. If you want to raise your leadership quotient, become an active learner by reading about leadership and discussing leader-ship stories with your friends and teammates.

SO WHAT IS LIBERTY?

For most of recorded history men and women have lived under despots. Ex-cept for brief glimpses of limited liberty in ancient Greece and the Roman Republic, it has been but a whispered word. Most human beings have lived and died under the rule of kings, emperors, dictators, or oligarchs.

Aristotle, the great Athenian philosopher of the 3rd Century BC, argued, "The basis of a democratic state is liberty."

Marcus Porcius Cato Uticensis (95 BC–46 BC), called Cato the Younger, was a Roman senator who lived in the time of Julius Caesar and believed, "By liberty, I understand the power which every man has over his own actions, and his right to enjoy the fruits of his labor, art and industry, as far as by it he hurts not the society, or any members of it, by taking from any member, or hindering him from enjoying what he himself enjoys. The fruits of a man's honest industry are the just rewards of it, ascertained to him by natural and eternal equity, as is his title to use them in the manner which he thinks fit: And thus, with the above limitations, every man is sole lord and arbiter of his own private actions and property . . . no man living can divest him but by usurpation, or by his own consent."

The limited freedoms of the Roman republic gave way to the absolutism of the Roman empire. For centuries after the Romans mankind knew only the rule of autocrats, theocrats, and kings, until the Magna Carta was conceived. In 1215 A.D., British King John was forced by rebellious noblemen to limit his power and abide by a charter, which proclaimed that his power was not arbitrary but was bound by common law and that free men had liberties. The Magna Carta gave *free men*, the nobility, legal status that made them freemen. The Magna Carta, also known as *Magna Carta Libertatum*, was an extraordinary document for its time as it sought to limit the king's power. More than five centuries later the Magna Carta would have an important influence on the American Revolution. From this important parchment a precedent was set. The Magna Carta was the seed that after much toil, conflict, and blood would eventually grow to become the rule of constitutional law in Great Britain. From the development of British constitutional law the Liberty Tree would take root and grow in the American colonies.

John Locke (1632–1704), English philosopher and political theorist who is considered the ideological progenitor of the American Revolution, wrote, "Freedom of men under government is to have a standing rule to live by, common to every one of that society and made by the legislative power vested in it and not to be subject to the inconstant, uncertain, arbitrary will of another man." Locke believed they every person was born with the natural rights of life, liberty, and property.

Edmund Burke (1729–1797), Irish statesman, orator, author, political theorist, and philosopher, was a champion of individual liberty. A member of the British parliament, Burke led the debate that questioned the executive authority of the king and championed constitutional limits to the government's authority. Burke supported the cause of liberty in the British colonies and tried to repeal the Tea Tax. In 1774 he said Americans love liberty : "Slavery they can have anywhere. It is a weed that grows in every soil." He went on to say, "The true danger is when liberty is nibbled away, for expedience, and by parts."

Jean-Jacques Rousseau (1712–1778), a Genevan political philosopher who influenced the Enlightenment in the 18th Century and had a major impact on the French Revolution, wrote, "I prefer liberty with danger to peace with slavery."

According to Samuel Adams (1722–1803), known as the Father of the American Revolution, "The liberties of our country, the freedom of our civil

Constitution, are worth defending at all hazards; and it is our duty to defend them against all attacks.

Thomas Paine (1737–1809), whose writings greatly influenced the American Revolution and the United States Declaration of Independence, said in his treatise *The American Crisis*, "A man can distinguish himself between temper and principle, and I am as confident, as I am that God governs the world, that America will never be happy till she gets clear of foreign dominion. Wars, without ceasing, will break out till that period arrives, and the continent must in the end be conqueror; for though the flame of Liberty may sometimes cease to shine, the coal can never expire."

Benjamin Franklin (1706–1790) loved Liberty above all things. He said: "Where Liberty is, there is my country."

John Adams (1735–1826) realized how fragile a blessing Liberty is. He warned, "Liberty cannot be preserved without general knowledge among the people."

Liberty is so precious that Thomas Jefferson believed, "Liberty is to the collective body, what health is to every individual body. Without health no pleasure can be tasted by man; without liberty, no happiness can be enjoyed by society." He also proclaimed, "The tree of liberty must be refreshed from time to time with the blood of patriots and tyrants."

George Washington (1732–1799), believed that Liberty's sacred fire was an "experiment entrusted to the hands of the American people." He went on to say, "The preservation of the sacred fire of Liberty, and the destiny of the republican model of government, are justly considered deeply, perhaps as finally, staked on the experiment entrusted to the hands of the American people."

In 1776 the world witnessed something remarkable. Born of the Enlightenment of philosophers like Locke and Rousseau, nurtured by a rugged individualism that was necessary to tame the wilderness in a strange new land, and forged in fire by a war for independence, America became a beacon for millions of people. That beacon's brightest light is Liberty.

Liberty is centered on individual freedom: *Liberty is the inalienable right of the individual for independent action; to make choices, as long as those choices do not harm others.*

Liberty is the opposite of collectivism. Liberty releases the individual to work, create, build, and prosper. As Ayn Rand so aptly wrote in her essay *The Only Path To Tomorrow*, "Degrees of human ability vary, but the basic principle remains the same: the degree of a man's independence and initiative determines his talent as a worker and his worth as a man. . . . While men are still pondering upon the causes of the rise and fall of civilizations, every page of history cries to us that there is but one source of progress: Individual Man in independent action. Collectivism is the ancient principle of savagery. A savage's whole existence is ruled by the leaders of his tribe. Civilization is the process of setting man free from men."

AND WHAT WAS THE AMERICAN REVOLUTION ALL ABOUT?
The American Revolution was about Liberty and *leadership*. By 1765 the thirteen British colonies in America no longer needed English rule from the home country and felt they would be more effective and more prosperous—for the benefit of themselves and the British empire—if left to govern themselves. The British believed they had the authority to control America's wealth without the consent of the Colonists. Taxation without representation was the method employed by the British empire. Americans called this tyranny and rebellion was the American answer. The British replied with invasion, occupation, and war. Revolution was the consequence.

It took courage, perseverance, and leadership to win that Revolution. It took men like George Washington, Henry Knox, and Daniel Morgan to beat the British Army. It took organizers like Sam Adams and statesmen like John Adams, Ben Franklin, and Thomas Jefferson to lead the fledging American government and form a republic. It took the leadership of countless other Americans to win independence and form a new government. These leaders had to solve a myriad of problems, from simple, to complicated, to complex, to chaotic and do so with too-few people and extremely limited resources. None of these leaders was perfect. All of them were human, with human biases, failings, and faults. They didn't have time to be perfect; they were doing their best to win a revolution. As Pulitzer Prize winning author David McCullough wrote in his essay *The Glorious Cause of America*: "They rose to the occasion as very few generations ever have."

American Liberty was born in revolution and was based on the right of the individual to "Life, Liberty and the pursuit of Happiness." Kings and aristocrats were no longer in charge merely because of the "divine right of kings" or the station of their birth. In the United States, the government served the citizen. Alexander Hamilton said in a speech to the New York Ratifying Convention of the Constitution on June 17, 1788: *"Here sir, the people govern."*

Today, the current generation of Americans faces challenges as tumultuous as those present in 1775. We are the most powerful nation on earth, yet we are bogged down in endless wars. We have the most individual liberty of any people on the planet, yet we have an emerging nanny state and more individuals incarcerated than any developed country. We have landed men on the moon, yet Congress cannot pass a budget—a budget that is required by law to be passed every year—in order to manage our financial affairs. We have the richest economy on earth, yet we are so deep in debt, with nearly $17 trillion borrowed as of this writing, that we may never be able to pay off the balance. Will we leave this burdensome debt to our children and future generations? If so, our national debt is really a matter of national character and speaks volumes about the kind of people we have become and the leadership we have failed to exercise. Our nation faces an enemy as never before: our greatest enemy . . . and that enemy is *us*. Abraham Lincoln may have been right: "America will never be destroyed from the outside. If we falter and lose our freedoms, it will be because we destroyed ourselves."

Leadership is required to reverse this damaging course. In the months and years ahead every citizen of our Republic will have hard choices to make: to lead or to follow, to be active or to be passive, to be a part of the solution or to ride along oblivious to the impending disaster, to embrace individualism or clasp the false fairness of collectivism, to choose Liberty or accept tyranny, to support statism or defend the American Republic.

Every citizen will be affected. Every person will experience the changes. Will you be prepared to take action? Will you lead others to meet the challenges that lie ahead?

Liberty transformed America into one of the most successful nations in history. Today Liberty is in danger. The liberties that the founders of the United States of America held in so much esteem are being slowly, methodically but surely, transformed into tyranny.

Ronald Reagan, the fortieth president of the United States, put it best when he said, "Ours was the first revolution in the history of mankind that truly reversed the course of government, and with three little words: 'We the people.' 'We the people' tell the government what to do, it doesn't tell us. 'We the people' are the driver, the government is the car. And we decide where it should go, and by what route, and how fast. Almost all the world's constitutions are documents in which governments tell the people what their privileges are. Our Constitution is a document in which 'We the people' tell the government what it is allowed to do. 'We the people' are free."

In short, our Liberty is ours to keep or ours to lose. Retaining Liberty requires action and leadership.

INDIVIDUALS MATTER

America was founded upon the rights of the individual, not upon the supremacy of the state. As John F. Kennedy said in his inaugural address, "The rights of man come not from the generosity of the state, but from the hand of God." Maintaining those rights requires leadership. Raising your individual leadership quotient can make a difference in your life and in the lives of others. And no matter your age or experience, through dedicated study you can always raise your leadership quotient. Benjamin Franklin once said, "a frequent recurrence to fundamental principles . . . is absolutely necessary to preserve the blessings of Liberty and keep a government free." Read the stories of the leaders described in *7 Leadership Lessons of the American Revolution* and revisit some of the fundamental principles of leadership.

President Ronald Reagan also said, "Freedom is never more than one generation away from extinction. We didn't pass it on to our children in the bloodstream. It must be fought for, protected, and handed on for them to do the same, or one day we will spend our sunset years telling our children and our children's children what it was once like in the United States where men were free." In the pages of this book you will learn about and study the leadership of a select few who changed the course of human events and helped birth an exceptional nation. Inspired by their stories, you can become a leader who changes the course of your personal history and helps makes the United States of America a more just, prosperous and free nation. Today, we need leadership more than ever. Your leadership can help fuel the fire that will keep alight the torch of Liberty for generations to come.

Samuel Adams pointing to the Massachusetts Charter that described the rights of citizens in a 1772 (portrait by John Singleton Copley).

Chapter **I**

THE FIRST TEA PARTY
The Leadership of Samuel Adams

If our trade be taxed, why not our lands, in short, everything we posses? They tax us without having legal representation.
—SAMUEL ADAMS

No taxation without representation!
—MOTTO OF THE SONS OF LIBERTY

LEADERSHIP IS THE ART OF *INFLUENCE.*

In 1770 two regiments of British soldiers occupied Boston. On a clear and cold winter night on March 5th, an angry mob of colonists heckled a guard outside the Custom House on King Street. A squad of British soldiers soon reinforced the sentry. As the squad stood their ground, boys threw snowballs and oyster shells at the Redcoats. The soldiers shouted at the boys and more citizens of Boston assembled to join the commotion. The crowd grew. Many in the crowd exchanged insults with the British and taunted them to fire. The boys continued to throw snowballs and icicles. A boy got too close and a soldier struck the boy in the head with the butt of his musket. The angry crowd surged forward shouting and cursing as the British soldiers came to arms. Suddenly, a British soldier was knocked down, his musket discharged, and in the confusion the rest of the Redcoats fired a volley into the throng of angry civilians. When the smoke cleared, five Boston men lay dead on the snowy street.

The incident was quickly dubbed the Boston Massacre. Patriot Paul Revere created an etching of the event that depicted the British firing line mercilessly blasting away at the crowd of unarmed citizens. Nineteen-year-old Henry Knox, a local bookstore owner, was there at the scene of the shooting and vowed that the Redcoats would hang for the murder of innocent citizens. The newspapers carried the story to every colony in America. The cry rang out, near and far, that the British Regiments had to leave Boston.

After the killings, over three thousand citizens of Boston and the surrounding villages gathered in and around the Old South Church to demonstrate their resentment at the British occupation. The size of the crowd was not lost on Royal Governor Thomas Hutchinson, who was charged with keeping order in the king's colony. The last thing the governor wanted was to resort to force.

Samuel Adams, a member of the Massachusetts Legislature, carried the people's petition to an audience with the Governor. The petition demanded that the British troops leave Boston. Hutchinson and Adams were bitter enemies. Adams was the leader and organizer of the patriot group called the "Sons of Liberty," a major thorn in Hutchinson's side. Adams's Sons of Liberty opposed the Crown's intolerable policies that regulated the colonies and taxed their industry. The Sons of Liberty showed their disdain for British rule by hanging effigies of royal officials from the "Liberty Tree," a tall elm tree that stood in the Boston Commons. Over the years the tree became a rallying point for protests against the Crown. The Sons of Liberty also threw stones at royalist homes, and even tarred and feathered tax collectors. In general, Adams and his rowdy rabble were the governor's nemesis and, now that blood had been shed, an angry force that must be carefully reckoned with.

Demonstrating the power of his office, Hutchinson sat serenely in a large chair, flanked by members of his staff, facing the assembly of disgruntled patriots. Hutchinson calmly gazed at the rabble-rouser who was causing him so much trouble: Samuel Adams. The two men could not be more different. Adams wore a very plain set of clothes and a coat that looked as if it had been slept in. Dressed in his finest clothes, Hutchinson expected to diffuse the situation with a demonstration of his authority by granting an audience with Adams. He hoped that this would boost the man's ego and be enough to calm the mob. From his commanding position in the assembly hall the Governor looked at Adams and tried hard not to sneer.

To Adams, the governor's chair looked like a throne, a throne that stood for an abusive and unaccountable government that Adams had grown to despise. Next to the Governor sat a British army officer, a lieutenant colonel resplendent in his immaculate red uniform, who represented the military power behind the throne. The officer commanded the British soldiers garrisoning Boston and was responsible for the men who had fired on the crowd. Instead of being impressed or overawed, Adams saw Hutchinson on the defensive.

Without hesitation, Adams stepped boldly forward, arms folded across his chest, and addressed Hutchinson. He looked the governor firmly in the eyes and insisted that all British troops be withdrawn immediately. Adams knew that he had the people on his side and most of the population of Boston was outside the building and filled the streets. Adams wanted Hutchinson to realize that he was resolute and that the people would not be deterred. "I am in fashion and out of fashion, as the whim goes. I will stand alone," Adams announced with defiance. "I will oppose this tyranny at the threshold, though the fabric of liberty fall, and I perish in its ruins!"

The crowd supported Adams with applause and shouts. The noise of the crowd echoed from outside. Governor Hutchinson sensed that the meeting was going poorly and he feared the citizens of Boston might riot. He tried to compromise with the drably dressed firebrand standing in front of him by offering to remove one regiment, leaving the other in place. "If you have the power to remove one regiment, you have the power to remove both," Adams countered, his gray eyes flashing as he pressed his point. "It is at your peril if you refuse. The meeting is composed of three thousand people. They have become impatient. A thousand men are already arrived from the neighborhood, and the whole country is in motion. Night is approaching. An immediate answer is expected. Both regiments or none."

Hutchinson's face paled. Adams smiled as he saw the governor's knees twitch. After a moment of silence the governor nodded, looked away and then, in a sullen voice, agreed that both regiments would leave Boston the following day.

Later, when an ardent British supporter in the Massachusetts Legislature asked Governor Hutchinson why he had not tried to sweeten Samuel Adams's disposition by offering him a paid position in the governor's office, an office from which he could exert control over Adams, he replied: "Such is the obstinacy and inflexible disposition of the man, that he never would be conciliated by any office whatever."

Samuel Adams was not a man to be trifled with. An agitator for liberty, he was not a contented man. Contented men do not lead rebellions. In most governments, and especially in the thirteen British colonies in America, fomenting a rebellion was a crime punishable by death.

Long before the Boston Massacre and the meeting with Governor Hutchinson, Samuel Adams had attended the prestigious Boston Latin School and graduated from Harvard College, paying his way by waiting on tables in a restaurant. He tried his hand at brewing beer, failed in business, and went on to earn a masters degree. His thesis foretold his future: "*Whether it be lawful to resist the supreme magistrate if the commonwealth cannot otherwise be reserved.*" In January 1748 Adams started a newspaper, the *Independent Advertiser*. The paper was entirely about politics and very critical of the king's policies in the Thirteen Colonies. Adams was acting editor and wrote most of the material. The paper's theme was consistent: Massachusetts or any other free society should govern itself. Many of the ideas in Adams's articles were based on the theories of John Locke (1632–1704), an English philosopher and physician regarded as one of the most influential of Enlightenment thinkers, who wrote extensively on the rights of common man and liberty. Locke wrote that government is morally obliged to serve people by protecting life, liberty, and property. Armed with Locke's Enlightenment ideas, Adams became devoted to politics and spent most of his time discussing opposition to British rule. Although the *Independent Advertiser* failed as a business, Adams had found his calling.

In 1764 Adams vigorously opposed the Sugar Act, a tax imposed by Parliament on sugar. He was elected to the Massachusetts legislature in 1765 and was reelected annually to the legislature until 1775 when the American Revolution broke out and the legislature was dissolved. His passion for liberty drove him to oppose the British government at every turn. He believed it folly to hope for reconciliation and compromise with the king's officials, particularly with the royal governor, Thomas Hutchinson.

Adams believed that Great Britain's administration over its American colonists was arrogant, heavy-handed, and unjust and should be ended. In his eyes Great Britain had betrayed existing laws and had broken its political compact with the colonists, a compact that had promised a system of limited government and noninterference by the Crown in internal colonial affairs. By 1773 many Americans were angry with the British for a series of intolerable laws and decrees, but few called for open rebellion or armed revolution. For most, Great Britain was still their country, King George their sovereign and revolution the farthest thing from their minds. Many hoped that the British Parliament would listen to the colonists' grievances and change the laws to fit the character and special circumstances of the American colonies.

Adams believed that there was never a *right time* for dramatic change.

Years of studying politics caused him to believe that only a combination of vigorous leadership and dramatic action could bring about change. He was determined to supply both the vigorous leadership and the dramatic action.

His greatest strengths lay in his passion for Liberty and his ability to communicate his passion to others. He was also a skillful leader and organizer. He was not the finest orator in the colonies, but he could write clearly and became one of the preeminent journalists in America. He used his talent for writing and his classical and religious education to report on the important issues of the day. He was an ardent proponent of a free press and had a nose for news. He was not rich, in fact he was habitually poor, but he was extremely skilled in inspiring and motivating people. Significantly, he had an uncanny ability to understand the needs, wants, and dreams of his fellow colonists. He wrote "mankind is governed more by their feelings than by reason." He was one of the first investigative journalists to use his understanding of emotions to great political advantage.

Passion was Samuel Adams's most powerful attribute. When charged with passion, his penetrating gray eyes could animate anyone caught in his gaze. Embittered by what he considered inconsiderate and arrogant British rule, he leveraged his passion to fuel his effort to organize networks of like-minded patriots. He then linked the networks so they could operate with unified purpose. He called these networks "committees of correspondence." The correspondence generated by these committees, in the form of pamphlets and newspapers, spread information about American dissatisfaction with British rule. Adams went one-step further by declaring to the committees that if the British imposed taxes without the consent of the colonists, it would lead to rebellion.

The correspondence circulated in Massachusetts and throughout the Thirteen Colonies via the remarkable postal service created by Benjamin Franklin, the first postmaster in the colonies. Franklin was appointed postmaster of Philadelphia in 1737, joint postmaster general of the colonies for the Crown in 1753, and postmaster for the United Colonies in 1775. His organizational genius created one of the most efficient and rapid postal services in the eighteenth century. The postal routes he instituted moved correspondence hundreds of miles throughout all the colonies in days rather than weeks. Samuel Adams and his committees of correspondence took advantage of this excellent communication system to fan the fires of dissatisfaction against the Crown.

One of the principal networks Samuel Adams helped organize in 1765 was a group called the Loyal Nine. The Loyal Nine agitated against the British Stamp Act. As this group grew in numbers it became known as the Sons of Liberty. The Sons of Liberty met to oppose the Coercive Acts and heavy-handed British Rule. They met under an old elm in Boston that Adams named The Liberty Tree. It became a rallying site for patriots. Some of the more famous Sons of Liberty were Patrick Henry, John Hancock, James Otis, Paul Revere, and Dr. Joseph Warren. The Massachusetts governor suspected the Sons of Liberty of plotting to overthrow the government, but the Sons insisted that they were standing up for their rights as British subjects and had the right as British subjects to protest unjust laws. Sons of Liberty groups soon sprouted in each of the colonies and many royal governors feared them, for many of these men were also members of the colonial militias. As the Crown tightened its grip through regulation and taxation, the Sons of Liberty adopted the motto: "Taxation without representation is tyranny."

Taking action, the Sons of Liberty and other like-minded organizations agitated against the royal governors and harassed and intimidated British tax collectors. Unwelcome in nearly all American communities, tax collectors, Stamp Act officials, and other Crown officials were easy targets for the practice of tar-and-feathering. Samuel Adams led the effort to boycott British goods and deny the tax collectors revenue. As the actions of the Massachusetts colonists grew into open rebellion with the Crown, King George III decided to teach the unruly Americans a lesson.

On May 10, 1773, a new Tea Act was authorized by Parliament. It allowed the British East India Company to import half a million pounds of tea into the colonies without paying tax, duties, and tariffs. The foremost objective of the Tea Act was to establish the supremacy of Parliament to levy taxes on the American colonies. Its secondary purpose was to support the troubled British East India Company that had tea it was unable to sell. This privileged status gave the nearly bankrupt British East India Company a monopoly to sell tea directly to its own agents in the colonies who had a surplus of tea that needed a market. With this monopoly the British East India Company could disrupt the established supply chain for tea. They could legally bypass the established colonial middlemen, undercut the price of smuggled Dutch tea into the colonies, and undersell American merchants. With cheap British tea shipped directly to agents favored by the Crown, American businessmen involved in the tea trade were out of a job. All across the colonies, Colonial merchants were furious about the Tea Act.

The act levied only a three-penny tax per pound on tea arriving in the colonies. The cost was paid by the British agent and passed on to the customer, but the tea was still cheaper than smuggled tea. The money generated by the tax, however, went directly into the royal coffers to pay for British officials living in America, thereby making these officials dependent on the Crown for their livelihood and independent of colonial control. Previous to this, colonial officials were paid by local taxes and were beholding to the local citizenry. This gave the Crown tighter control over the leaders of the colonies. The Tea Act therefore, was less about taxing tea to raise income for the British government than in proving the Crown's right to arbitrarily raise taxes on Americans.

Many colonists felt that their rights as Englishmen were being usurped. The Tea Act angered Americans all across the Thirteen Colonies and each colony found its own way to oppose it. The ports of Philadelphia and New York City refused to let British ships laden with tea unload their cargoes and turned the ships back in protest. In Boston, however, the royal governor of Massachusetts allowed the tea ships to dock and ordered that the tea be unloaded and the taxes paid.

Governor Hutchinson had several good reasons to support the tea tax. First, he was a loyal British official who always obeyed the king and Parliament; he was demonstrating his loyalty to his superiors. Second, he had invested substantially in the East India Company and would profit nicely when the tea were unloaded and sold in Massachusetts. Third, his two sons and his son-in-law were three of only five people who were licensed to handle shipping and sales for the East India Company in Boston and their fortunes were tied up in the sale of this tea.

Samuel Adams and many other colonists believed that if the British could get away with the arbitrary tax on tea, without discussing this with the citizens who had to pay the tax, they could do the same for other commodities. Adams spread the word through the Sons of Liberty organizations in Boston, New York, and Philadelphia that this new tax posed a direct threat to the livelihood of all Americans, that it was another example of taxation without representation and an act of tyranny. On November 2, 1773, the patriots held a town meeting. Led by Adams, they voted to stop the tea from being unloaded.

In late November, ships laden with tea docked in Boston harbor. The day following their arrival the Sons of Liberty posted notices all over Boston: "Friends! Brethren! Countrymen! The worst of plagues, the detested TEA ... is now arrived in this harbor. The hour of destruction, or manly opposition to the machinations of tyranny, stares you in the face. Every friend to his country, to himself and posterity . . . is now called upon . . . to make a united and successful resistance to this last, worst, and most destructive measure of administration." Although Samuel Adams did not sign these notices, few doubted who was the author. Once the ships arrived he fired up the populace with speeches as the Sons of Liberty guarded the wharf day and night to stop anyone from unloading the tea.

Hutchinson defied Adams and the mob. Unable to unload their cargoes and facing threats from the Sons of Liberty guarding the wharfs, the captains of the three ships laden with tea considered sailing out of the harbor. Determined to take charge of the situation, Governor Hutchinson took action to prevent the ships from sailing away before the tea was unloaded. On December 14th, he ordered Admiral John Montagu to place two armed ships in Boston harbor with orders to fire on them if the tea laden ships tried to depart. He also wrote to Parliament for permission to arrest some of the leaders of the Sons of Liberty for high crimes and misdemeanors for interfering with the unloading of the tea ships.

Confrontation between the patriots and the British officials was imminent. The East India Company's tea was contained in 342 chests distributed aboard three ships—*Dartmouth, Beaver,* and *Eleanor*—all docked at Griffin's wharf. The patriots had stood guard at the docks for weeks and prevented the merchant seamen from unloading the tea. As tensions mounted, the warships bristling with cannons anchored near the docks in a show of force to insure the offloading of the tea. The Governor declared that the tea would be unloaded on December 17, 1773, and any interference would not be tolerated.

Samuel Adams realized that if the Crown had the power to tax without the consent of the colonists, it had the power to take any and all of their property. The power to tax is the power to destroy. Without representation, this power becomes an exercise in tyranny. Adams said, "If Taxes are laid upon us in any shape without our having a legal Representation where they are laid, are we not reduced from the Character of free Subjects to the miserable State of tributary Slaves?"

Led by Adams, the Sons of Liberty demanded that the tea be sent back to London and refused to allow the tea tax to be paid. The patriots held meetings to determine the fate of the three cargo ships. On the night of December 16, 1773, nearly eight thousand Bostonians gathered to listen to Samuel Adams speak at the old South Meeting House. Adams had organized the meeting and prepared his followers to act when he gave the signal. He told the crowd he had sent word to the governor that the people of Boston were united in their desire to have the tea ships return to England with their cargoes. The tea would not be unloaded and the tax would not be paid.

During the meeting, a messenger arrived with a letter from the governor. Adams read the letter and then announced to the crowd that Hutchinson had refused their demands and that the British East India Company ships would not leave Boston harbor until their cargo had been unloaded and the tax paid.

At this point Adams said, "This meeting can do nothing more to save the country." As if on cue, men in the crowd responded, with wild Indian hoops and hollers. Suddenly, fifty or so men disguised in Indian garb, carrying hatchets and tomahawks, appeared among the crowd, their faces obscured with charcoal and paint to hide their identities. They shouted, "To the docks!"

The crowd cheered, shouting, "To the docks! Boston harbor [is] a teapot tonight!" as they tramped off to Griffin's Wharf. In the brisk December air, near 9 P.M., as the moon lit the harbor, the throng of patriots boarded the tea ships. They were not an unruly mob, but a group of patriotic citizens who performed one of the most symbolic acts of rebellion against British rule ever witnessed in the American colonies. Like-minded citizens watching from the dock cheered them. The British warships did not interfere, being unwilling to shoot into the mass of civilians. The ship's company aboard each of the tea ships did not resist the "Indians."

An eyewitness account by shoemaker and patriot George Robert Twelvetrees Hewes recalled the actions of his fellow "Indians" during the Boston Tea Party: "Having painted my face and hands with coal dust in the shop of a blacksmith, I repaired to Griffin's Wharf where the ships lay that contained the tea. . . . When we arrived at the wharf, there were three of our number who assumed an authority to direct our operations, to which we readily submitted. . . . We then were ordered by our commander to open the hatches and take out all the chests of tea and throw them overboard, and we immediately proceeded to execute his orders, first cutting and splitting the chests with our tomahawks, so as to thoroughly expose the tea to the effects of the water. . . . In about three hours from the time we went on board, we had thus broken and thrown overboard every tea chest to be found in the ship, while those in the other ships were disposing of the tea in the same way, at the same time. We were surrounded by British armed ships, but no attempt was made to resist us."

Samuel Adams had instructed his Indians to respect all private property on the ships, except the tea. Thousands of Bostonians watched from the dock as the tea was dumped into the harbor. The patriots worked quickly, dumping the tea but taking great care to do no damage to the ships. When the Indians accidentally broke a padlock on one of the ships, they later replaced it. They even swept the decks of the ships before they left and made the first mate of each ship attest that no damage had been done to anything other than to the crates of tea.

As they left the ships, many of the Indians were singing a song that some say was written by Samuel Adams. The song is titled "Tea, Destroyed by Indians." One of the memorable lines read: "A NOBLE SIGHT—to see, the accursed TEA Mingled with MUD—and ever for to be; For KING and PRINCE shall know that we are FREE."

John Adams, cousin to Samuel Adams, wrote in his diary on December 17, 1773:

> Last Night 3 cargoes of Bohea Tea were emptied into the Sea. This Morning a Man of War sails. This is the most magnificent Movement of all. There is a Dignity, a Majesty, a Sublimity, in this last Effort of the Patriots, that I greatly admire. The People should never rise, without doing something to be remembered—something notable and striking. This Destruction of the Tea is so bold, so daring, so firm, intrepid, and inflexible, and it must have important Consequences, and so lasting, that I can't but consider it as an Epoch in History. . . . Many persons wish that as many dead carcasses were floating in the harbor, as there are chests of tea. What measures will the ministry take? Will they punish us? How? By quartering troops upon us? By annulling our charter? By laying on more duties? By restraining our trade? By sacrifice of individuals?

When the news of the Boston Tea Party reached London, the British were furious. The notion that the whole dispute was about the denial of the right of Great Britain to tax the Thirteen Colonies without their consent was lost in the act of the destruction of the East India Company's private property: the tea. The House of Lords reacted like a "seething caldron of impotent rage" and King George III remarked, "The colonies must either submit or triumph. . . . vigorous measures appear to be the only means left to bringing the Americans to a due submission to the mother country, the colonies will submit. . . . That with firmness and perseverance America will be brought to submission."

The other American colonies sympathized with Massachusetts. A Virginian named Theodorick Bland wrote, "The question is, whether the rights and liberties of America shall be contended for, or given up to arbitrary powers." Submission was not in the American character and King George was in for a shock that would change the world.

The definitive defense for the Boston tea Party was written by a nineteen-year-old patriot and college student named Alexander Hamilton, who signed his work as "A Friend of America." Hamilton's first major political treatise, "A Full Vindication of the Measures of Congress," was published on December 15, 1774, almost on the anniversary date of the Tea Party. His words bear repeating:

> But some people try to make you believe, we are disputing about the foolish trifle of three pence duty upon tea. They may as well tell you, that black is white. Surely you can judge for yourselves. Is a dispute, whether the Parliament of Great Britain shall make what laws, and impose what taxes they please upon us, or not; I say, is this a dispute about three pence duty upon tea? The man that affirms it, deserves to be laughed at.
>
> It is true, we are denying to pay the duty upon tea; but it is not for the value of the thing itself. It is because we cannot submit to that, without acknowledging the principle upon which it is founded, and that principle is a right to tax us in all cases whatsoever. . . .
>
> But being ruined by taxes is not the worst you have to fear. What security would you have for your lives? How can any of you be sure you would have the free enjoyment of your religion long?
>
> Would you put your religion in the power of any set of men living? Remember civil and religious liberty always go together, if the foundation of the one be sapped, the other will fall of course.
>
> Call to mind one of our sister colonies, Boston. Reflect upon the situation of Canada, and then tell me whether you are inclined to place any confidence in the justice and humanity of the parliament. The port of Boston is blocked up, and an army planted in the town. An act has been passed to alter its charter, to prohibit its assemblies, to license the murder of its inhabitants, and to convey them from their own country to Great Britain, and to be tried for their lives.

What was all this for? Just because a small number of people, provoked by an open and dangerous attack upon their liberties, destroyed a parcel of Tea belonging to the East India Company. It was not public but private property they destroyed. It was not the act of the whole province, but the act of a part of the citizens; instead of trying to discover the perpetrators, and commencing a legal prosecution against them; the parliament of Great Britain interfered in an unprecedented manner, and inflicted a punishment upon a whole province, "untried, unheard, unconvicted of any crime." This may be justice, but it looks so much like cruelty, that a man of a humane heart would be more apt to call it by the latter, than the former name.

Signed: A friend of America

For Samuel Adams the Boston Tea party was a shining moment of freedom and a protest against the tyranny of arbitrary government that failed to represent its citizens. On December 31, 1773, Samuel Adams wrote the following New Year's Eve message in the *Boston Gazette*: "To all Nations under Heaven, know ye, that the PEOPLE of the AMERICAN WORLD are Millions strong—countless Legions compose their ARMY OF FREEMEN."

There is no doubt of the significance of the Boston Tea Party to the patriot cause nor the hand that Samuel Adams played in making this important event take place. No one can say if Samuel Adams was actually with the Indians who dumped the tea into the harbor during the Boston Tea Party, but his hand in organizing the circumstances that led to this brazen act of rebellion was clear. Later, when British General Gage threatened to imprison Adams if he did not stop his opposition to the Crown, Sam replied, "Sir, I trust I have long since made my peace with the King of kings. No personal consideration shall induce me to abandon the righteous cause of my country. Tell Governor Gage it is the advice of Samuel Adams to him no longer to insult the feelings of an exasperated people."

So clear and so well known to the British was Adams's reputation as a rebel and agitator that on April 19, 1775, when the British soldiers marched to Lexington, they had orders to arrest him.

Revisionist historians have tried to paint Samuel Adams as a cynical propagandist, a plotter whose self-interest was more consuming than his patriotism. The historical record does not support this narrow view. Samuel Adams believed that cynical means would only produce an end that was counterproductive; that strong measures were only sanctioned when all other means of protest and petition failed. Adams became the Father of the American Revolution due to his passion, strong-willed leadership, organizational skill and take-charge attitude.

He realized that reconciliation with the Crown would lead nowhere. He hungered for a complete separation from the mother country. He believed that America should be a place where no man bowed to royalty; where there were no kings, princes or dukes; where every man and woman could have the freedom to make as much or as little of his life as he wished. He dreamed of an America where Americans ruled themselves, where the American virtues of rugged individualism and self-reliance would thrive. His leadership was decisive in setting the conditions for what was to come: The war that would decide if Americans were to be free or would remain the subjects of kings.

After the Boston Tea Party a fiery Virginian orator named Patrick Henry pronounced, "The distinctions between Virginians, Pennsylvanians, New Yorkers, and New Englanders are no more. I Am Not A Virginian, But An American!"

LEADERSHIP LESSONS FROM SAMUEL ADAMS

- **Leadership is the art of influence.** Samuel Adams influenced Americans, not just in Massachusetts, but in each of the Thirteen Colonies, to organize for the cause of American Liberty. He became the father of American Independence and the spark that touched off the flame of revolution. Others would lead the cause to its conclusion, but Samuel Adams was the *essential* leader of the birth of American Liberty. In 1766, ten years before American independence, Adams wrote a letter published in the *Massachusetts Circular* that attacked "taxation without representation," and called for all of the colonies to resist unjust British laws. His writings electrified the colonial population and raised political awareness across America. If you want to lead you must find ways to influence people to join your team, participate in your cause and share a common vision.
- **Commitment makes all the difference.** To act, to do, to be committed to the cause is everything. People do not follow leaders who are not committed. Adams felt that citizens of a free society were duty bound to stand up for their political rights. Adams believed that "Among the natural rights of the colonists are these: First a right to life, secondly to liberty, and thirdly to property; together with the right to defend them in the best manner

they can." He epitomized the idea that leaders must be committed to overcoming obstacles and getting the job done.

- **Leaders organize for success.** Adams's development of the "committees of correspondence" and organizations like the Sons of Liberty gave crucial form and structure to the cause of Liberty. Adams believed that "It does not require a majority to prevail, but rather an irate, tireless minority keen to set brush fires in people's minds." To lead effectively, you must organize for success and motivate team to act.

- **Leaders Shape the Culture of their Organizations.** You cannot lead effectively unless your organization understands your vision and acts upon it. The single purpose of Samuel Adams's life was to encourage his fellow colonists to stand up for their rights as free men. He was the quintessential revolutionary. He was constantly at work writing letters and articles for newspapers, organizing meetings, and holding discussions for the cause of Liberty. He became the soul of the Sons of Liberty by articulating their struggle as a struggle of free men against oppressive government. He organized people and led them to action in the streets of Boston. His efforts to repeal the Stamp Act, his determination in front of Governor Hutchinson to remove the British troops from Boston after the Boston Massacre and his actions during the Tea Party were critical acts of leadership. His influence was felt from Boston to London. He gave the struggle for freedom direction and purpose and ignited the torch of Liberty.

- **Leaders understand that they must appeal to people emotionally as well as intellectually.** Adams believed that people are governed more by their feelings than by reason. You can implore to logic, but if you do not appeal to people's feelings you may never reach them. Adams's ability to inspire the citizens of Boston to launch the First Tea Party, then called simply "the destruction of the tea," engaged the feelings of the colonists and focused their rage against unjust British rule. The lesson here is that a leader must make his team members *feel* the cause as much as understand it.

*Patrick Henry's "Give me Liberty or give me death!" speech before the
Virginia House of Burgesses* (painting by Peter F. Rothermel, 1851).

Chapter 2

IF WE WISH TO BE FREE
The Oratory of Patrick Henry

If this be treason, make the most of it. —PATRICK HENRY

LEADERSHIP REQUIRES *PASSION*.

The Age of Enlightenment was changing Europe. Political philosophers, such as, Montesquieu, John Locke, and other European intellectuals, were writing pamphlets and books that questioned the divine right of kings and discussed the rights of man. Enlightenment writers championed the concepts of religious tolerance, democracy, republicanism, and liberty. These books were read with great intensity in the Thirteen Colonies by men like John Adams, Ben Franklin, Thomas Jefferson, and Patrick Henry.

In the seventeenth century many of the first colonists to America made the hazardous trip across the Atlantic Ocean at their own expense to escape excessive government control, high taxes, and religious persecution. They struggled in a harsh environment against the Indians, surviving hardships, scarcity, pestilence, and famine. In those early days their government was small and local. The struggle for survival was paramount and individual self reliance was a requirement. The pace of communication between the Crown and the British colonies in America was set by the three weeks or more it took a wooden sailing ship to make the perilous journey across the Atlantic Ocean. They cherished their independence and many colonists considered it a birthright; a reward for the dangers and sacrifice they incurred as pioneers in the New World. Their survival and success in America was dependent upon their own efforts. Far away from the politics of the empire, the colonists created a new life in a new world, establishing their homes, farms, and industries in an atmosphere of independence.

Although subjects of the Crown, the colonists had no direct representation in Parliament, but still believed they possessed all the rights of citizenship held under English Common Law. This loose relationship between the colonies and Great Britain caused the American character to develop, built upon rugged self reliant, self sufficient, and self confident individualism. In this atmosphere the seeds of American *exceptionalism* were planted, engendering an attitude where merit counted more than birth and action more than status. Life was hard, brutal, and short. Mortality rates were high, especially for children. Large families were needed both to work the land and to ensure the survival of a few offspring. No one could count on help from the mother country for his or her daily existence. Colonists banded together for protection and to provide for a common defense but soon found that a communal economy led to ruin and death. If you wanted to survive and thrive in the New World, you grew your own crops and hunted your own food. You persisted and flourished through your own sweat, toil and tears.

By the eighteenth century the colonies were thriving and most Americans proudly considered themselves British citizens, loyal subjects of the Crown. They were accustomed to being part of the British Empire, which ruled them with a light touch. In America they enjoyed an extraordinary degree of independence from "big government," more so than their counterparts in England. Independence and the ideas of the Enlightenment converged in the minds of many colonists causing them to look at their situation differently from the people back in England who saw themselves as subjects of the Crown and therefore entitled to the benefits of the British Empire.

Americans thought of themselves, not as Americans, but as Virginians, Pennsylvanians, Carolinians or New Yorkers. Each colony created local governments, generally based on the rules of British Common Law. Many colonials felt a greater bond to their neighbors, local governments, and state legislatures than to the home country. As a result of this special situation the colonists developed a character and culture that was different from that of the subjects of the kings of Great Britain and other European countries.

By 1750, if there was one thing that typified colonists in America more than anything else it was their resentment of outside authority in all its forms. American loyalty could not be mandated or legislated; it could not be ordered; it had to be earned and earned utilizing a careful blend of self-interest and self-worth.

Since Americans had governed themselves for years and were in the habit of making their own decisions about how to live their lives, direct involvement by the British Government in the 1760s put Great Britain and her

Thirteen Colonies on a collision course. The trouble developed shortly after the French and Indian War, which was part of a much wider and costly British-French conflict lasting from 1756–1763. Great Britain won the war, captured all of Canada, and secured a dominant position of power in North America, but the costs of this victory were steep. In 1763, Great Britain faced a serious financial crisis. She thought to work her way out of the crisis by generating revenue wherever possible, specifically by taxing her prosperous colonies. To many in Parliament it was right and fair for the mother country to ask its colonies to help pay the costs of the war. Since they had no representation in Parliament, politicians could safely point a finger at the colonists for living the good life under the protection of the British military, and force them to pay. Under British mercantilism, a form of strict governmental regulation of the entire national economy where colonies were expected to support the mother country, the interests and needs of British subjects living on English soil had the highest priority. Therefore, when necessary, the interest and liberties of colonists living away from England were subordinated to those of the empire. The long-term consequence of this policy was the root cause of the American Revolution.

In 1763, in part to solidify control, prevent trouble with the Indians, and negate the high cost of posting British troops to protect the new lands they had acquired from the French, Parliament decreed that the colonists could no longer settle lands on the western frontier. This infuriated the colonists on the frontier who viewed these lands as theirs for the taking. The colonists resented being told that they could not clear and farm land they already lived on and had made their homes. They considered this interference in their affairs as an attempt to restrict their opportunities to grow and prosper and many openly disobeyed this decree.

As the British imposed their will, Americans resisted, and called this meddling in their affairs "tyranny." As the British debt soared, so did the need for the Parliament to raise taxes. Colonists harassed tax collectors and obstructed them from gathering revenue. In 1768, the British sent four thousand British soldiers to Boston to maintain control and enforce the collection of taxes imposed by the Townshend Acts. The city of Boston had a population of twenty thousand; a garrison of British Regulars that amounted to 20 percent of the city's population was an overt act of belligerence by the Crown against its unruly subjects. Even so, few colonists were ready at this time to declare open rebellion against the Crown. Fewer still harbored thoughts of a war for independence from Great Britain. This mindset was about to change dramatically.

The mismanagement of the American colonies continued, coming to a climax in Boston on March 5, 1770, when protestors clashed with a detachment of British troops. Outside of Boston's Old State House on King Street, a squad of British soldiers was confronted by a gang of youths who threw snowballs and oyster shells at them. Soon a large crowd emerged shouting insults at the "lobster backs" as the Redcoats were derisively called. The crowd quickly got ugly and challenged the lobster backs to go back to England. Some in the enraged crowd shouted for the British to shoot, if they had the courage. The situation soon got out of hand. Confused and surrounded by a large angry mob, British soldier Private Hugh Montgomery was struck and his musket went off. Upon hearing the shot, Montgomery shouted to his mates "Damn you, fire!" and other British soldiers fired into the unarmed crowd. A black patriot, Crispus Attucks, was hit by several musket balls and died instantly, becoming the first casualty for the patriot cause. The crowd shouted, "Murderers! Murderers!" at the British soldiers. Other colonists killed on the spot by the volley of British musket fire were Samuel Gray and James Caldwell. Samuel Maverick and Patrick Carr were wounded and died later, Maverick the next morning and Carr within two weeks. Christopher Monk was wounded just above the groin, but lived another ten years. The tragic incident became known as The Bloody Massacre in King Street and later as the Boston Massacre. Afterward, patriot John Hancock stated, "Let this sad tale of death never be told without a tear; let not the heaving bosom cease to burn with a manly indignation at the barbarous story." For those Americans thinking of rebellion, the Boston Massacre became a vivid example of all that was wrong with Great Britain, King George, and Parliament.

The Incident on King Street, as the Boston Massacre was called by the British, and other unruly and insubordinate actions of their American subjects incensed the king and Parliament. Nevertheless, in an attempt at conciliation, Governor Thomas Hutchinson met with Samuel Adams and ordered British troops withdrawn to Castle Island. Additionally, Governor Hutchinson promised an inquiry and trial of the British soldiers involved. John Adams, a cousin of Samuel Adams, was asked to defend the eight British soldiers involved in the incident. In a dramatic court hearing John Adams was able to get six acquitted, with the remaining two soldiers convicted of the lesser crime of manslaughter.

This quieted things down until May 10, 1773, when Parliament enacted the Tea Act and sent more troops to enforce it. The Boston Tea Party that resulted in American defiance over the Tea Act was a defining moment in the colonists' relationship with Great Britain. With the army garrison mostly confined to Castle Island because of the Boston Massacre, and few British soldiers on the streets, the patriots were able to dump the tea into Boston harbor in protest. Most Americans agreed that the demonstration in Boston harbor on December 16, 1773, sent a powerful message to King George and Parliament: The colonists were determined to stand up for their rights. Many in the American Colonies and some in Great Britain agreed with the spirit and actions of the Tea Party patriots and felt that their appeals had not been addressed.

Massachusetts was the tinderbox and the king viewed the colony as a contagion. In 1774, the other colonies seemed manageable. Georgia, South Carolina, North Carolina, Virginia, New Jersey, New York, Massachusetts, and New Hampshire were already designated Crown colonies, regulated by direct oversight of a royal governor who followed royal instructions and was appointed by the king. Delaware, Maryland, and Pennsylvania were designated proprietary colonies and were ruled by governors appointed by the local legislatures. Connecticut and Rhode Island were designated charter colonies whose governors were elected by qualified voters in each of those colonies.

For King George and many in Parliament the Boston Tea Party was the last straw and it became clear to them that they had to rule America with a firmer hand, no matter what the previous governing relationship with each colony had been. Prime Minister Lord Frederick North (April 13, 1732– August 5, 1792) considered Boston to be the epicenter of the trouble in the colonies and he wanted to punish Bostonians for the Tea Party. If his men could quell the problem in Boston he was convinced that a demonstration of force would stop these infernal protests from erupting throughout the colonies. On April 22, 1774, Lord North reported to the king, "The Americans have tarred and feathered your subjects, plundered your merchants, burnt your ships, denied all obedience to your laws and authority; yet so clement and so long forbearing has our conduct been that it is incumbent on us now to take a different course. Whatever may be the consequences, we must risk something; if we do not, all is over."

Parliament acted quickly on Lord North's report and dictated a series of Acts of Parliament specifically aimed at Massachusetts, targeting the rebellious Bostonians where it would hurt the most: in the pocketbook. The patriots called these decrees the Intolerable Acts or the Coercive Acts. The acts included:

- **The Boston Port Act,** established on March 31, 1774, closed the port of Boston until the British East India Company had been repaid for the tea destroyed during the Boston Tea Party. Americans objected and considered this act unjust as it punished everyone in Boston rather than just the people who had dumped the tea into the harbor. The citizens of Massachusetts felt that this was mass punishment without legal representation. Many in the other colonies saw it as an abuse of British power over Americans.

- **The Massachusetts Government Act,** established on May 20, 1774, placed the government of the Colony of Massachusetts under direct British control and appointed a governor selected by the king. This act was the most egregious. It took away the right of the citizens of the Colony of Massachusetts to elect their own representatives and "the said method of annually electing the counselors or assistants of the said Province should no longer be suffered to continue." The act also restricted the rights of citizens to assemble in town meetings and in groups. Citizens of the other colonies were alarmed that the Crown could exercise these same unilateral actions in their colonies. Patriots realized that the colonies needed to unite in the cause of Liberty or fall separately to an arbitrary tyranny imposed by the force of British arms.

- **The Administration of Justice Act,** established on May 20, 1774, reinforced the king's power by permitting the governor in Massachusetts to change the location of a trial of officials charged with a crime derived from their enforcement of British law or the suppression of riots, to another British colony or to Great Britain. After the Boston Massacre soldiers had been given a fair trial in a Boston court and were defended by none other than John Adams, a cousin of Samuel Adams. Adams had the case against the soldier's commander dismissed and the charges against the soldiers reduced. Two British soldiers were convicted of manslaughter and had the punishment of their thumbs branded. Despite this fair treatment, the Administration of Justice Act made the future trial of any British official, army officer or soldier by a local court unlikely. Some colonists called this the "Murder Act" as it provided the local population no accountability over British officials.

- **The Quartering Act,** established on June 2, 1774, applied to all thirteen colonies and required them to provide housing and provisions for soldiers deployed there. If suitable barracks or other buildings were not available, the colony's governor could commandeer "so many uninhabited houses, outhouses, barns, or other buildings as he shall think necessary to be taken (making a reasonable allowance for the same) and make fit for the reception of such officers and soldiers, and to put and quarter such officers and soldiers therein for such time as he shall think proper."

On June 12, 1774, Gen. Thomas Gage declared martial law in Massachusetts. All Thirteen Colonies responded with emphatic indignation. They realized that a distant and arbitrary government was trampling their rights as British citizens. Acting together, the colonies formed the Continental Congress, a daring and monumental step that showed their disapproval of Lord North's policies and Parliament's Intolerable Acts. Forming a congress was an act of rebellion, as the assembly was not authorized by the Crown and operated contrary to the authority of the Crown's colonial governors. The First Congress assembled at Carpenter's Hall in Philadelphia on September 5, 1774. There were fifty-six delegates appointed by their respective legislatures with Virginian Peyton Randolph presiding as President of the Congress. Each of the Thirteen Colonies was represented except for the newest colony, Georgia. The First Continental Congress declared the rights of all American colonists to "life, liberty and property" and that "the foundation of English liberty, and of all free government, is a right in the people to participate in their legislative council." The delegates believed that Parliament was acting against the wishes of King George and hoped to convince him to stop the Coercive Acts, to secure their common rights under British law, and to reverse the abuse of royal authority in the American colonies.

Congress also petitioned the Crown for a redress of grievances and the repeal of the Intolerable Acts. Congress's aim was reconciliation not rebellion. Nevertheless, the delegates of the First Continental Congress were practical men who understood power and realized that they must act in order to secure their rights. Congress declared its opposition to the repressive acts of Parliament saying they are "not to be obeyed," and then took a decisive step in urging the formation of local militias.

Lord North and Parliament viewed the creation of militia units under the command of the Continental Congress with great alarm. The British government did not recognize the legitimacy of the Continental Congress and did not respond to the Americans' petition. By 1775, economic and military tensions between the colonists and the British escalated to the breaking point. In February 1775 a provincial congress was held in Massachusetts during which John Hancock and Joseph Warren began defensive preparations for a state of war. Parliament learned of these preparations and declared Massachusetts to be in a state of rebellion.

During these tumultuous times, and knowing what was going on in Massachusetts, the legislatures of the various colonies met to decide what to do. The Virginia legislature knew that war clouds were forming and felt it necessary to address in public debate the issue of rebellion against the unreasonable acts of the Crown and Parliament. Virginia, which at the time was the largest colony in America, held a meeting of delegates on March 23, 1775, at St. John's Church in Richmond. One of the members of the Virginia legislature was a patriot named Patrick Henry.

Patrick Henry (May 29, 1736–June 6, 1799) was a man of extraordinary talents. He was an attorney, a planter, a failed merchant, and a successful politician. Imbued with a belief in Liberty, in 1765 Patrick Henry began his opposition to Parliament's meddling in American affairs by leading fellow colonists against the hated the Stamp Act. Henry strongly believed that the colonial assemblies were the only legal power that could impose taxes and that Parliament could not usurp that right. His fiery oratory often had his opponents accusing him of treason to the Crown.

Patrick Henry's most important speech was made on March 23, 1775, during a session of the House of Burgesses at Saint John's Church in Richmond. Rebellion was in the air, largely because the Continental Congress's petitions were being completely ignored by King George. Every member of the Thirteen Colonies knew that the British intended to enforce their rule by the power of the British Army and more British soldiers were arriving in Boston. Conflict seemed inevitable. Resolutions were presented by Patrick Henry to prepare Virginia for conflict with the intent of "embodying, arming, and disciplining such a number of men as may be sufficient for that purpose."

Before the vote was taken Henry delivered one of the most impassioned and famous speeches in American history. He implored the delegates to vote in favor of preparing for war against the Crown. Going to war with Great Britain, the greatest superpower of the time was a serious act. The colonies had no army, navy, nor even a central government. They did not have factories with which to create muskets or cannons. They did not have a tenth of the wealth of Great Britain. The idea of opposing Great Britain must have seemed both incredibly brave and suicidal, but war was exactly what Patrick Henry was proposing. He believed there was no choice but to fight or to surrender all rights as freemen.

Henry spoke without notes. Eyewitness accounts tell us that his voice started low and calm and rose loudly as he reached the culmination of his speech. Patrick Henry's stirring speech to the House of Burgesses was recorded as follows:

No man thinks more highly than I do of the patriotism, as well as abilities, of the very worthy gentlemen who have just addressed the House. But different men often see the same subject in different lights; and, therefore, I hope that it will not be thought disrespectful to those gentlemen, if, entertaining as I do opinions of a character very opposite to theirs, I shall speak forth my sentiments freely and without reserve.

This is no time for ceremony. The question before the House is one of awful moment to this country. For my own part I consider it as nothing less than a question of freedom or slavery; and in proportion to the magnitude of the subject ought to be the freedom of the debate. It is only in this way that we can hope to arrive at truth, and fulfill the great responsibility, which we hold to God and our country. Should I keep back my opinions at such a time, through fear of giving offense, I should consider myself as guilty of treason towards my country, and of an act of disloyalty towards the majesty of heaven, which I revere above all earthly kings.

Mr. President, it is natural to man to indulge in the illusions of hope. We are apt to shut our eyes against a painful truth, and listen to the song of that siren, till she transforms us into beasts. Is this the part of wise men, engaged in a great and arduous struggle for Liberty? Are we disposed to be of the number of those who, having eyes, see not, and having ears, hear not, the things which so nearly concern their temporal salvation?

For my part, whatever anguish of spirit it may cost, I am willing to know the whole truth—to know the worst and to provide for it. I have but one lamp by which my feet are guided; and that is the lamp of experience. I know of no way of judging of the future but by the past. And judging by the past, I wish to know what there has been in the conduct of the British ministry for the last ten years, to justify those hopes with which gentlemen have been pleased to solace themselves and the House?

Is it that insidious smile with which our petition has been lately received? Trust it not, sir; it will prove a snare to your feet. Suffer not yourselves to be betrayed with a kiss. Ask yourselves how this gracious reception of our petition comports with these warlike preparations, which cover our waters and darken our land. Are fleets and armies necessary to a work of love and reconciliation? Have we shown ourselves so unwilling to be reconciled that force must be called in to win back our love? Let us not deceive ourselves, sir. These are the implements of war and subjugation—the last arguments to which kings resort. I ask gentlemen, sir, what means this martial array, if its purpose be not to force us to submission? Can gentlemen assign any other possible motives for it? Has Great Britain any enemy, in this quarter of the world, to call for all this accumulation of navies and armies?

No, sir, she has none. They are meant for us; they can be meant for no other. They are sent over to bind and rivet upon us those chains which the British ministry have been so long forging. And what have we to oppose to them? Shall we try argument? Sir, we have been trying that for the last ten years. Have we anything new to offer on the subject? Nothing.

We have held the subject up in every light of which it is capable; but it has been all in vain. Shall we resort to entreaty and humble supplication? What terms shall we find which have not been already exhausted? Let us not, I beseech you, sir, deceive ourselves longer.

Sir, we have done everything that could be done to avert the storm which is now coming on. We have petitioned; we have remonstrated; we have supplicated; we have prostrated ourselves before the throne, and have implored its interposition to arrest the tyrannical hands of the ministry and Parliament.

Our petitions have been slighted; our remonstrances have produced additional violence and insult; our supplications have been disregarded; and we have been spurned, with contempt, from the foot of the throne. In vain, after these things, may we indulge the fond hope of peace and reconciliation. There is no longer any room for hope.

If we wish to be free—if we mean to preserve inviolate those inestimable privileges for which we have been so long contending—if we mean not basely to abandon the noble struggle in which we have been so long engaged, and which we have pledged ourselves never to abandon until the glorious object of our contest shall be obtained, we must fight! I repeat it, sir, we must fight! An appeal to arms and to the God of Hosts is all that is left us!

They tell us, sir, that we are weak—unable to cope with so formidable an adversary. But when shall we be stronger? Will it be the next week, or the next year? Will it be when we are totally disarmed, and when a British guard shall be stationed in every house? Shall we gather strength by irresolution and inaction? Shall we acquire the means of effectual resistance, by lying supinely on our backs, and hugging the delusive phantom of hope, until our enemies shall have bound us hand and foot?

Sir, we are not weak, if we make a proper use of the means which the God of nature hath placed in our power. Three millions of people, armed in the holy cause of Liberty, and in such a country as that which we possess, are invincible by any force which our enemy can send against us. Besides, sir, we shall not fight our battles alone. There is a just God who presides over the destinies of nations, and who will raise up friends to fight our battles for us.

The battle, sir, is not to the strong alone; it is to the vigilant, the active, the brave. Besides, sir, we have no election. If we were base enough to desire it, it is now too late to retire from the contest. There is no retreat but in submission and slavery! Our chains are forged! Their clanking may be heard on the plains of Boston! The war is inevitable—and let it come! I repeat it, sir, let it come!

It is in vain, sir, to extenuate the matter. Gentlemen may cry, "Peace! Peace!"—but there is no peace. The war is actually begun! The next gale that sweeps from the north will bring to our ears the clash of resounding arms! Our brethren are already in the field! Why stand we here idle? What is it that gentlemen wish? What would they have? Is life so dear, or peace so sweet, as to be purchased at the price of chains and slavery? Forbid it, Almighty God! I know not what course others may take; but as for me, give me Liberty, or give me death!

The Virginia legislature voted immediately after Patrick Henry's rousing oration. The vote for rebellion was not taken without reservation; all knew the seriousness of declaring that they would oppose Great Britain, but the resolution passed by a narrow margin. Henry's persuasive voice helped to convince the Virginia delegates to side with the patriot cause. Word of his compelling oratory and his impassioned demand for "Liberty or death!" spread across the colonies like wildfire. Several weeks later, on April 19, 1775, the first shots, shots "heard 'round the world," marking the start of the American war for liberty were fired at Lexington, Massachusetts. Overnight the hearts and minds of many Americans changed from hesitation to action. Because of Patrick Henry thousands of Americans rallied to the cause and readied to battle the most powerful military, political, and economic force in the world.

—◦◦◦—

LEADERSHIP LESSONS FROM PATRICK HENRY

- **Leadership requires passion.** Effective leaders must have fire in their bellies. Enthusiasm is contagious. Passionate leaders motivate their followers. Motivated followers make all the difference in achieving success. Patrick Henry was intensely committed to the goal of Liberty. He inspired people with his eloquence and passion. He clearly articulated what was at stake in the looming conflict. His vision became the leadership vision for thousands during the American Revolution. His call to arms was a rallying cry that set the goal for a future where every American would always have the blessings of Liberty. His passionate ability to inspire leaders of the Virginia legislature and his fellow Americans set him apart and earned for him the sobriquet "Trumpet of Liberty." His "Give me Liberty or Give me Death" speech is as inspiring, relevant and actionable today as it was more than two centuries ago. It is worth reading and rereading.
- **Leadership without enthusiasm usually fails.** Leaders without passion, without enthusiasm, usually fail in any serious test. Patrick Henry's passion to oppose the tyranny of Great Britain infused determination and commitment in many Americans. As the famous nineteenth century writer and philosopher Ralph Waldo Emerson said: "Enthusiasm is one of the most powerful engines of success. When you do a thing, do it with all your might. Put your whole soul into it. Stamp it with your own personality. Be active, be energetic and faithful, and you will accomplish your object. Nothing great was ever achieved without enthusiasm." Patrick Henry would have agreed with Emerson. He was passionate for the cause of Liberty and knew that enthusiasm is key to leadership.
- **Leadership is about effective communication.** Patrick Henry's vision declared that the American colonies should be free and independent of Great

Britain. He artfully articulated this vision for everyone to see. He wasn't afraid to say so, even when saying so was considered treason and treason was punishable by death. He believed that Liberty was worth fighting for. Forty years after the American War for Independence, John Adams reflected that the American Revolution was more than just a war; it was a change in the hearts and minds of the people. When Patrick Henry said: "Three millions of people, armed in the holy cause of Liberty, and in such a country as that which we possess, are invincible by any force which our enemy can send against us," he correctly envisioned courage and victory where most only saw fear and defeat.

- **The leader must want to lead and be ready to fight for what he is passionate about.** Leaders either rise to the challenge or fall flat. Effective leaders have enthusiasm for the cause and the team. Patrick Henry's words at the Virginia Legislature on March 23, 1775 communicated his passion for Liberty and his desire to fight for that Liberty at all costs, even unto death. Do you have the same passion for Liberty? Today many Americans find themselves in circumstances similar to those faced by Patrick Henry. Many wonder where our nation is headed. Will we surrender our Liberty to an ever-encroaching big-government bureaucracy or choose the path of limited government and self-reliance? With each passing year Americans are pressed to choose between freedom and a "soft" tyranny where the "nanny state" increasingly limits individual liberty, the welfare state continues to grow, and government stealthily assumes ever more responsibility for its subjects from cradle to grave. Isn't that what our Forefathers fought against? When Patrick Henry said: "The battle, sir, is not to the strong alone; it is to the vigilant, the active, the brave," he declared not only his determination to be vigilant, active and brave in the cause of Liberty, but his willingness to fight for Liberty, and his understanding that passion and enthusiasm are enablers that help leaders accomplish goals. The actual American Revolution was born in a transformation of the hearts and minds of the American people before the first shots at Lexington and Concord were fired.

General Henry Knox (portrait by Charles Willson Peale, 1784).

Chapter 4

A BOSTON BOOKSELLER
The Accomplishments of Henry Knox

---

*The want of them [cannon] is so great that no trouble or
expense must be spared to obtain them.*—General George
Washington to Colonel Henry Knox November 16, 1775

LEADERSHIP REQUIRES *KNOWLEDGE.*

"**F**orward!" Lines of red-coated British grenadiers stepped forward as if
they were not individual soldiers but part of a well-oiled, deadly and
unstoppable machine.

June 17, 1775 was a hot day. Captain Henry Knox looked down on the
advancing Redcoats. The disciplined ranks of men marching toward him were
professional soldiers. The regiments of the king in North America were some
of the best in the British Army. Unlike the militiamen he led, the attacking
British infantry were known for their unflinching determination under fire
and fierce bayonet assaults.

It was but eight weeks after the stinging British retreat from Lexington
and Concord. Gen. Thomas Gage, replacing Thomas Hutchinson as military
royal governor, had sent a force of British regulars to take decisive action
against the rebellion and secure suspected weapons stockpiles in Lexington
and Concord, Massachusetts. Gage was convinced that his show of force
would intimidate the growing insurrection, make the hotheads cower at the
might of British military power and bring the rebellious population back to
their senses.

The colonists learned of the British plans and Paul Revere and other patriot riders alerted the local militia to assemble: "The regulars are coming!
The British regulars are coming!" When the seven hundred British Army

regulars under the command of Lt. Col. Francis Smith reached Lexington on April 19, 1775, they met a company of eighty local militiamen under the command of Captain John Parker. Parker had deployed his men in the open on Lexington Green. He told his men: "Stand your ground; don't fire unless fired upon, but if they mean to have a war, let it begin here."

There was a tense standoff as the British regulars moved into formation. As the standoff continued, more British soldiers continued to move into Lexington. A shot was fired—to this day no one knows who fired that shot—but it triggered a volley of shots. When the smoke cleared, eight colonial militiamen lay dead on Lexington Green. That shot unleashed the "dogs of war." On that fateful day in April the American war for independence began in earnest!

The surviving colonial militiamen fled. The king's troops seized Lexington and searched every building but found no caches of rebel arms or munitions. Lieutenant Colonel Smith pressed on to his secondary objective, marching another six and a half miles to Concord. At Concord the British were similarly disappointed. The Massachusetts militia had removed all military stores and scattered them among several hiding places in nearby farms and villages. Aroused, patriot "Minutemen" gathered from nearly every farm, hamlet and village in Middlesex County. The British force had stirred up a hornet's nest.

While the British busied themselves searching Concord for rebel arms, militiamen from nearby counties converged on the Redcoats. The colonials were angry and pressed the fight for their homes and farms against an invading army. Without any real organization or formal command colonial militias swarmed the British and fired from every stone wall and tree. Outnumbered nearly six to one and met by rebel militiamen at every turn, the British beat a hasty retreat to Boston, harassed all the way by musket fire. The British force suffered 73 men killed, 174 wounded, and 53 missing in skirmishes with the rebels along the seventeen-mile route of withdrawal. The patriots counted 49 killed and 39 wounded, but they had stood up to 700 British regulars and dramatically demonstrated their determination to fight.

When the sun rose on Boston April 20, 1775, the British found themselves surrounded by nearly fifteen thousand armed patriot militiamen. The British were bottled up in Boston as patriot militia blocked all escape routes from the town except those by sea. General Gage wrote of his surprise at the number of Americans surrounding Boston: "The rebels are not the despicable rabble too many have supposed them to be. . . . In all their wars against the

French they never showed such conduct, attention, and perseverance as they do now."

On May 10, 1775, a fleet carrying forty-five hundred fresh British troops under Maj. Gen. William Howe arrived in Boston harbor to reinforce the garrison. General Howe (10 August 1729–12 July 1814) was a brilliant, courageous, and ambitious officer who was appointed as Gage's second in command. A professional soldier with powerful political connections, Howe was a hero of the Seven Years War—known in America as the French and Indian War—he had gained a reputation for bravery and fortitude in the Battle of Quebec against the French in 1759.

Patriot spies learned that General Gage intended Gen. William Howe's infantry to launch an amphibious attack to occupy the area near Bunker Hill on the Charlestown Peninsula overlooking the city of Boston. This force would break the siege and start a land offensive calculated to clear the patriots from the approaches to Boston.

But the patriots were one step ahead of General Gage. Patriot Gen. Artemis Ward gave orders to Gen. Israel Putnam to fortify the area near Bunker Hill immediately. Henry Knox was ordered to reconnoiter the Charleston Peninsula around Bunker Hill and select the best places to dig fortifications. Although only 25 years old, Knox was widely trusted for his character, energy, and military knowledge and was a perfect fit for the job. His reconnaissance efforts eventually led to the occupation of a hill just down the slope from Bunker Hill called Breed's Hill. Under the guidance of senior commanders Col. William Prescott and Dr. Joseph Warren, and junior leaders like Knox, the patriots planned their defenses. In all, about fifteen hundred patriots had assembled. On the night of June 16 they dug extensive defensive trenches, parapets, and breastworks in anticipation of a British attack. Breed's Hill was a natural defensive position. It was surrounded by water on three sides.

Henry Knox was used to overcoming adversity. He was born in Boston on July 25, 1750. His father died when Henry was only twelve. Without the means to survive on his own, Henry was apprenticed to a Boston bookseller to make his way in life. He thrived in this new occupation, developed a love for books and literature, and worked diligently to become a self-educated man. He particularly enjoyed reading books on military science and military history. He dreamed of being a soldier.

In 1771, at the age of twenty-one, Knox used his savings to become an entrepreneur and opened his own bookstore. The store developed into a prosperous business due to Knox's drive and energy and was soon the rage of Boston. It became an eighteenth century version of our modern day Starbucks, contained many of the latest books from England, and was the place to be and be seen for young Bostonian sophisticates.

In 1772, to pursue his love of the military, Knox joined the Boston Grenadier Corps, an amateur hometown defensive militia that was distinguished for its good discipline. The Grenadiers drilled every week in the Boston Commons to the delight of the local townsfolk who took great pride in their town's militia. Knox was rapidly promoted due to his military inclinations and leadership abilities and the men of his company voted for him to become an officer. He also became an ardent patriot, a member of the Sons of Liberty, and a close friend of another young man with a taste for military service, Nathaniel Greene, who later served as second-in-command to George Washington

Life was good for Knox. His bookstore was thriving, he had found satisfaction in the Boston Grenadier Corps, and had even won the fancy of the love of his life, a pretty Boston socialite named Lucy Flucker. But confrontation with Great Britain was looming. The Boston Massacre, an event that Knox witnessed firsthand, the Boston Tea Party and the conflict at Lexington and Concord changed his life and the lives of his fellow colonists forever.

So it was at dawn, on June 16, 1775 that Henry Knox, leader of a company of hastily assembled and poorly armed militiamen, looked down on Boston from the breastworks on Breed's Hill and wondered how the day would end. Could they expect to stop the British forces? The militiamen were hardly soldiers. Except for a few who saw the fighting at Lexington and Concord, most of them had never fired a shot in anger at another man. Few had any formal military training. Fewer still had bayonets for their muskets and hunting rifles. As he stared at the massive British fleet poised for attack, each ship armed with the latest cannon and manned by the best gunners in the world, a lump formed in his throat. He had studied the British Army. Knox knew the British gunners would do their utmost to smash the militia defenses with a fierce cannonade. Then the well-drilled and professionally led British infantry would be ferried from the ships, land on the shore and conduct a relentless attack. He knew the British would not give up until they had taken the hill. There would be hell to pay but the patriots would not back down.

On the British warship *Lively*, anchored in the Charles River, General Gage peered through a brass spyglass and was stunned to see that the rebels had fortified Breed's Hill overnight with a 160-by-30-foot earthen defensive line. Gage knew that he had been beaten to the punch and the patriots had occupied the high ground before he could land his infantry. The secret was out, but the attack must continue. Angry at this infuriating development, Gage ordered the naval bombardment to begin.

The *Lively* fired the first cannon shots at the patriots shortly after sunrise. The shots landed short of the defenses, but rattled the untrained and undisciplined militiamen. Henry Knox, now the captain of a company of musketmen, reassured his men and did his best to keep them steady. Other British ships also bombarded the defenders, hoping to scatter the rebels. Eventually a thundering fire developed from a total of 128 guns. Several cannonballs crashed into the rebel defenses, but the British guns had trouble ranging the trenchline. Most cannonballs fell short of the breastworks and caused few patriot casualties. The ineffectiveness of the British Navy's guns raised patriot morale, but Henry Knox was nonetheless impressed with the potential of British firepower.

General Gage was not amused as he scanned the rebel lines. It seemed that the only way to move the rebels off Breed's Hill would be to send his infantry up the hill in a direct frontal assault and push them off with the bayonet. Losing patience with the naval bombardment, Gage ordered Howe to launch the amphibious assault, carry on the frontal attack, and storm the rebel defenses. At 1 P.M. on June 16, British infantry disembarked from the ships into longboats. For most of the afternoon, twenty-two hundred British soldiers were slowly rowed from ship to shore. Howe assembled his regiments on the beach south of Breed's Hill and sat down to eat a meal, all in clear view of the tired and hungry rebel force. Then, the red-coated infantrymen put on their packs, formed lines and marched forward in splendid, well-disciplined ranks.

General Howe vowed that he would defeat the rabble on Breed's Hill in one dramatic battle that would revenge British losses from the withdrawal from Lexington and Concord and end the curse of rebellion in the American colonies forever. He had nothing but contempt for the rebels and expected them to run at the sight of his men marching up the hill in tight formation. The spectacle of his twenty-two hundred disciplined regulars, with their red coats blazing and long steel bayonets gleaming, would surely frighten the rabble away.

On command, the red line of soldiers stepped off as one man. Each soldier wore a heavy, red-wool coat. His pack weighed sixty pounds and his Brown Bess musket weighed an additional twelve. With drums beating and the Union Jack flag snapping in the breeze, the most feared infantrymen in the world moved forward in the heat of the afternoon with quiet, professional determination to obey their orders and crush the rebels.

Henry Knox watched in awe as the British marched steadily up the hill. He had worked all night without rest alongside the militiamen digging trenches. His men were tired and hungry. Few of them had thought to bring water and food when they left Boston the night before. Yet with determination they stood their positions and braced for the attack.

"Hold your fire men!" Their commanding officer, Colonel Prescott, ordered.

"We haven't much powder and ball," another patriot officer shouted. "We must make every shot count. Aim low, aim for the officers in the fancy uniforms. Don't shoot until you see the whites of their eyes!"

The British marched forward at a steady, ominous pace, drums drumming and regimental flags flying. The red-coated soldiers held their muskets at the carry position against their right shoulders. The shiny steel bayonets that tipped each musket glistened in the sun like thousands of tiny mirrors. The effect inspired awe and fear.

Knox watched as the British came within fifty yards of the patriot trenches.

"Fire!" Colonel Prescott ordered.

Musket fire erupted from the militia line sounding like jagged thunder, growing into a storm of noise. The militiamen fired, reloaded, and fired again. Redcoats fell. The first British line melted like snow on a warm spring day. Huge gaps showed in the red line. The patriot defenders fired with deadly accuracy downhill at their targets. Red-coated soldiers from the second rank moved forward to replace the fallen but patriot musket-balls struck many of them as well. Primary targets for the militia muskets, several British officers were hit while urging their men forward. The dead and wounded lay in the tall grass. As their officers fell to the Yankee fusillade, the British line stopped. Amid the blast of muskets and the cries of the wounded, Howe gave the order and a drummer beat the call for retreat. The red-coated soldiers broke ranks and ran back down the hill.

Knox and his fellow defenders cheered. The patriot rabble had defeated an attack from the greatest army on earth but the battle was not over. He knew and understood the awful power of musketry and rifles, but he wondered what would have been the effect against the British if he had had a battery of cannon. A volley of case shot, loose metal or stones fired from a cannon, would have devastated the British ranks. How he wished for even one cannon!

British military professionalism was not to be denied. General Howe vowed to have his victory. He reformed his ranks and they came up the hill again. In the humid June afternoon, the British had a hard time climbing the hill, but they came on. In this second attack the disciplined crimson line of infantry again closed to within fifty yards of the breastworks. The militiamen waited for the British to close the distance and then let loose another shower of musket balls. Patriot lead tore into flesh as one Redcoat after another fell. Rifles and muskets barked and the second attack was shattered, much like the first. The Redcoats staggered back in retreat.

Again the patriots cheered. Knox checked his men's supply of ammunition. They were almost out of ball and powder. With cool assurance he walked the trenchline and encouraged his men.

Watching the attack from the bottom of the hill, General Howe could not believe that the finest infantry in the world was being decimated by a citizen rabble. He ordered his men to take off their heavy packs. He ordered in all his reserves. He told them that they would make another assault and that this time there would be no retreat. Leading the third attack himself, Howe commanded his men to press forward with the bayonet.

The patriots were nearly out of ammunition and only a few had bayonets. Few had any skill or training with the bayonet. Fewer still had ever met a bayonet charge. As the British advanced the patriots opened fire. Knox tried valiantly to keep his men at their posts but all along the line, as their powder ran out, the militiamen fled in panic. Minus ammunition, they saw little reason to wait behind the breastworks to be skewered by British steel. Knox watched as the patriots along the ever-thinning line fired their last volley. Dozens of British soldiers fell, but the Red Line did not halt. Patriot muskets were reloaded and fired but the militiamen had lost all sense of fire discipline and no longer followed orders. The British line stoically took losses from the patriot fire and kept moving uphill in grim determination. Near the summit, British officers shouted to charge with the bayonet. The red line screamed "huzzah!" and the British regulars rushed forward the last ten yards, leaped over the parapet, and lunged with cold steel.

The sight of the advancing Red Line and the blood curdling shouts of the bayonet charge were more than the untrained patriots could stand. Out of ammunition, a few militiamen bravely stood against the British and used their rifles and muskets as clubs, but it was futile. Others fled outright. Without bayonets, training, or discipline to stand by their officers, it was an unequal fight. The patriots could not match the British steel for steel and did not have the training required to hold a defensive position as a unit. Colonel Prescott stood his ground and was killed by a British bayonet in the melee. In the fury and confusion of the bayonet attack the militia's defense of Breed's Hill dissolved. The surviving patriots fled in full retreat. Led by the courageous Dr. Warren, small clumps of patriots held together to attempt to cover the retreat, but a volley from British muskets cut Warren down and a final push of British bayonets broke the patriot's resolve. Knox tried to rally his men, but it was pointless. No one was listening. He barely escaped with his life.

Exhausted from their climb and horrified by the casualties from the difficult attack in the face of withering fire, the British did not pursue the fleeing militia very far. As the smoke cleared on the battlefield, the British counted their dead and recovered their wounded. Several wounded patriots were bayoneted on the spot as the British were in no mood to show mercy. Although the British won the three-hour battle, it was one of the deadliest of the war and the Redcoats were in a foul mood. The British took Breed's Hill at the cost of 226 British soldiers and 19 officers killed and 828 wounded, from a force of 2,200 men, a casualty rate of 38 percent. General Howe was the only officer among his field staff who was not wounded, and he was covered in blood. Officers had been shot all around him. General Gage called the fighting for Breed's Hill, "A dear bought victory, another such would have ruined us."

In the Battle of Bunker Hill, as the combat for Breed's Hill became known, the patriots suffered 115 killed and 305 wounded from a force of 1,500 defenders, but 70 percent of the force retreated to fight another day. Despite departing the field in broken order, the Massachusetts militiamen took pride in the fact that they stood up to the British in battle and made the Redcoats pay dearly for their victory. The fledgling patriot army had proven itself in a true stand-up fight and vowed to do better the next time. The British, especially General Howe, were horrified at their losses. Howe vowed to avoid future frontal attacks against fortified patriot positions at all costs.

Due to the heavy casualties and his failure to break the siege of Boston, Gage was removed from command and replaced by General Howe. In his report to King George, General Gage declared "a large army must at length be employed to reduce these people." Gage also recommended that a large enough force would require "the hiring of foreign troops."

The Battle of Bunker Hill was a moral victory for the patriots. They had proven they could stand up to the best of the British Army. For Henry Knox it was a baptism of fire, and he learned a very valuable lesson: they would not beat the British in battle until they increased their firepower, training, and discipline. The best way to do this was to create and train a corps of artillery. With few forges in the Thirteen Colonies capable of making cannon barrels, the question was where could the fledgling patriot army find cannon?

On June 14, 1775, the Second Continental Congress in Philadelphia voted to create the Continental Army out of the militia units around Boston. The next day Congress appointed Congressman George Washington of Virginia as commanding general. Washington respectfully accepted the challenge, declared that he would serve without pay, and stated that he felt himself unworthy to the task ahead, but would do his duty to his utmost. He set off to create an American Army and lead it against the British in Boston. On July 3, 1775, Washington arrived at Boston and took command of all American forces.

After the Battle of Bunker Hill, the British occupied Boston but patriot militia still surrounded the town and prevented the British forces any means of movement except by sea. Washington's first tactical move was to reinforce the siege defenses around Boston with improved earthworks. Under Washington's careful supervision, trenches and strong redoubts were sited and speedily constructed. As the earthworks advanced, the British realized their position on Bunker and Breed's hills gave them no advantage and withdrew their men back to Boston. Washington quickly reoccupied Breed's Hill, enhanced the defenses there, and extended his siege line.

As vital as improving the defenses was to the patriot cause, weapons, ammunition, and gunpowder were even more needed commodities if Washington expected to push the British out of Boston. He requested supplies of muskets, ammunition, and gunpowder from Congress, but there was no organization to support these requests. Supplies trickled in from the other colonies, but the most powerful battlefield weapon—field cannons—was wanting. With only a few small artillery pieces, the newly formed Continental Army could only depend on muskets, shovels, and courage to defeat the British. Washington knew he needed more; he desperately needed more and heavier artillery.

Henry Knox was well aware that artillery was an essential ingredient of eighteenth century battle. Muskets and rifles fired at close range could cause tremendous numbers of casualties against unprotected enemy infantry, but the firepower of muskets and rifles paled against that of cannon. Artillery was the greatest killer on the battlefield. At far range, cannon balls could smash down defenses and sink ships. At close range a case shot, or canister, a shell consisting of small projectiles or nails that had the effect of a large shotgun shell, could wipe out an entire rank of enemy infantry. The American siege of Boston would not succeed without cannons and Washington's Continental Army could not win without artillery.

Knox sought an audience with Gen. Washington and in short order they had gained a mutual respect. Knox was inspired by the general's calm, confident, and determined personality. Standing six-foot-three, dressed in a splendid blue-coated uniform, with piercing blue-gray eyes, Washington not only looked like a leader, but acted the part. Washington's firm grasp of the military situation, his leadership and exemplary character exceeded Knox's expectations. In Washington, Knox had found a role model. Washington was similarly impressed with Knox's understanding of military affairs, particularly with his knowledge of artillery.

Washington was creating an army from scratch and had problems that needed solving in every department. The discipline, training, supplies, field sanitation, and leadership of his enthusiastic but amateur troops were a constant concern. His officers were just as devoted to the cause as the men *and* were just as unlearned in the art of war. Washington knew that he needed to train a professional army to oppose the British and he knew that he would have to do so without the luxury of a break from the fighting. He desperately needed officers with an understanding of the art and science of war who could lead men in battle. When his artillery commander became ill, Washington looked for a man with knowledge and energy to lead his artillery. On November 8, 1775, Washington wrote to Congress asking them to appoint Knox artillery commander of the Continental Army and recommended his promotion to the rank of colonel. Although nearly all of Knox's understanding of war was self-taught, his reputation for remaining cool under fire and his knowledge of artillery quickly advanced him to a key position on Washington's staff.

As summer passed into fall, the siege of Boston became a stalemate; the British were unwilling to attack and the Continental Army was unable to launch a successful all-out assault. Washington hoped for another defensive battle, another Bunker Hill, but Howe was unwilling to risk his troops in an attack against rebel defenses. By November 1775, when it was clear that

Washington did not have the artillery needed to break the stalemate, Colonel Knox approached the general with a plan to get some cannon.

Shortly after the skirmish at Lexington and Concord, a small patriot force called the Green Mountain Boys led by Ethan Allen, linked up with a Colonel Benedict Arnold, and boldly attacked the strongest fortress in North America, Fort Ticonderoga, which is located at the south end of Lake Champlain in upstate New York. The fort was held by a token force of British defenders, but contained the largest armory of cannons anywhere in America. Ethan Allen and the Green Mountain Boys quickly overpowered the British and captured the fort.

Inside Fort Ticonderoga they captured sixty cannons of various calibers and sotres of ammunition. Knox had learned of this cache and realized that if these captured guns could be sighted on the heights around Boston, they could drive the British fleet out of Boston harbor. That would leave the British garrison without hope of resupply and reinforcement, and unable to withdraw.

Knox met with Washington and recommended that he go to Fort Ticonderoga and haul as many cannon as he could from the fort to Boston. Washington enthusiastically agreed. He believed that if anyone could drag the guns from Fort Ticonderoga to Boston, it would be Henry Knox.

There was a slight problem with this idea. Fort Ticonderoga is located more than three hundred miles from Boston. There were no major roads along the route and few bridges across the numerous waterways that would have to be crossed. In many cases, there were no roads or bridges at all. There was also no readily available means of transport. To add to the challenge, winter was fast approaching.

On November 17, 1775, the twenty-five-year-old bookseller, newly promoted to brevet colonel in the Continental Army by George Washington, pending the approval of Congress, headed off for Fort Ticonderoga on horseback accompanied by his nineteen-year-old brother, William. He carried with him $1,000 in freshly printed Continental currency and a note from General Washington to Gen. Philip J. Schuyler. The Continental Congress had placed Schuyler in command of the militia in the area designated as the Northern Department of New York in what is now upstate New York. In the letter Washington asked Schuyler to assist Knox in his quest for the cannons.

The trees were bare and a cold wind blew from the north as the riders traveled to Fort Ticonderoga; two men on a mission that could decide the fate of the American cause. They headed to New York City and then rode north along the Hudson River, making good progress. On December 4, a heavy snowstorm slowed their progress as they reached Fort George, just south of Lake George, and only a day's journey from Fort Ticonderoga. At Fort George, Knox's organizational skills immediately kicked in and he worked with the Continental Army garrison to arrange for men, sleds, oxen, and supplies to haul the guns from Ticonderoga to Boston.

When Knox arrived at Ticonderoga on December 5, he selected fifty-nine cannons for transport, including a number of 11-foot guns that weighed five thousand pounds each. He also took a large supply of several tons of heavy cannonballs, twenty-three hundred pounds of bullet lead, and thirty thousand gunflints from the fort's arsenal. The total weight of the cannon and ball he intended to drag to Boston was nearly sixty tons. All of it would have to be placed on dugout boats and canoes, shipped across Lake George and then loaded onto large wooden sleds to be pulled by teams of oxen or draft horses.

To say that this was a monumental task would be a gross understatement, yet Knox proceeded undaunted. He energetically planned every step of the move, coordinated support, led by example, and made things happen. As the temperature dropped and more snow fell, the foul weather became a major problem. Forest trails turned to ice and his men had to lower the heavy guns down steep hills using ropes and pulleys to slow their descent. Icy streams and creeks, swollen with rain and snow, had to be planned for and boats had to be carried forward to float the guns across. Few of Knox's men could swim. In the icy waters the chances of survival after immersion were low. Knox personally directed each water crossing and carefully looked after each cannon. The work was dangerous, cold, and slow.

Knox's column spread out quite a distance, one sled behind the other, as it inched south from Fort Ticonderoga, to Fort George, to Saratoga, to Albany, to Claversack, to Springfield, to Cambridge. Knox called his column the "noble train of artillery." Progressing about six miles a day, the sleds made deliberate and steady progress. Knox overcame one adversity after another. When his men would go no further, he halted, built fires to warm them, and, once they were rested and warm, inspired them to keep going, telling them that the entire patriot cause was in their hands. When the weather grew colder, the sledding got a bit easier as the ground hardened. But the trip that Knox thought would take a few weeks turned into a fifty-six-day ordeal.

At one point near Albany the river ice was too thin to cross and there were no alternate routes. Knox halted the column and in the evening, augured holes in the ice. As water rushed up it covered the ice and began to freeze. Just before sunrise, the ice was thick enough for his column to cross. In spite of his precautions a few of the heavily laden sleds cracked through the ice. Knox stopped the column and dredged up the ordnance from the icy river bottom. He kept a meticulous diary and noted: "Went on the Ice About 8 oClock in the morning & proceeded so cautiously that before night we got over three sleds & were so lucky as to get the Cannon out of the River, owing to the assistance the good people of the City of Albany gave, in return for which we christen'd her—The Albany."

Nothing was going to stop Henry Knox from bringing the cannons to General Washington. Knox and his brother arrived at Boston with all fifty-nine cannons and several loads of cannon balls, lead, and gun flints on January 24, 1776. Throughout the difficult and exhausting journey he had not lost a single piece of artillery. When Knox reported to an admiring General Washington in Cambridge, his fellow officers greeted him with admiration and applause. He also learned that Congress had officially approved his promotion to colonel. Still, Knox did not stop long to rest. He got to work placing the guns to support Washington's goal of driving the British from Boston. Within days of the arrival of the "noble train of artillery," Knox had expertly placed the cannons at key points to engage the British in Boston and aimed them at British ships in the harbor. By March 2 the guns were supplied with powder and shot. Then Knox began the bombardment of Boston and any British ships that ventured into range. During the night of March 4, Knox's men manhandled their heaviest cannons onto Dorchester Heights, a piece of key terrain overlooking Boston harbor, and emplaced ingeniously crafted improvised entrenchments using fascine baskets made of sticks and wicker that where then formed into a wall and filled with earth. The next morning the British saw the American heavy artillery emplaced in strong defensive positions on the high ground overlooking the city, commanding the town and Boston harbor. Overnight, the Americans had done what seemed to the British to be impossible. The British had two options: attack and seize Dorchester Heights, resetting the same conditions as the attack on Breeds Hill and the horrendous casualties that ensued, or ask General Washington for terms. Howe realized that the casualties he would suffer to take Dorchester Heights and capture Knox's cannon would be higher than the men he had lost in the fight to take Breeds Hill. Not only were the rebels defending behind strong earthworks, now they had cannon. As Howe vacillated the weather changed and a violent storm swept over Boston, making any movement by boat nearly impossible. Within a few days, General Howe acknowledged that any further defense of Boston was futile and offered Washington terms to withdraw his men.

Howe proposed that his army would depart Boston by ship and would not torch the city if Washington let his men depart without any shooting. Washington, not wanting to see Boston razed and its population put in jeopardy, agreed. More importantly, Washington knew that his army was woefully short of gunpowder. The new American nation, with no treasury and a total lack of military industrial structure, did not have the means to supply Washington's army. Unbeknown to the British, Washington only had enough gunpowder for a few shots from each cannon and not enough to bombard the British out of Boston. Knox's cannons were mostly bluff.

Washington agreed to terms. On March 17, Saint Patrick's Day, eighty-nine hundred British soldiers and eleven hundred loyalists boarded British ships and left Boston for Nova Scotia. Gen. Washington had won a brilliant victory and driven the British from Boston. He reported to Congress that the liberation of Boston was largely due to the energetic efforts of a portly, twenty-five-year old bookseller named Henry Knox. Knox's achievement of securing and transporting the cannons and supplies from Fort Ticonderoga to Boston and placing the guns on Dorchester Heights demonstrated his boldness, determination, expertise, and creative mind. Most importantly, it vindicated Washington's faith in selecting a leader so young and inexperienced

Washington's victory brought hope and renewed spirit to the cause of Liberty. It is clear that without the victory at Boston in March 1776, the idea of American independence and the signing of a Declaration of Independence a mere four months later in July 1776 would never have happened.

—◆◆◆—

LEADERSHIP LESSONS FROM HENRY KNOX

- **Leadership Begins with Study:** Henry Knox was a bookseller by profession and a life-long learner. Like many of the leaders of the American Revolution, Henry Knox was an autodidact, spending hours in self-directed learning. He devoured information about anything that interested him, especially anything relating to the military. He learned almost exclusively about artillery and cannon from his self-study of British books. He secured the latest books that contained the detailed information he required. He researched the selected subject and mastered that information. He learned the art of fortification, the building of earthworks, and military drill, and became the preeminent expert on artillery in America, all from books he purchased at his own expense. He practiced with whatever was at hand, as a leader in the local militia or by talking with British soldiers prior to the Revolution about artillery drills and tactics. He also learned on the job, listened to experts who had more skill than he did, and never let his lack of expertise stop him from learning. Today, with a plethora of available books and access to the Internet you have an unlimited free library at your fingertips. Take a cue from Henry Knox and raise your leadership quotient by studying leadership. Make leadership studies a part of your own self-directed learning program. If you want to become an effective leader, study and master the skills that you will need to be effective in your efforts.

- **Determination to Succeed Is the Price of Success:** The ancient Carthaginian military genius Hannibal is credited with saying, "We will either find a way, or make one!" Hannibal crossed the Alps Mountains in winter in 218 B.C. with a Carthaginian army and thirty-seven war elephants. No army had ever before crossed the Alps in winter. Hannibal was determined and to the great surprise of his Roman enemy successfully made the passage. Hannibal's exhortation could just as well have been Henry Knox's. During the difficult trek from Fort Ticonderoga to Boston, Knox never faltered. In every case he found a way to motivate his men to overcome the difficult and make the impossible possible. Like Hannibal, Knox overcame geography and weather through leadership and determination. Initially, Knox believed it would take two weeks to retrieve the cannon, but it took more than six weeks. In spite of the delay and the arduous effort required to move heavy cannon by boat and sled across extremely difficult terrain, Knox persisted. Historian Victor Brooks, who penned the book *The Boston Campaign* called the transportation of the guns from Fort Ticonderoga to Boston "one of the most stupendous feats of logistics" of the entire war. If you want to succeed, take on the motto of Hannibal and the actions of Knox and "Find a way or make one!"
- **Think Out of the Box:** Henry Knox was only twenty-five years old when he proposed the plan to Washington to lead an effort to secure guns from Fort Ticonderoga in the dead of winter. There were more senior and experienced leaders in the young American army, but Knox was the man who came up with the idea, crafted a plan, and convinced Washington to back him. The extraordinary accomplishment of moving his "noble train of

artillery" across such a vast distance under such difficult circumstances required creative problem solving of the highest order. When his sleds could not cross frozen rivers because the ice was too thin, Knox solved the problem. He bored holes in the ice, allowing water to come up from below, and freeze overnight, thereby increasing the thickness enough for his sleds to cross over. *This is thinking out of the box!* If you want to lead effectively, remember the grit that Henry Knox demonstrated in transporting the cannons from Fort Ticonderoga to Boston. Like Knox, think of new ways to accomplish your task and don't be afraid to try what hasn't been done before.

- **Leaders Must Have a Positive Attitude:** Few people will follow a pessimist for long. If you believe you can't do something, and put that in your head as a fact, then you are probably right. On the other hand, the first step to finding a way to do something is to believe you can. A positive approach is vital in leading any team. Teams need inspiration and the leader's attitude can quickly become the attitude of the group. Henry Knox had an infectious, positive attitude. He firmly believed he could retrieve the cannons from Fort Ticonderoga regardless of the difficulties. Many of his contemporaries, whom we might call average men, thought this was an impossible task. Henry Knox, however, wasn't average. He was determined and was sure he could succeed. When he started on his journey he had with him only his younger brother, a letter of authorization, and a small amount of nearly worthless paper Continental currency: two men, two horses, a letter, and some funny-money to facilitate dragging sixty tons of cannons and ammunition over three hundred miles across icy hills, mountain passes, and frozen rivers. Yet, he fully expected to develop the situation as he went along. His positive attitude fueled his drive to succeed and helped him create a vision for success. Henry Knox believed in only one possible outcome: *Success!* His positive attitude was crucial to overcoming a mountain of troubles and inspired those he met and enlisted in the effort. When his men's spirits lagged he found ways to urge them on. When they were cold, he made sure they got warm. If you wish to lead, take on a positive attitude in all things as Henry Knox did. Believe that you cannot succeed, and you will generally prove yourself right. Firmly believe that you can do the task and you have half the game already won.
- **Choose Leaders Based on Merit:** Leaders come in all shapes and sizes. If Henry Knox had been a book, you would be wise not to judge him by his cover. Knox wouldn't make it today as the hero in a Hollywood movie, but

he played a vital role in securing American Liberty. Plainly put, Henry Knox was fat. He was known as "Fat Henry Knox." He stood six feet tall but weighed over 250 pounds. That didn't matter to George Washington. Washington selected Fat Henry Knox as a leader and made him a colonel because of the merit of his ideas, the strength of his determination, and his loyalty to the cause of Liberty. Washington needed leaders who were willing to step up and take on responsibility forming an army. Nearly everyone in the fledgling American army was new to this trade, and there were very few experienced soldiers within General Washington's ranks. Washington didn't need dandies, he could find plenty of them. Washington needed leaders. Knox's merit, determination, and loyalty were more important than anything else. When you select leaders, keep that in mind.

A depiction of (left to right) Franklin, Adams, and Jefferson working on the Declaration of Independence (painting by Jean Leon Gerome Ferris, 1900).

Chapter 4

OUR LIVES, OUR FORTUNES, AND OUR SACRED HONOR

The Collaboration of Benjamin Franklin, John Adams, and Thomas Jefferson

---

When in the Course of human events it becomes necessary for one people to dissolve the political bonds which have connected them with another and to assume among the powers of the earth, the separate and equal station to which the Laws of Nature and of Nature's God entitle them, a decent respect to the opinions of mankind requires that they should declare the causes which impel them to the separation. The Preamble of the Declaration of Independence, signed July 4, 1776

LEADERSHIP REQUIRES *PERSUASION, VISION,* AND *A TALENT FOR COMMUNICATION.*

The British withdrawal from Boston was not the end of the colonies' war for independence, far from it. While the patriots euphorically celebrated their success at Boston, the British brooded and schemed how to reconquer Massachusetts and maintain control of their other American colonies. Having expected a quick victory, King George did what most kings do after things go badly: fire someone. He replaced Gen. Thomas Gage with Gen. William Howe.

Howe, an influential member of the British parliament, was considered by many British soldiers to be the best commander in the British Army. He believed that the key to controlling the American colonies was winning New York, not Boston. In the summer of 1776 Howe made preparations to crush the rebellion with overwhelming force. The largest invasion force Britain had ever assembled headed for New York harbor. General Howe was determined to land an army in New York, smash the colonial rabble in arms and bring the leaders of the insurrection to England in chains. He expected to end the rebellion in one good season of campaigning.

The only impediment to Howe's plans was Gen. George Washington's newly formed Continental Army.

By British standards Washington's force was hardly an army but it was the best the colonies could produce in such a short time. It was entirely composed of proud self-reliant men willing to fight. Washington's band of enthusiastic volunteers was determined to resist invasion. Washington knew that defeating the vaunted British Army, supported by the powerful Royal Navy, was a lot to ask of his men, especially if they were fighting merely for reconciliation with Great Britain. Why fight for half-measures? Why risk your life in battle against the most powerful force in the world just to continue living under the rule of a despotic sovereign and an unjust Parliament? Was that a cause worth sacrificing, fighting or dying for?

What the situation required was a dramatic break from Great Britain and a statement of the causes that explained the reasons for that dissolution. Patrick Henry had articulated the concept clearly. What was on the lips of nearly every patriot who held a rifle or musket in Washington's army was the word "*Independence!*"

The Second Continental Congress met in June in Philadelphia. One of the pressing issues was how to proceed. Should the colonies declare independence from the mother country or should they seek reconciliation?

The drafting and subsequent approval of the Declaration of Independence is a remarkable story of leadership. The document was crafted in just three weeks and the extraordinary "Declaration" would not exist today but for the preeminent leadership of three men.

The consideration of a declaration of colonial independence from Great Britain was a monumental idea, contrary to the dictates of conventional thought and world history. The idea was *revolutionary*. For the delegates to the Second Continental Congress it was unnerving, dangerous, and an act of desperation. Kings, czars, sultans, emperors and shoguns ruled the great civilizations of the world. The notion that provincial New World colonists would attempt to overturn the traditional political order of the Old World's most powerful empire with full intent to rule themselves was nothing short of astonishing. To openly and unashamedly call attention to that position in a published document was a declaration of treason in the eyes of the British king and Parliament.

As we have seen in previous chapters, the journey toward American independence and liberty was a long one. It began with the founding of the first colonies and continued through the serious mishandling of colonial affairs following the French and Indian Wars (1763–1764) and the imposition upon them of British taxes including The Revenue Act (sugar tax of 1764), the Quartering Act (1765), the Stamp Act (1766), The Townshend Acts (1767), the Tea Act (1773), the Boston Massacre (March 5, 1770), the Boston Tea Party (1773), the Intolerable Acts (1774), and the garrisoning of Boston by four regiments of British troops (1774). Understandably the idea of independence was well advanced by the time the First Continental Congress met at Carpenter's Hall in Philadelphia, Pennsylvania in 1774.

Once the first shots were fired at Lexington and Concord in April 1775, it appeared to many Americans that any hope of reconciliation with Great Britain was futile. Thomas Paine captured that sentiment in his wildly popular pamphlet *Common Sense*, wherein he passionately explained America's cause against British rule, argued for independence, and laid out a continental charter of union. He said, "No man was a warmer wisher for reconciliation than myself, before the fatal nineteenth of April, 1775 (Massacre at Lexington), but the moment the event of that day was made known, I rejected the hardened, sullen tempered Pharaoh of England for ever; and disdain the wretch, that with the pretended title of Father of his people, can unfeelingly hear of their slaughter, and composedly sleep with their blood upon his soul."

On August 23, 1775, the king pushed many loyal colonists into the patriot camp when he issued "A Proclamation by the King for Suppressing Rebellion and Sedition." The proclamation decreed that any colony in open rebellion with the King's authority was considered traitorous and would be dealt with accordingly. Furthermore, the rebellion would be suppressed by force. The die was cast. The official break with the Old World was only a matter of time, though the outcome of such a break was as yet unknown.

With sentiment among Americans mounting against British rule, the Second Continental Congress looked to the future. Something had to be done to establish the legitimacy of the American cause. Repeated petitions to the Crown had been rejected, but what should they do?

On May 4, 1776, the General Assembly of the Colony of Rhode Island declared independence from Great Britain. Virginia followed Rhode Island's lead. The mood for independence was growing but at least a third of all the people in the Thirteen Colonies wanted to remain a part of the British Empire. With some colonies declaring independence and others not, the British might try to pit one against the other in a strategy of divide and conquer. What was needed to strengthen the cause was a powerful treatise for independence that would bring all of the colonies into one united confederation of states.

A committed group of men in the Continental Congress pushed the argument for declaring the independence of the united colonies. On June 7, 1776, Richard Henry Lee of Virginia offered a resolution "that these United Colonies, are, and of right ought to be, free and independent states." John Adams seconded the motion, but due to the uncertainty of the positions of many delegates, the vote was delayed for three weeks. On June 11, Adams suggested that a committee be formed to write down grievances and explain the case for independence. The motion carried and a five-member committee was formed to prepare a paper: Benjamin Franklin, John Adams, Thomas Jefferson, Roger Sherman, and Robert Livingston. The committee appointed Jefferson to create the first draft. The draft was then edited by the other committee members and was submitted to Congress on June 28. Thirty-nine changes were made to the final document.

Overall, the Declaration of Independence was the end product of the cooperation and agreement of fifty-six men who were lawyers, jurists, merchants, farmers, and large plantation owners. The *reason* it was created was largely due to the preeminent leadership of three of the fifty-six: Franklin, Adams, and Jefferson. Franklin persuaded the delegates to work together; Adams supplied the vision for independence, and Jefferson provided an unparalleled talent for written communication.

Benjamin Franklin persuaded the delegates to work together. The prestige of this self-made Renaissance man, who was a worldwide celebrity, cannot be overstated. Franklin was a successful printer, author, publisher, entrepreneur, scientist, inventor, philosopher, politician, postal chief, team-builder, and much more. He had mastered five languages, all self-taught and was one of the wealthiest men in America. He was also a master diplomat, one of the most creative thinkers of the eighteenth century and, until 1770, an ardent supporter of the British Empire.

Unlike many of the American-born delegates to the Second Continental Congress, Franklin had lived in England, was personally acquainted with many influential British leaders, and traveled in circles that were usually restricted to the aristocracy.

He was serving in London as an agent of the Massachusetts legislature when news arrived of the Boston Tea Party. On January 29, 1774, Franklin was officially summoned before the Privy Council, a formal body of advisers to the king. The issue was as much about the growing American rebellion in Massachusetts as it was about the private letters from Royal Governor Hutchinson that Franklin had provided to patriots in Boston and Sam Adams had made public. The letters concerned the governor's belief that American liberties must be curtailed to prevent rebellion. Franklin stood erect, in silence, in the "cockpit" of the Privy Council for an hour as the king's solicitor-general excoriated him for making these private letters public. This episode was a defining moment for Franklin. Following this incident, when Franklin returned to Philadelphia in 1775, he become an ardent revolutionary, and worked to turn opinion in Pennsylvania against King George and Parliament.

King George responded to the Boston Tea Party exploits by asking Parliament to pass laws that became known in America as the Intolerable Acts. The Port Act closed Boston harbor until Bostonians paid for the tea destroyed in the Boston Tea Party. Other laws restricted the rights of the citizens of Massachusetts and granted the Crown dictatorial powers.

Two weeks after the skirmishes at Lexington and Concord, the Pennsylvania legislature chose Franklin as a delegate to the Second Continental Congress.

In June 1776, as the senior member of the declaration committee, Franklin declined the job of writing the declaration and passed the task to Adams and Jefferson. He was seventy years old and told them that he had vowed to refrain from writing anything that was expected to be edited by others. Instead, in the final weeks of 1776 Franklin focused his energy and skills on supporting the cause of independence and the approval of the declaration, first by establishing trust among his fellow delegates and then by convincing them to join in the vote for independence.

Using his distinctive style of optimism, charisma, clever wit and keen sense of human nature, Franklin quietly won over those delegates who were apprehensive about openly declaring independence. Perhaps Franklin's most significant edit to Jefferson's draft was to change the phrase "sacred and undeniable" to "self-evident." After signing the Declaration of Independence, Franklin was quoted as saying: "There must be no pulling different ways. We must all hang together, or assuredly we shall all hang separately."

John Adams supplied the vision and oratory for independence. The pugnacious Adams was a firm believer in the cause of independence and one of its greatest champions. He was convinced that all ties with Great Britain must be severed in order to secure Liberty for Americans and the sooner those ties were broken, the better. He tirelessly articulated a clear vision of an American government established *by* Americans and *for* Americans. In later years, recognition of Adams's unflinching and ceaseless crusading for the cause of independence caused him to be dubbed the "Atlas of Independence."

In 1765, eleven years before the Declaration of Independence, Adams wrote: "[L]iberty must at all hazards be supported. We have a right to it, derived from our Maker. But if we had not, our fathers have earned and bought it for us, at the expense of their ease, their estates, their pleasure, and their blood."

Adams knew his own limitations, particularly those displayed by his direct and earthy style. He had scrutinized Thomas Jefferson ever since the thirty-three-year-old Virginian had arrived in Philadelphia that June. Earlier that year Jefferson had written "A Summary View of the Rights of British America." Adams had read Jefferson's work, approved of his talents as a writer and knew they were superior to his own and to those of his fellow committee members.

Adams's letters, which were published in 1850, explain it like this:

> When Jefferson proposed to me to make the draft I said, "I will not," "You should do it." "Oh! no." "Why will you not? You ought to do it." "I will not." "Why?" "Reasons enough." "What can be your reasons?" "Reason first, you are a Virginian, and a Virginian ought to appear at the head of this business. Reason second, I am obnoxious, suspected, and unpopular. You are very much otherwise. Reason third, you can write ten times better than I can." "Well," said Jefferson, "if you are decided, I will do as well as I can." "Very well. When you have drawn it up, we will have a meeting."

Once the declaration was edited, in the debate that followed Adams was its most vocal supporter. In a letter written in 1813, Thomas Jefferson acknowledged John Adams's role in securing the adoption of the Declaration of Independence: "No man better merited, than Mr. John Adams to hold a most conspicuous place in the design. He was the pillar of its support on the floor of Congress, its ablest advocate and defender against the multifarious assaults it encountered. For many excellent persons opposed it on doubts whether we were provided sufficiently with the means of supporting it, whether the minds of our constituents were yet prepared to receive it & etc. [sic.] who after it was decided, united zealously in the measures it called for."

The day after the adoption of the Declaration of Independence, John Adams wrote to his wife Abigail: "Yesterday, the greatest question was decided that was ever debated in America; and greater, perhaps, never was or will be decided among men. A resolution was passed, without one dissenting colony, 'That these United States are, and of right ought to be free and independent states.'... I am well aware of the toil, and blood, and treasure that it will cost to maintain this declaration, and support and defend these states; yet through all the gloom, I can see the rays of light and glory. I can see that the end is worth more than all the means; and that posterity will triumph, although you and I may rue, which I hope we shall not."

Thomas Jefferson's brilliant talent for composition was employed to its fullest to provide the most important, single document of the American Revolution. Jefferson was a quiet and sensitive man. He was not an effective orator, but as Franklin and Adams recognized, he excelled at the written word. More than just a writer, Jefferson was a voracious reader and had earned a reputation as an authority on the law, political philosophy, and world history. He possessed an enlightened understanding of the rights of man, the principles of liberty, and the meaning of political independence. In drafting the Declaration of Independence he meticulously communicated in imperishable language the conditions for revolution, explained the cause for separation, and offered facts to prove the tyranny of the sovereign.

Jefferson worked diligently between June 11 and June 28, 1776, to complete the first draft. Benjamin Franklin and John Adams made corrections and edits. The document went through three stages: the original draft by Jefferson; changes made by Franklin and Adams submitted to the committee of five, and the final version that was edited and adopted by Congress.

Jefferson reasoned from self-evident principles of government and articulated the cause for liberty, equality, and the right to self-determination. He stated that the declaration was an "expression of the American mind." The declaration also listed what Samuel Adams called George III's "Catalogue of Crimes" against the people of America, laying each abuse of power at the foot of the king. Although Jefferson denounced the slave trade in his original document, his ideas did not survive the debate and sadly, in order to gain unanimity, were struck from the final document.

The Declaration of Independence signified the establishment of self-government in America and laid the foundation for the establishment of a republic. It was a vital first step for liberty for all Americans. It established a new nation of *free people*. It declared that the colonies were free and independent states, no longer part of the British Empire. It masterfully outlined the principles of free government. It dignified the American Revolution as a proclamation of principle against a tyranny that oppressed the rights of man. It designated the Thirteen Colonies as one American nation and one people, separate from the people of the British Empire. It is a remarkable document that continues to inspire us today as the embodiment of the American spirit, and beckons us to continue the epic struggle for individual liberty for all people, regardless of race, color, creed or sex. We should rededicate ourselves to the principles of liberty and always remember that our freedoms have been purchased at the cost of much blood, sweat, toil and tears.

THE DECLARATION IS PRESENTED

With a clean break from Great Britain as their goal, the pro-independence delegates waged a difficult political struggle to revise Congressional instructions to ensure that the delegates of the Second Continental Congress had the authority from their colonies to vote for independence.

Once the Declaration was written, more hard work had to be accomplished to secure its unanimous approval by the delegates. During the last week of June 1776, John Adams, Benjamin Franklin, and many other delegates of the Second Continental Congress went into overdrive prior to the vote on independence. They were determined to convince the delegates to turn toward the cause of declaring independence from Great Britain. Georgia, Massachusetts, North Carolina, Vermont, and Virginia were firmly behind Independence. So the main effort was focused on winning over the middle colonies of New York, New Jersey, Maryland, Pennsylvania, and Delaware. Franklin was suffering from a bad attack of gout and was absent from many of the sessions during the first three weeks of June. He asked Thomas McKean (March 19, 1734–June 24, 1817), an influential Pennsylvania lawyer and a delegate from Delaware to the Continental Congress, to help bring Delaware on board.

The effort to bring Delaware to vote for independence is an example of what it took behind the scenes to secure the vote. Delegations to the Continental Congress from the colonies consisted of anywhere from two to seven men. Delaware had three delegates: Thomas McKean (March 19, 1734–June

24, 1817), George Read (September 18, 1733–September 21, 1798) and Caesar Rodney (October 7, 1728–June 26, 1784). A majority vote of the delegates of any colony was required to cast a vote. Caesar Rodney was ardent for independence, but because of his military experience he was away in Dover countering loyalist raids in Sussex County when he received word from McKean that he and Read were unexpectedly deadlocked on the vote for independence. Rodney, who was in poor health and suffering from cancer, rode eighty miles to return to the Congress and vote yes. Thanks to McKean and Rodney, Delaware voted for independence.

Franklin then worked the members of his own Pennsylvania delegation, John Dickinson and Robert Morris. Franklin maneuvered Dickinson into abstaining and persuaded Morris to vote in favor of independence. Adams, Franklin, and others also convinced New Jersey and Maryland delegates to vote yes. That left the colonies of New York and South Carolina who could block a vote in favor of independence. How would they vote? New York was divided in its support for the declaration as it contained a large population of Tories, who favored reconciliation over revolution. South Carolina wavered over the issue of slavery.

There are no transcripts of what was said during the debates, but one can imagine Franklin whispering to the New York delegates: "Those who trade liberty for security have neither." Through persistence, persuasion, and compromise, the Declaration of Independence was unanimously adopted on July 2, with New York abstaining as their legislature had not yet authorized them to vote on independence as it had fled New York City as British forces approached on June 30. With the vote settled, Congress worked to finalize the wording of the declaration, which was approved and sent to the printer on July 4, 1776. The New York delegation signed a week later.

THE DECLARATION IS APPROVED

The men who signed the Declaration of Independence on a hot July day in Philadelphia knew that should the revolution fail they were signing their own death warrants. Nevertheless, on July 2, 1776, the declaration was unanimously adopted, with twelve colonies concurring and New York abstaining. President of the Congress John Hancock signed the document with an oversized signature so that even "fat King George can read it without his glasses." The other members of Congress signed the declaration as well, making it an official action of the Congress of the newly declared United States of America.

The concluding words of this masterful document have a power that still reaches us today and clearly shows what was at stake in 1776, what each generation of Americans might one day face to maintain their liberty:

> *For the support of this declaration, with the firm reliance on the protection of the Divine Providence, we mutually pledge to each other our lives, our fortunes, and our sacred honor.*

—————

LEADERSHIP LESSONS FROM BENJAMIN FRANKLIN, JOHN ADAMS AND THOMAS JEFFERSON IN THE PROCESS OF DECLARING INDEPENDENCE:

- **Teamwork Wins.** Effective teams *are* greater than the sum of their parts. The team of Franklin, Adams, and Jefferson, enthusiastic for the cause of independence, committed to a common purpose, and working together to apply their complementary skills, created one of the most powerful proclamations in the history of mankind. Although Jefferson was the primary writer and deserves credit for authorship, without the work of Franklin and Adams the Declaration of Independence would not have turned out as it did and might not have been adopted. Many American declarations against the Crown's rule had been written in 1775 and 1776, but this one was special. Under the direction of an effective team, Jefferson's seminal declaration evolved into America's exceptional Declaration of Independence.

- **Complex Tasks Often Require Collaborative Teamwork.** Some problems can be solved by individual genius, but many complex tasks require collaborative teams. The problem that Franklin, Adams, and Jefferson faced required that they selflessly combine their individual gifts to gain their ultimate goal. They had to think creatively and bring forth what had never before existed: a convincing argument made to a world ruled by kings and autocrats that would declare in clear language why their revolution was right and legal. Franklin delivered the political integration, persuasion, and coordination; Adams provided the passion, convincing oratory and grit; and Jefferson furnished the genius that transcribed one of the most important documents in history. Much more was needed than just superb writing and eloquent prose. The declaration had to be unanimously adopted by all the colonies represented at the Continental Congress. If one colony, for any reason, opposed, the declaration would not pass. Delegates had to be convinced that the declaration was the right step on the road to independence. Working together, each member of the team—Franklin, Adams and Jefferson—brought his special leadership and skills to the crafting *and* acceptance of the Declaration of Independence.

- **Develop a Clearly Defined Common Goal.** Franklin, Adams and Jefferson embraced a common quantifiable performance goal: independence. They had to state the purpose clearly and write an argument for independence that was so sharp and convincing that Congress would unanimously approve the document, take the daring step to declare independence from Great Britain, and convince all thirteen Congressional delegations to vote yes or abstain. They had to compromise to achieve this goal, but kept true to the ultimate goal, realizing that without first declaring independence, other freedoms could not occur.

- **Focus on Strengths, Not Weaknesses.** Franklin, Adams and Jefferson expertly employed their complementary skills to accomplish the task, focusing their individual strengths to accomplish the goal. Congress agreed that the vote for independence must be unanimous, that no colony could oppose the declaration. The delegates from New York and South Carolina were of particular concern as they had spoken against a hasty decision for independence. New York, with a significant Tory population and a British army bearing down on their capital city, hesitated to break from the mother country for fear of reprisals. South Carolina feared financial ruin if independence were declared. The New York and South Carolina delegations had to be converted to the cause, or persuaded to abstain, before the vote took place. Ben Franklin paved the way for the declaration's adoption and approval by quietly winning over the Congressional delegates one delegate at a time. Debating on the floor of the Congress, John Adams convincingly argued for the reasons that independence must be declared and championed each section during the editing process. Thomas Jefferson provided the "happy talent" for composition that drafted the masterpiece and distilled the arguments for independence into the eloquent prose that inspired a new nation and continues to inspire each new generation of Americans.

- **Use the Best Person for the Task.** Recognizing individual talent is a skill of effective leaders. Franklin, Adams, and Jefferson worked together, each applying their best talents in different areas to secure the vote for independence. Franklin, for example, was the consummate politician and persuader. He reacted swiftly and reached out to Thomas McKean, who was a native Pennsylvanian but a delegate from Delaware, to work with Caesar

Rodney to secure the Delaware vote. Quiet and introverted Thomas Jefferson was the person with the best skills to act as primary author of the declaration. John Adams set the conditions for success through political organization and oratory. Together, all three men were essential in leading the Congress to vote for independence.

- **Rely on Discussion and Persuasion Rather than Authority.** Adams, Franklin, and Jefferson knew that the members of the Continental Congress were the most accomplished people of their colonies. Each delegate was an accomplished lawyer, businessman, or politician and each delegate had strong views on the matter of breaking away from Great Britain. These men could not be ordered around like clerks, but had to be treated with respect, persuaded, and convinced. Understanding their points of view and gaining their trust was an important part of the job of securing the Declaration of Independence.

General George Washington after the Battle of Princeton
(painting by Charles Willson Peale, 1799).

Chapter 5

VICTORY OR DEATH! *Washington at the Battles of Trenton and Princeton*

If every nerve is not strained to recruit the New Army with all possible Expedition I think the game is pretty near up. . . . No Man I believe ever had a greater choice of difficulties & less the means of extricating himself than I have-However under a full persuasion of the justice of our Cause I cannot but think the prospect will brighten.—General George Washington in a letter to his brother Samuel on December 18, 1776

LEADERSHIP REQUIRES *DETERMINATION*.

The cause never looked more in doubt. Disaster. Defeat. Dishonor. These phantoms haunted Gen. George Washington as he rode his horse through the cold mud of a worn-out New Jersey thoroughfare and his depleted army marched to the Delaware River. He knew that some of his men doubted the capabilities of their commander and, considering the string of disasters they had endured, he couldn't blame them.

As the year 1776 came to a close, catastrophe loomed before the young American Republic. The army's spirit was nearly broken. Morale was teetering on the edge of an abyss dug ever deeper by defeats and retreats. Casualties were high and setbacks occurred everywhere. The fervent patriotism, which had burned bright in the spring and summer, cooled under the freezing winds of adversity. In some cases it was non-existent as some turned coat, sold their freedom for security and pledged their loyalty to Britain's King George.

After the British evacuation of Boston on March 26, 1776, Washington immediately moved his forces to New York to defend that important city from British attack. He ordered his men to prepare trenches and earthworks to defend Manhattan Island. America had bravely declared independence from Great Britain on July 4, 1776. The British read the declaration and came back with a vengeance.

During July and August, the British under General Howe, supported by a British fleet, landed thirty-two thousand British and Hessian regulars on Staten Island without a fight. By late August Washington had gathered a combined force of roughly eighteen thousand men, some who signed up to serve in the Continental Army for a six-month enlistment and militia soldiers who served a much shorter time and expected to make frequent trips home. They were untrained but enthusiastic volunteers. Strong defenses alone, however, are not sufficient to win wars.

On August 22, Gen. William Howe landed an unopposed force of twenty thousand British regulars and Hessian mercenaries on Long Island. As Howe marched his men northeast it became clear that the Americans had fortified the high ground. Howe had experienced the great cost of frontal attacks against rebel trenches at Bunker Hill (Breed's Hill) and made up his mind to find a way around the rebel defenses. Moving at night to an unguarded spot on the American left flank, Howe attacked and turned the American defenses. Outgeneraled, Washington barely staved off catastrophe by withdrawing his battered army to Brooklyn Heights. With his army penned up on the high ground at Brooklyn Heights and the British Navy controlling the water around Long Island, Howe's victorious troops appeared poised to destroy the American army.

But Washington coolly performed a miracle. He ordered Colonel John Glover's sturdy fishermen from Marblehead, Massachusetts, known as Marbleheaders, to collect every craft that could float. During the pitch-dark night of August 29–30, Washington ordered his rear guard to build the campfires high to deceive the British and make every indication that the army was digging-in and preparing for a tough defense of Brooklyn Heights.

Quietly, while the British army rested in preparation for battle in the morning, the Americans thinned their lines, and moved to boats waiting for them along the shore of the East River. Glover's militiamen were expert boat handlers and rowed the army safely across the river to Manhattan right under the noses of the British Navy. When Howe's men attacked Brooklyn Heights on the morning of August 30, they found nothing but empty trenches. The American army, numbering about nine thousand, had escaped without losing a man!

Howe was astonished that Washington had escaped, but rather than launching a vigorous pursuit he paused, possibly because he thought the

Americans were beaten and would just melt away. Washington's leadership ability at this time became indispensable and it was clear to those who fought with him that he was the only person who could hold the rag-tag American Army together. In mid-September he won a narrow defensive victory at Harlem Heights in New York when the British infantry buglers sounded the fox hunting call "gone away" and so insulted the Americans by this act—the hunting call was used to signal that the fox was running away—that Washington turned about and forced the British to retreat. A month later at White Plains the American forces were defeated, which coupled with a later defeat at Fort Washington, resulted in their retreat into New Jersey.

By November 19 Gen. Lord Charles Cornwallis had forced American Maj. Gen. Nathanael Green's army to evacuate Fort Lee, the last American stronghold on the Hudson River in New Jersey. The evacuation of Fort Lee on November 19, 1776, was a debacle that left behind large stores of sorely needed supplies and munitions. Washington was forced to retreat farther into New Jersey toward Pennsylvania. It was clear to Washington and his generals that his untrained recruits and militia were no match for the superbly trained British and Hessian troops. By December 1776, the unhappy Continental Army appeared to be permanently beaten and it looked as if the Glorious Cause of Liberty was destined to be skewered on the cold and deadly steel of British and German bayonets. Disaster, defeat, and dishonor loomed.

As the six-foot-three-inch General Washington rode alongside his tired, bedraggled troops, he reviewed the events of the past few months. There was very little to feel good about. His army was on the run, his supplies were nearly exhausted and the cause of Liberty seemed an impossible dream. His senior officers, Generals Horatio Gates and Henry Lee, openly criticized his generalship and remarked to their officers that Washington was unfit for command. With the British expected to attack Philadelphia, the American Congress, which had so proudly declared independence five months earlier, abandoned the city and fled to Baltimore. Before fleeing Philadelphia, Congress conferred on Washington *all* governmental powers, in essence making him a dictator.

The fate of the Republic was now entirely in Washington's hands. There was no one left to report to. He was forty-four years old.

Morale was very low. Nothing sinks the spirit of an army more than defeat and retreat. To add to the misery, uniforms and equipment were wearing out from months of hard campaigning. The Continentals marched everywhere. Horses and wagons were in short supply and Washington's troops, largely infantry, were expected to walk and carry their own equipment. Shoe supplies were so poor that many lads marched barefoot. Bullets, gunpowder, food, water, and provisions of nearly every type required to keep an army in the field were nearly exhausted. To add crisis to calamity, most soldiers' enlistments were expiring December 31, 1776, or shortly thereafter. With the war going badly, many soldiers were counting the days until their duty was up and they could honorably return home. If Washington was going to maintain his army, he needed a victory.

The British Army on the other hand, was a well drilled, excellently equipped, and superbly led professional force considered to be the best army in the world. It consisted of infantry, some companies of dragoons (mounted riflemen), and artillery. General Howe had assembled a combined arms force consisting of more than eight thousand soldiers to finish off Washington's depleted ranks. Some of Howe's best troops, the Hessians, were the much feared German mercenaries Jefferson described in preparing the Declaration of Independence when he wrote: "He is at this time transporting large Armies of foreign Mercenaries to complete the works of death, desolation, and tyranny, already begun with circumstances of Cruelty & Perfidy scarcely paralleled in the most barbarous ages, and totally unworthy of the Head of a civilized nation."

With the British in close pursuit of the rag-tag, ill-equipped, ill-fed Continental Army, Washington retreated as quickly as possible, often only a few steps ahead of Howe's forces. During the retreat to the Delaware River, the American rear guard was so closely pursued by Redcoats that they could hear the music of the British advance guard.

Washington hated retreating, but he knew there could be no revolution without an army to fight for it. He would not quit; he refused to let the cause die; he believed vehemently in American independence, calling it the "Glorious Cause." Washington understood that as long as the Continental Army survived, there was hope for independence. He did not believe his army was defeated. As long as he was able to muster one regiment against the foe he vowed to fight on. During the retreat he yearned to find the right circumstances whereby he could turn his army around, attack, and pay the British back for past defeats.

Attack, however, usually required an advantage over the defender. Prudent tacticians recommend a three-to-one numerical advantage in order to launch a successful attack. Washington's army, numbering only about two thousand men, was a shadow of the force he had commanded in New York several months earlier. Many of his soldiers were sick and unfit for duty. Some were as young as fourteen and some as old as sixty. Badly outnumbered, he was unwilling to risk a battle on British terms against superior British forces. He knew that if he could cross the Delaware and put the river between his force and Howe's pressing legions, he could gain a short respite. Washington ordered his reliable Colonel Glover to secure every floatable boat and barge and carry his men across the Delaware River to the relative safety of the Pennsylvania shore. Glover's Marbleheaders pulled off another miracle, and Washington moved his small army to the other side of the river in the nick of time.

The British were forced to pause in their pursuit of the rebels because the Massachusetts fishermen had left too few boats on the east bank of the river to carry the Redcoats across. By the middle of December, with the weather already turning icy and the promise of a hard winter ahead, General Howe decided to move his troops into winter quarters in Bordentown and Trenton. Howe planned to renew the fight against the Americans from these "jumping off points" when the weather improved. He had little doubt that it would be the final campaign of the war and vowed to send his forces across the river in the spring of 1777, crush Washington's feeble "rabble in arms" and settle the issue of independence once and for all.

By December 8, Washington's army was safely positioned on the Pennsylvania side of the Delaware River. He ordered his men to camp and scour the area for food and supplies. While his men foraged, Washington regrouped and made organizational changes. He had learned the value of leadership at the small unit level during the battles fought in the previous five months. If he wanted to mount a successful counterattack, he would have to shift his basic combat organizational system from regiments to brigades. His brigades would contain fewer men than the older regimental organization but would have a higher percentage of leaders. Washington believed having more leaders at the troop level would set an example for his raw soldiers and improve command and control. He also organized artillery companies to act in direct support of each brigade.

One of Washington's most admirable qualities was his ability to learn from his mistakes. Despite the acknowledged prowess of the British and Hessian soldiers, Washington burned to turn the tables on them and avenge the cruel defeats of the previous six months. As the army, rested, reorganized and resupplied, Washington remembered the lessons of the past months fighting and contemplated his next move. He had learned crucial lessons from the difficult combat in New York and New Jersey. He knew that his foes were not supermen and recognized their weaknesses, few though they were. He understood the enemy's tactics and knew that if he could prevent the British and Hessians from forming the battle formations from which they drew their striking power, he could gain a significant advantage over them. The enemy's power came from his ability to form appropriate fighting formations—line, column, or square —rapidly on command. Washington realized that the Hessian formations, especially, were rigid, requiring open ground and close command and control. Cracking the enemy's discipline, denying him time to deploy into his combat formations, and targeting his leadership were key to their defeat.

Washington understood he must employ flexible tactics, avoid the enemy's strengths and hit them where they were weakest. Whenever possible he would use surprise to his advantage. If he could not surprise the enemy, he would try to maneuver his army to a position where the British would be forced to attack him. Once in position he would entrench his men so they could fire at the attacking Redcoats from *behind cover*.

Washington had also learned that the enemy forces, particularly the Hessians, held his soldiers in utter contempt. He would use their arrogance to his advantage.

Most importantly, he knew that the fundamental state of his army's spirit was a preeminent factor in winning a victory. The Continental Army's esprit de corps could not be maintained in defeat. He knew that his soldiers would not stay under arms long without a victory, large or small, to embolden it. Washington's army needed a dramatic victory to rally new recruits to the "Glorious Cause," or the war would be lost and the bold concept of an independent American Republic would become a sad historical footnote about a failed rebellion.

PLANNING AND PREPARATION

During this crisis of spirit, the fiery and eloquent author Thomas Paine turned in his pen in favor of a musket and marched with the American army as a common soldier. Paine had written the famous treatise *Common Sense*, published January 10, 1776, the same time the transcript of King George III's October 27, 1775 speech to Parliament calling for harsh measures against the traitors in the rebellious colonies arrived in America. The seventy-nine-page pamphlet became an immediate best seller, selling thousands of copies in its first months of publication. *Common Sense* reinforced American's desire for independence from Great Britain, clarified what was at stake in the conflict, and denounced proponents of a negotiated peace.

Recognizing Paine's contribution to the cause, some officers persuaded him to use his talents to write a piece that would raise troop morale. Paine got to work, writing by candlelight during the freezing nights of the retreat across New Jersey and by December 19, 1776, his second pamphlet, *The Crisis*, was complete. It began with the immortal line: "These are times that try men's souls; the summer soldier and the sunshine patriot will, in this crisis, shrink from the service of his country; but he that stands it now, deserves the love and thanks of man and woman. Tyranny, like hell, is not easily conquered; yet we have this consolation with us, that the harder the conflict, the more glorious the triumph."

On December 22, morale kicked up a notch when Washington received reinforcements. Gen. Horatio Gates arrived with eight hundred men; Gen. John Sullivan came with about two thousand, and Gen. John Cadwalader brought in nearly a thousand Pennsylvanians. These reinforcements and militia volunteers increased Washington's army to nearly six thousand fighting men. He selected twenty-four hundred men for the main assault force for the planned attack, and deployed some of his remaining to guard the sick and wounded, secure supplies, and occupy key positions on the American side of the Delaware River.

That same day, Washington called his officers together for a council of war. A council of war was a traditional process used to explain intent, to discuss courses of action, to inspire consensus, and, lastly, to issue orders. Washington always listened carefully to his officers and regularly changed his opinions based on their expert suggestions. In this case, however, Washington was resolute; the situation was dire, and no advice would sway his desire to attack the British.

Although there is no official record of what was said at the council of war, the outcome was clear. Washington proposed a night crossing of the treacherous Delaware River from three locations, with assembly on the enemy side, followed by an attack on the Hessians at Trenton. Washington would lead the core of the Continental Army, a force of nearly twenty-four hundred men and cross at McConkey's Ferry. Simultaneously, Brig. Gen. James Ewing would cross south of Trenton with seven hundred militia to seize the key bridge over the Assunpink Creek, while Brig. Gen. John Cadwalader would land further south near Bordentown with nearly eighteen hundred men, twelve hundred from Pennsylvania and six hundred from New England. Cadwalader's attack on Bordentown would block a Hessian retreat from Trenton. Ewing, who was born in Trenton, would attack with his militia to block a Hessian retreat from Trenton across Assunpink Creek. The main force commanded by Washington and his subordinate commanders Gen. John Sullivan and Gen. Nathanael Greene, would assault the enemy garrison with the hope of taking the Hessians by surprise.

During the council of war Washington asked General Gates what he thought of the plan. Gates had extremely hard words for Washington and considered the plan folly and suicidal. He argued against the attack, directly questioned Washington's leadership and military competence and refused to support the plan. After a short but heated exchange, Washington "excused" General Gates from his camp. That night Gates left his troops and departed for Baltimore in search of Congress.

Unruly, unwilling, and disobedient senior officers were only part of Washington's worries. His greatest concern were the soldiers of the chief target of his attack: the Hessians at Trenton. From spies that worked under Washington's direct control, he learned that the fifteen hundred Hessians quartered in Trenton were under the command of Colonel Johann Gottlieb Rall. The dashing Hessian commander was a battle experienced fifty-six-year old career soldier with a reputation as a tough disciplinarian, a fierce fighter, and a hard drinker. Rall requested quartering at Trenton, the most forward and exposed British outpost in New Jersey, considering it an honor for his regiment to be posted to the most dangerous position. He was respected by his men and was considered to be a fair and extremely capable commander, one of the best in the Hessian force.

Rall's Hessians also had a bloody reputation. His men had fought and won against Washington in the Battle of Long Island, the Battle of White Plains, and the storming of Fort Washington. With the exception of the assault on Fort Washington, where his Hessian Regiment lost nearly 177 men, Rall thought the battles against the rebels were easy victories. He viewed the American soldier and especially George Washington with scorn. One Hessian officer, Colonel Heerigen who commanded a regiment that fought at the Battle of Long Island, typified Hessian opinion of Americans: "If we would be opposed by a brave enemy, they would maybe attack us when we are occupied fetching our provisions and tents. To our luck we are fighting a nation which does not know what a real war means."

The Hessian's treatment of prisoners during the Battle of Long Island, where they bayoneted American wounded and those who attempted to surrender, and reportedly pinned the bodies of dead patriots to trees and barn doors, was particularly heinous to Washington and his men. After taking heavy losses to American musket fire at Fort Washington on November 14, 1776, the Hessian soldiers took revenge and beat and bayoneted prisoners until Hessian and British officers interceded and restrained them. Washington never forgave the Hessians for what they did to his men at Long Island and Fort Washington. It became a very personal matter for Washington. He had a big score to settle with Rall and the Hessians.

When Rall's officers drew up plans to create defensive works for Trenton, Rall disregarded them. He considered the Americans to be nothing more than rabble and country bumpkins and saw no need to fortify Trenton or build the usual defensive redoubt. When asked what his men would do if Washington attacked, Rall replied: "Shit upon shit! Let them come. . . . We will go at them with the bayonet."

With this intelligence information in mind, Washington completed final plans for the attack on Trenton, including all possible means to raise his soldiers' morale and faith in the cause. On December 23, Paine's pamphlet, *The Crisis*, was read aloud to the troops as they stood in brigade formations.* Certain lines of the treatise fired up the men's spirits, such as this one:

> There are cases which cannot be overdone by language, and this is one. There are persons, too, who see not the full extent of the evil which threatens them; they solace themselves with hopes that the enemy, if he succeeds, will be merciful. It is the madness of folly, to expect mercy from those who have refused to do justice; and even mercy, where conquest is the object, is only a trick of war; the cunning of the fox is as murderous as the violence of the wolf, and we ought to guard equally against both. . . . By perseverance and fortitude we have the prospect of a glorious issue; by cowardice and submission, the sad choice of a variety of evils—a ravaged country—a depopulated city—habitations without safety and slavery without hope—our homes turned into barracks and bawdy-houses for Hessians.

When the reading of the entire pamphlet was over, the men cheered. Thomas Paine's words had hit the mark.

---

* *The Crisis* was the first of a series of thirteen pamphlets known as *The American Crisis*, which extended into 1783.

Washington held a final planning session on Christmas Eve, with all senior officers present. Colonel Glover's men gathered boats of every kind and secretly gathered them at the crossing sites on the Pennsylvania side of the Delaware River. This ad hoc fleet included a number of large flat-bottomed Durham boats, normally used to haul cargo, not people. Washington was ready. He planned to cross his army over the Delaware River on Christmas night and attack around 5 A.M. on December 26, the morning after Christmas, hitting the Hessians just before sunrise. He didn't have the recommended three-to-one advantage needed for a successful attack, but he counted on catching the Hessians napping. Surprise was everything.

On Christmas Day he issued the orders for the attack to his key officers. The watchword for the attack succinctly reflected General Washington's mood: "Victory or Death."

THE BATTLE OF TRENTON

On Christmas Day the ground was covered in snow. A cold, chilling rain fell as Washington's soldiers made last minute preparations. At 3 P.M. Washington's main force assembled in columns, eight men abreast. The men were ordered to remain quiet and stick to their units. As evening approached, officers marched their tightly packed columns unit-by-unit to the crossing point at McConkey's Ferry. Every man, even the officers, carried a heavy pack with three days' rations and a rifle or musket. By sunset, the weather turned more miserable with freezing rain striking the soldiers as they waited to be ferried across the river. Most of the men had not eaten anything all day except for a quick breakfast. Officers placed a white paper in their caps so the men could follow them in the coming darkness. The rain-soaked men, unprotected from the storm except for their meager clothing, were wet, cold, hungry, and tired. Never faltering, they followed their officers and sergeants and pressed on, lining up to board the boats.

Colonel Henry Knox commanded the river crossing operation while Colonel John Glover's Massachusetts Marblehead Militiamen handled the boats. Around 5 P.M. it was dark enough for the loading to begin. The weather worsened as sleeting rain turned horizontal, stinging the men's faces. Delays occurred. In the dark, everything became harder and the men shivered, slipped, and cursed. By the time the first boats cast off from the Pennsylvania shore the operation was behind schedule. Colonel John Fitzgerald, Washington's aide-de-camp wrote: "It is fearfully cold and raw and a snowstorm is coming. The wind northeast beats into the faces of the men. It will be a terrible night for those who have no shoes. Some of them have tied only rags about their feet—others are barefoot, but I have not heard a man complain."

Washington led by example. He joined the first wave of boats, along with a company of Virginia troops. As the boats navigated the frigid water, no one knew for sure if the Americans would achieve surprise. Many people knew about the preparations for the attack and Washington feared the attack might be discovered and the Hessians waiting. Secrets were very difficult to maintain. If the Hessians were alert, if their patrols had discovered Washington's intentions and were ready and waiting for them in their well-drilled formations, his brave American lads would be rowing into a trap to be slaughtered without hope of defense or retreat.

The Delaware River at McConkey's Ferry was about eight hundred feet wide and the current was swift. The water was dotted with large chunks of ice and the steersman could not see the far shoreline. Into the black, sleet and snow of Christmas night the boatmen rowed their big, flat-bottomed Durham boats across the icy river. Sleet and hail hampered the crossing and gale-like winds pushed against the boats. Most of the men crossed the river standing up as the bottoms of the boats were filled with icy water. The majority of Washington's soldiers had never learned to swim, and their fear of capsizing into the turbulent waters of the Delaware was palpable.

The experienced Marbleheaders maneuvered their boats as best they could in the hazardous conditions, avoiding large chunks of ice floating down the river. The largest Durham boats were 65 feet long and 8 feet in the beam. They were designed to transport up to 20 tons of iron or 150 barrels of flour. Four men and a steersman manned each boat, using long "setting poles" and oars to move them along.

The enemy shoreline remained quiet with no hint of activity. The first boat landed on the New Jersey side of the river and a group of American skirmishers jumped into the frigid water and ran toward the trees. The leader of the advance party quickly passed word that the landing site was unopposed. There was no enemy in sight. Washington's boat landed just behind the lead boat. The Virginians fanned out and set up a picket line to secure the landing site. Although they were behind schedule, the first step in Washington's plan was attained.

As soon as the first troops disembarked, the boats immediately headed back to the Pennsylvania shore for another load. Col. Henry Knox, General Washington's hefty, but indispensable artillery commander, diligently took charge of the landings on the New Jersey shore. Wrapped in his thick, blue wool cloak, Knox worked throughout the frigid, tempestuous night, guiding boats to the landing site. His booming voice may have saved the day, as visibility fell to only a few feet in the blinding snow, and the Marbleheaders guided their boats shoreward to the sound of Knox's voice.

As Knox shouted in the distance, Washington pulled the collar of his coat up to cover his neck from the icy air. He tugged out his watch-chain in the dim light and checked the time. He had planned to have the entire army on the New Jersey side by midnight of Christmas Day. In spite of his planning, in spite of Knox's energetic leadership and Glover's skill, the weather delayed the crossing. Vital minutes were lost as each boat took longer to load and unload. Vital time was wasted as blinding snow and chunks of floating ice bumped the boats and slowed the crossing. The oarsmen began to tire, but carried on in spite of the wet and cold. Washington had planned to attack the Hessians at dawn on December 26 but the delays were wrecking that plan. It would take more time to assemble the army and daylight was fast approaching. If Washington were to win a Christmas present for his nascent country he would have to attack in daylight.

The difficult river-crossing operation continued. By 3 A.M. the entire American infantry arrived on the New Jersey banks of the Delaware River. Then Glover's weary boatmen rowed the boats back across the river to ferry the artillery over. Washington waited patiently as Knox continued working to get his heavy and unwieldy cannons onto the boats and across the Delaware. He contemplated the option of running a daylight attack against the feared Hessians. By 4 A.M., without losing a single gun, Knox had the artillery and some horses across.

Although the entire American force of infantry and artillery was now assembled on the New Jersey side of the river, the men still had to march about nine miles to Trenton in blinding snow. Daylight would occur in a few hours, too soon for Washington to keep to the original plan's schedule. Just before he ordered his men to move out, a scout arrived with word that the intolerable weather, the swift current and huge chunks of ice had stopped Ewing from making the crossing at Trenton Ferry. The scout also reported that Cadwalader had crossed near Bordentown, but was unable to ferry his cannon across due to the impossible weather conditions. Reluctantly, Cadwalader had reloaded the boats with his force and rowed back to the American side of the Delaware.

In darkness on the New Jersey shore, Washington wrapped himself in his cloak and sat upon an old wooden box and deliberated. The failure of

Ewing and Cadwalader to cross the Delaware was a devastating setback. His carefully rehearsed plan was in ruins. Instead of three powerful American forces hitting the Hessians in Trenton in a simultaneous surprise attack, Washington had only one column of soldiers consisting of twenty-four hundred cold, wet men and a dozen cannon. To make matters worse, the crossing was three hours behind schedule. Washington was on his own. All of his men were not yet across the river, and the sun would soon be up. He would have to attack in broad daylight. With his plan coming apart and the weather worsening, another leader might have called it quits. A lesser man might have rowed his men back to Pennsylvania. But with enlistments running out and the bad effect on morale another setback would generate, Washington believed wholeheartedly that the only course of action he could take would be to go on. It *would* result either in victory or in death: Victory bespoke conquest and triumph; death bespoke death to the revolution, death to the notion of American liberty and independence, and probably death for himself.

Washington, however, was not just "another leader." He held true to salvaging the remnants of his plan, he held true to his watchword—Victory or Death—and issued orders to press on. Viewed from his current position, two roads led to Trenton; the southern River Road leading to the west end of town and the northern Pennington Road leading to the east end of town. He calculated the time needed to make the march and changed the time of attack from dawn to 8 A.M. He and General Greene would lead half the men along the Pennington Road, while General Sullivan led the rest along the River Road. The two columns would divide at Bear Tavern at a fork in the road leading to Trenton. At 8 A.M. Washington and Greene would hit the Hessians from the north as Sullivan attacked them from the southwest and cut off their retreat. Within minutes of Washington's issuing the new time of the coordinated attack the men began to march.

The main Hessian force of fifteen hundred men was divided into three regiments, housed in buildings scattered throughout Trenton. The Hessians considered their posting at Trenton hard duty as they were always wary of an American attack. According to a Hessian officer's diary: "We are obliged to be constantly on our guard, and do very severe duty . . . our people begin to grow ragged. . . . We have not slept one night in peace since we came to this place. The troops have lain on their arms every night, but they can endure it no longer."

On Christmas night there was no drunken revelry in the Hessian camp

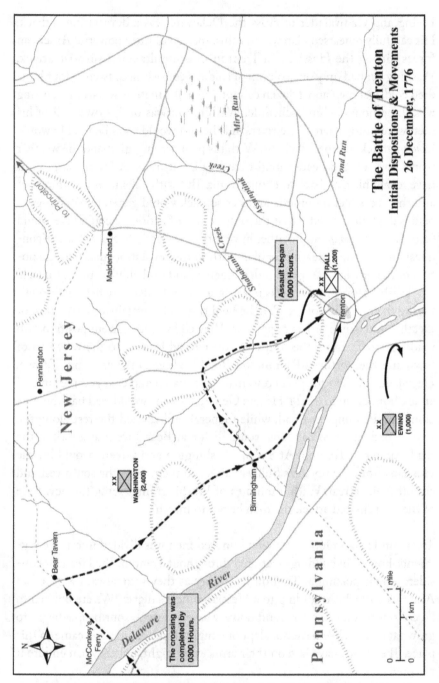

Map of Washington's Crossing and the Battle of Trenton.

as there was no time for drinking. Instead of a celebration, there was great deal of confusion for the weary Hessian garrison when a small New Jersey partisan band raided one of the Hessian guard posts. The partisans, on their own initiative and completely unaware of Washington's plans, fired a few shots at close range at the enemy outpost, killing a Hessian, and then fled into the darkness. The alarm was sounded, Colonel Rall ordered the regiment to arms, mounted his horse and sent out patrols to kill or capture the rebels. The small band of Americans was never found, but Rall and his men, after several hours of patrolling in dark, wet, cold and snowy weather, returned to barracks in the early hours of the morning. Rall ordered his men to rest and cancelled morning stand-to formation. Except for a few tired pickets on the outskirts of town, Rall was blind to Washington's moves.

Typically, every morning at dawn Rall's men assembled in formation, ready to fight in case of an American attack. This procedure known as "stand-to," is a tactical method still used today by professional armies. Due to the partisan attack, the weariness of his men, and the terrible weather, Rall cancelled stand-to for the morning of December 26.

In the cold, darkness of the early morning, the long column of American soldiers, musket and rifles pointed skywards in the carry-arms position, looked more like a refugee column than an army on the attack. Complete uniforms were few among the Continentals. Homespun clothing was the norm for the militia. Few were dressed for winter conditions, and as mentioned, some of the soldiers had cloth wrapped around their feet, as they had no shoes. Two men had already died of the cold after the crossing. Washington rode his horse along the line, offering encouragement and inspiration. The wet and freezing soldiers continued silently toward Trenton, buoyed by the presence of their general and staying warm by keeping on the march.

As Washington neared Trenton a courier from General Sullivan rode up and reported that the rain and cold had reduced the effectiveness of their muskets and rifles. Some of their flintlocks would not fire in those conditions. Washington looked sternly at the courier and replied, "Tell General Sullivan to use the bayonet. I am resolved to take Trenton."

Washington's advance guard surprised a company of Hessian soldiers who were billeted in a house on the Pennington Road about a mile northwest of Trenton. George Washington, astride his horse, led the assault on the Hessian company. Those Hessians who were not killed or captured fled into Trenton, firing as they fell back, with Washington's men hot on their heels.

The Hessians had raised the alarm, waking from their short sleep after chasing partisans in the night, but it was too late. It was 8 A.M. and the column led by Greene and Washington arrived at Trenton. Knox and his artillery, representing Washington's greatest firepower, traveled with Washington. The snow was still blowing hard. The wind was freezing, especially to men whose clothes were wet. The men moved from column into line formation at quick time and as quietly as possible. The line formed and stopped at a slight rise at the edge of town.

Washington nodded to Colonel Knox to deploy the artillery. Washington knew that Knox's cannons would be the key element of this fight, especially since the powder in many of the soldier's flintlocks was wet from the wet snow. Knox jumped into action and quickly ordered his men to manhandle the cannons into position. The guns were loaded and primed. Knox stood by for the order to fire.

The sleepy town lay before them, quiet and peaceful; the Hessians were nowhere to be seen. Washington smiled, savoring the moment. He realized he had achieved the surprise he had so desperately needed and hoped for. He heard the sound of cannon fire to the south and his face lit up. General Sullivan's guns were greeting the Hessians from the other side of Trenton. A squad of Hessians stumbled out of a barn. It was time to launch the attack.

"Now Henry! Fire!" Washington announced.

Knox nodded and turned to his gun crews. "*Fire!*"

The cannon boomed, smashing into the barn occupied by a Hessian squad.

"Advance and charge!" Washington ordered in a commanding voice.

The Americans cheered and advanced on Trenton. Knox's cannons fired again. A few Hessians stumbled out of buildings to see what was happening and then shouted the alarm. The sleeping Hessians woke and rushed to the battle, half-dressed and bleary-eyed. "The out guards made but small opposition, though, for their numbers, they behaved very well, keeping up a constant retreating fire from behind houses," Washington later wrote. "We presently saw their main body formed; but, from their motions, they seemed undetermined how to act." The Americans charged through the town, firing from house to house, rousting some Hessians from their beds and catching many of them, literally, with their pants down.

Hessian drums and bugles continued to sound the alarm. Colonel Rall quickly dressed, cursing at the confusion, and shouting orders to his aides. He rushed outside. His orderly brought him his horse. Rall mounted, shouted commands and tried to rally his beleaguered men. The Americans were soon all around him. He broke away, rode off to the east of town and tried to form any men he could find into a firing line. A company of well-trained Hessian soldiers did their best to assemble and form up in the blinding snow. Hessian officers yelled and cursed but to no avail as the Americans were upon them, stabbing with bayonets and swinging musket butts before many of the stunned Germans knew what was going on. A Hessian gun crew tried to ready their cannon for battle, but the rampaging Americans quickly captured them.

Rall was not about to give up. He thought that a determined counterattack might still win the day. Believing that he was surrounded and finding American forces already deep inside in Trenton, Rall directed every Hessian grenadier he could find to an open area where he intended to counterattack and drive the rebels from the town. He led his men forward, but right into a wall of cannon and musket fire. Surprised, Rall's men recoiled from the American fusillade as a dozen of their comrades fell. Some of Washington's men had managed to keep their powder dry after all. The Americans then charged with the bayonet, sending the Hessians reeling. In the melee, one of Washington's riflemen spotted Rall sitting on his horse through the falling snow, shouting commands. The American aimed, fired and hit the Hessian commander with a well-aimed shot. At nearly the same time, a second American rifleman saw Rall and fired, hitting Rall in the side. Hit twice, Rall fell from his horse seriously wounded and was unable to continue command. Their leader down, the remaining Hessians ran for a nearby orchard, hoping to make a heroic last stand. Facing volleys of musket balls fired from platoons of screaming Americans, and deafened by the roar of Henry Knox's cannons and the crash of cannon balls, the leaderless Hessians were quickly overwhelmed, and surrendered.

By 9:30 A.M. the fighting was over and the Hessians laid down their arms. The American victory was magnificent. In roughly ninety minutes of fighting amidst the hundred or so houses that made up the village of Trenton, Washington had defeated Rall's force, captured a thousand arms, several cannon, and taken nearly a thousand prisoners. "This is a glorious day for our country, Major Wilkinson," General Washington remarked to his young aide as the Hessians surrendered. "A glorious day!"

The Hessians suffered 22 dead, 92 wounded and 948 captured. Colonel Johann Gottlieb Rall, mortally wounded in the battle, was evacuated to a nearby house. Later the next day Rall died from his wounds. Before he died he knew that Washington had defeated him and had captured his entire force.

Washington's masterstroke had succeeded. His casualties were miraculously low. Only two men had died from over-exposure on the New Jersey bank of the Delaware River shortly after the crossing. Washington did not lose a single man to the enemy though two officers were wounded during the fighting: young Lieutenant James Monroe, a future president of the United States, and Capt. William Washington, the general's cousin.

By mid-day, Washington had swiftly moved his force back to the river-crossing site. The American army brought about nine hundred Hessian prisoners with them. Many a Continental soldier had heard stories of Hessians mercilessly bayoneting American wounded and prisoners. But under strict orders from General Washington the Hessian prisoners were treated according to the rules of war and were not harmed. Washington would not repay Hessian cruelty to American prisoners and wounded with cruelty. Before nightfall, Glover's Marlbleheaders rowed all of Washington's footsore army, captured booty and prisoners back across the Delaware River to the safety of Pennsylvania.

THE ENLISTMENTS ARE UP

Washington wrote to Congress on December 27, 1776, reporting the victory at Trenton and praising his officers and men: "In justice to the officers and men, I must add, that their behavior upon this occasion reflects the highest honor upon them. The difficulty of passing the river in a very severe night, and their march through a violent storm of snow and hail, did not in the least abate their ardor; but, when they came to the charge, each seemed to vie with the other in pressing forward and were I to give preference to any particular corps, I should do great injustice to the others."

Although the army was victorious at Trenton, it was also worn out. Rapid withdrawal to escape Redcoat reinforcements had taken its toll on the men and their equipment. Back in camp, Washington faced one of his most difficult challenges, not from the British, but from his own men. The men had served honorably under terrible conditions, without adequate food, supplies or weapons, while many of their countrymen stayed at home by hearth and fire, well fed and out of danger. The vast majority of army enlistments expired on December 31, 1776. Many soldiers felt they had done enough for the "Glorious Cause." They were proud of their victory at Trenton, but now they looked forward to going home.

Washington realized that the victory at Trenton was not nearly enough to keep his army together. He needed to drive the British out of New Jersey entirely to inspire new enlistments. To do this, he had to keep the army moving and hit the British hard once more. On December 29 he boldly re-crossed the Delaware River and landed at Trenton again, which the British had failed to secure after Colonel Rall's ignoble defeat. Once across the Delaware he occupied defenses along the high ground near Assunpink Creek.

On December 31, with enlistments about to expire, the units were ordered to form up and officers beseeched the men to reenlist. When the drums rolled the reenlistment tune, not a man stepped forward. Washington was alerted and appealed to one brigade in person, doing his best to persuade them. "My brave fellows, you have done all I asked you to do, and more than could be reasonably expected; but your country is at stake, your wives, your houses and all that you hold dear. You have worn yourselves out with fatigue and hardships, but we know not how to spare you. If you will consent to stay only one month longer, you will render that service to the cause of liberty and to your country which you probably never can do under any other circumstances."

A first, only a few stepped forward, but their example was enough and nearly the entire unit stepped forward to reenlist. Washington knew though, that appeals to patriotism and camaraderie would only go so far. When he took on the role of commander of the army in June 1775 he agreed to serve without pay. He knew that this sacrifice was too much to ask of his men. Washington had not received money from Congress to pay his soldiers for several months and the men knew they were reenlisting for patriotism alone. This was a bitter pill to swallow for those who had farm and family to take care of. Without a source of income, how would they and their families survive? Washington finally received help from Congress by way of a financier and signer of the Declaration of Independence, Robert Morris. Morris had stayed in Philadelphia when the rest of Congress left for Baltimore in December 1776. He secured $50,000 to pay Washington's troops, enough coinage to give every soldier who reenlisted a ten-dollar bounty to stay six weeks beyond the term of enlistment. This did the trick. Washington kept his army.

PRINCETON

British Lt. Gen. Charles Cornwallis, one of General Howe's most capable field commanders, was furious. Not only had the Americans stolen a victory at Trenton and then slipped back into Pennsylvania, but also they had crossed the Delaware again at Trenton and held the high ground along the Assunpink Creek. It was as if Washington were daring the British to attack him. Even more vexing to him, the Americans had wrecked his personal plans for a long-sought-after leave to return to England to visit his ailing wife. Recalled by General Howe after Rall's defeat at Trenton, and his leave cancelled, Cornwallis arrived in Princeton, assembled an army of eight thousand British regulars, and prepared to crush Washington's army. After receiving reports that the Americans were sitting on the high ground east of Trenton, Cornwallis left fifteen hundred men at Princeton and hurried toward Trenton to do battle with Washington.

The vanguard of Cornwallis's force arrived in Trenton in the waning hours of January 2, 1777. Hessian *jaegers* (*jaeger* is German for "hunter"—specially trained skirmish troops) and British light infantry brushed aside a weak screening force of American riflemen and the British occupied the town. Cornwallis arrived with the main body of his army and surveyed the terrain. The Americans were dug into a rise to the south of Trenton, on the south side of Assunpink Creek. The creek was swollen by rain and melting snow, and there were only three crossing sites available, the most important being the Assunpink Bridge. The American position was well sited, except for one key factor: the Delaware River was behind the American position. Cornwallis smiled. Washington had made a great blunder and was pinned on his hill with the river blocking his escape. Cornwallis had Washington just where he wanted him, locked into a decisive battle with no room to escape. Cornwallis ordered an immediate attack.

But Washington was ready. He had deployed his brigades carefully. Colonel Knox had sighted the crossing sites over the Assunpink with his artillery. In their hasty attack the British assaulted the most valuable crossing site, the sixteen-foot wide Assunpink Bridge, with a column of infantry. American rifles, muskets, and cannon focused their fire on the bridge and repulsed the attack, causing substantial casualties. As the British staggered back from the bridge, a cheer rose along the entire American line. Angry at their failure to force their way across the bridge, the British tried again, only to meet the same end. After three unsuccessful attacks, with dusk approaching and unwilling to take more casualties, Cornwallis called off the assault.

As darkness fell, Cornwallis ordered his men to bivouac in the streets of Trenton. He declared that he would renew the attack at first light and defeat the Americans once and for all. One of his staff officers, Sir William Erskine, replied, "Ah, in the morning Washington will not be here." Cornwallis raised his hand to silence the officer and responded: "Oh yes he will. I have got the old fox in a trap and he and his rag-a-muffins cannot escape me."

Washington had no intention of being trapped. Realizing that his defenses were not strong enough to stop five thousand Redcoats from crossing Assunpink Creek in full daylight, he called a council of war and issued new orders. Sensing an advantage offered by Cornwallis' mistake to halt the fight, Washington rapidly adjusted his plan. Rather than defend, he would withdraw from where the British were strong and hit them where they were weak. Through in-depth knowledge of the terrain and the benefit of excellent intelligence information provided by a host of spies and scouts, he knew of a trail leading east that would allow his army to slip by the British. The army would withdraw at night, leaving a few militiamen in position to keep campfires blazing to fool the British. Washington would then lead his army around Cornwallis' southern flank, bypassing Cornwallis' force and attack the smaller British forces at Princeton.

The withdrawal went according to plan. American campfires burned brightly all night and Cornwallis's force was unaware that Washington's entire army quietly and stealthily slipped past him. Without the aid of torchlight, with wagons and personal equipment muffled and the army under strict orders not to utter a sound, the Americans marched away through the cold, dark January night intent on attacking the British garrison at Princeton.

On the morning of January 3, Washington's column approached the outskirts of Princeton. The American advance guard, consisting of 120 riflemen, and 200 more following closely, was led by the able Gen. Hugh Mercer. Mercer was a doctor by profession, and had been an assistant surgeon in Scottish army of Bonnie Prince Charlie that fought the British for Scottish independence in the Battle of Culloden in 1746. Mercer fled Scotland for America and had served with Colonial forces in the French and Indian War (1754–1763). It was during the French and Indian War that Mercer became a longtime friend of George Washington.

As Mercer's men neared Princeton they were met head-on by a British column marching toward Trenton. The British force of about 276 men, commanded by Colonel Charles Mawhood, was as surprised to see American riflemen, as General Mercer was to see an advancing column of Redcoats. The two forces exchanged fire, and Mawhood ordered the British to charge with bayonets. The American advance guard discharged their rifles, but since they had no bayonets, retreated before the British charge. As brave Mercer tried to rally his men, the British overwhelmed him and he was bayoneted several times and mortally wounded.

Mercer's courageous sacrifice inspired Washington and his men, but that's the kind of man Mercer was. A little more than a century later, one of his decedents, Gen. George S. Patton Jr., would be born and go on to become a brilliant military commander in WWII.

General Washington saw Mercer fall and galloped to the front to aid his friend. The advance guard turned and counterattacked. Washington led more forces forward and charged into the fray, putting himself at great risk. Inspired by the sight of their commander, the Americans counterattacked. Winning the day, they defeated Mawhood's force and proceeded to capture Princeton. The battle took about forty-five minutes. Back at Trenton, Cornwallis found out he had been hoodwinked when he attacked the unmanned American defenses at Assunpink Creek. Enraged and hearing the echoes of cannon fire from the direction of Princeton, Cornwallis hastily turned his army around and headed toward the sound of the guns. By the time Cornwallis arrived at Princeton, Washington had escaped again and moved to Morristown, New Jersey. Washington's occupation of Morristown, a town surrounded by thickly wooded forest and easy to defend, forced the British to leave most of New Jersey to the Americans in order to protect their supply and communication lines to their forces in New York City.

After ten days of hard campaigning, Washington and his army of "rag-a-muffins" had won the day. The twin victories at Trenton and Princeton boosted American morale, opened up New Jersey for recruiting to the American cause and brought praise and much needed supplies to the Americans from France, Britain's perpetual enemy.

Frederick the Great, considered the greatest soldier of his time, was reported to have said that Washington's victories at Trenton and Princeton were the most brilliant campaign of the century. Outnumbered and on the verge of defeat, Washington reversed the course of the war and beat the best units the British could send against him. The victories were not strategic defeats for the British, the British losses could be replaced, but the resulting rise in morale and the ensuing political value were beyond measure to the Americans. It is no exaggeration to conclude that Washington's resolute leadership at Trenton and Princeton saved the fledgling United States of America.

—∿∿—

LEADERSHIP LESSONS LEARNED FROM GEORGE WASHINGTON AT THE BATTLES OF TRENTON AND PRINCETON

• **Leadership requires determination.** Washington was determined to win.

Death of General Mercer at the Battle of Princeton (painting by John Trumbull).

The strain of his responsibilities weighed on him, but Washington never gave up. He might lose a battle along the way, but he was adamant about winning American Independence. He put his heart, mind, body and soul into winning a victory that would save his army and the United States. Nothing could dissuade him from his goal and even in his darkest hours he looked for a way to turn the tide of defeat into a victory. During a chaotic time and one of the darkest periods of the war for independence, Washington's determination was decisive. He regrouped his tired and defeated troops and in ten days of hard campaigning, crossed the Delaware River multiple times, won two impressive victories, *and* kept his army together. This demonstrates Washington's talents as a consummate leader who could inspire people during the worst and most fearful of times. Without Washington's outstanding leadership there would not have been a victory at Trenton or Princeton and today the United States might still be a colony of Great Britain. In those ten days, from December 25, 1776, to January 4, 1777, George Washington saved the Glorious Cause of Liberty.

- **Effective leaders never stop learning.** Washington believed that leadership could be learned. He educated himself, worked to perfect his character, honed his interpersonal skills and consistently developed his leadership ability. Rather than brooding over his defeats in New York and New Jersey, Washington evaluated them and learned valuable lessons about his enemy, his own leaders, his troops and the terrain. He used this knowledge to pull off wins at Trenton and Princeton. He learned to increase his leadership quotient and raise the leadership quotient of everyone around him.

- **A leader's most powerful attributes are courage and self-confidence.** Fear is a reaction. Courage is a decision. Washington chose courage. He believed that self-confidence was essential for a leader and that courage enables all other leadership attributes, for without courage to carry on in the face of difficult odds, all is lost. At Trenton, the odds were stacked against success. Only a self-confident leader would consider counterattacking the most professional army on the planet, after enduring months of defeat and retreat, conduct a night river crossing in freezing weather, and launch a morning attack on one of the enemy's most feared formations. Only a leader of courage would lead from the front and turn a desperate gamble into a striking success. Washington was able to maintain confidence in himself, his army and the cause of liberty when everyone else was in despair. Prior to the crossing of the Delaware River and the Battle of Trenton, Thomas Paine wrote about George Washington in his pamphlet series *The American Crisis*: "There is a natural firmness in some minds which cannot be unlocked by trifles, but which, when unlocked, discovers a cabinet of fortitude; and I reckon it among those kind of public blessings, which we do not immediately see, that God hath blessed him (Washington) with uninterrupted health, and given him a mind that can even flourish upon care." Paine saw Washington's courage and self-confidence first-hand and foretold the cause and effect of one man's decisive leadership.
- **A true leader is honest.** Washington believed that only an honest man could bear the burden of leadership. He told it like it was. When he spoke, his soldiers believed him and they knew what he said was true. He earned their trust. This was a vital quality to have when the chips were down. When the enlistments ran out, his honesty and force of character convinced the army to re-enlist.
- **A true leader listens to others.** Washington believed that actions speak louder than words. In a council of war, or when visiting the troops at their campfires late at night, Washington listened and learned. He did not speak just to hear the sound of his own voice. When he spoke, others listened; they knew he was a man of few words and that he measured each spoken word for its weight and merit.

- **A true leader knows his team members.** Washington knew his soldiers and the officers who led them. He was with them, almost always at the front, leading by example. He inspired his soldiers to sacrifice for a greater cause, never missing the opportunity to tell them that they were serving for the greater good of all Americans. By knowing his people he knew how to appeal to them to make them believe that their noble sacrifices and worthy of greatness.

- **A true leader realizes that the leader is *always* on parade.** Washington understood that his soldiers watched his every move. When he appeared in front of them, his bearing, attitude, dress and deportment were on display. He inspired confidence and determination in his soldiers by his commanding presence. His courage inspired courage. At Trenton and Princeton he inspired his men by showing them exactly how to behave in the face of adversity, danger and death.

- **A true leader is Selfless.** Washington's devotion to the newly declared United States and his exemplarity civic virtue is a remarkable model of selfless leadership. Devotion to the Congress and the Glorious Cause of Liberty, above all personal motives, was Washington's driving force. His personal civic virtues focused on his individual behavior and responsibility, which he never shirked. When the Congress fled Philadelphia in December 1776 in fear of the British, they endowed Washington with unlimited powers. Imagine if Washington had been made of lesser stuff and had acted as a Caesar or a Napoleon! Washington never abused these powers and always deferred to the civilian authorities in Congress. His selflessness was a visible model for the Continental Army and helped earn the admiration and trust of his officers and men. Most importantly, Washington established the vital precedent that civilian-elected officials, not military officers, possessed ultimate authority over the American army.

Brigadier General Daniel Morgan
(portrait by Charles Willson Peale, 1794).

Chapter 6

"CHARGE BAYONETS!"
Daniel Morgan at the Battle of Cowpens

Great generals are scarce—there are few Morgans around.
—NATHANAEL GREENE

LEADERSHIP REQUIRES SETTING THE
CONDITIONS FOR SUCCESS.

"Delightful!" British Gen. Lord Charles Cornwallis exclaimed. "That bumpkin Greene has made an unforgivable mistake and divided his army. I shall send Tarleton to go after that backwoodsman Morgan and push him to the utmost! Once Morgan's rag tag militia is destroyed, I will turn on Greene and finish this damned rebellion."

Stalemated in the north, the British had adopted a new "Southern Strategy" intended to conquer the southern United States. In December 1778, a British force led by Lt. Col. Archibald Campbell bragged that he stripped the "first . . . stripe and star from the rebel flag of Congress" when he captured Savannah, Georgia. Charleston, South Carolina, the most important city and seaport in the South, fell to Generals Henry Clinton and Charles Cornwallis on May 12, 1780, after a two month long siege. The American cause was in ruins as American Gen. Benjamin Lincoln surrendered along with five thousand American soldiers. With the rebels reeling from these defeats, Clinton then left Cornwallis in charge and returned to New York to deal with French fleet menacing the nearby area. Cornwallis took charge of a veteran and victorious British army and a large force of Tories with orders to crush all rebels in the South. On August 16, 1780, at Camden, South Carolina, he defeated American Gen. Horatio Gates, the victor of the Battle of Saratoga (1777). Cornwallis's victory at Camden crushed the American southern army, inflicted over two thousand casualties and took a thousand prisoners. Gates fled from the defeat in panic, abandoning his army and covering 170 miles in three days on horseback, a remarkable ride for a fifty-three-year-old man. It seemed all the British needed to secure their Southern Strategy was to mop up a few companies of American militia and the war would be won.

One of Cornwallis's most trusted commanders was a twenty-six-year-old cavalier named Banastre Tarleton. Tarleton had earned a reputation as the best light cavalry commander in the British Army in North America. He commanded a mixed cavalry and light infantry force known as the British Legion, which was often called "Tarleton's Raiders." The fast moving force of 250 cavalrymen and 200 light infantrymen was composed mostly of loyalist Americans from Pennsylvania and New York. Rather than wear the red uniform of British regulars, Tarleton's men dressed in green jackets to distinguish themselves as a Tory regiment.

At the Battle of Camden, Tarleton's Raiders made a charge that broke the American line and scattered the American army. Tarleton's horsemen then pursued the broken, dispirited and leaderless Americans for twenty miles, sabering many of the fleeing survivors.

Because of this action and similar behavior in other skirmishes, Tarleton was *the* British officer Americans most feared. Militiamen and regulars alike feared Tarleton and his drgoons. One American militia fighter from a patriot guerrilla group led by Tarleton's nemesis, the American commander Francis Marion, observed that Tarleton and his men "not only exercised more acts of cruelty than anyone in the British army, but also carried further the spirit of depredation." What Tarleton lacked in subtlety and tactical foresight he made up for in dash and courage. Learning of American Gen. Daniel Morgan's presence in North Carolina, Cornwallis dispatched Tarleton at the head of twelve hundred men to bag Morgan and his "rag-tag" eight hundred man army. Tarleton, overconfident, expected a "fox chase."

The short, red-headed, dark-eyed, Tarleton had first gained fame when he captured American Gen. Charles Lee on December 13, 1776. Lee was considered by the British to be the most competent American General, more important than Washington. Operating on intelligence information from a Tory informant, Tarleton's horsemen surrounded a house in Basking Ridge, New Jersey, and forced Lee to surrender. General Lee became a prisoner of war and was later exchanged, but as the dashing cavalryman who had caught Lee, Tarleton basked in the notoriety. Tarleton relished his reputation as a cocky, daring, and utterly ruthless cavalry officer with a talent for war. His hard-riding British Legion acted as shock troops for Cornwallis. Tarleton earned his reputation for ruthlessness when his men killed Americans who surrendered after a skirmish on May 29, 1780. His Legion chased down a company of Virginia militiamen near a settlement called the Waxhaws, on the border between North and South Carolina, and annihilated it. Of the 350 men in the company 113 were killed and another 203 captured. Of those captured 150 were so badly wounded that Tarleton left them behind, and many of them died. The casualty rate in this fight was 75 percent prompting the Americans to call it the "Waxhaws Massacre."

Because of his actions at the Waxhaws, and his cut and slash tactics across the south where he burned houses and crops and killed livestock, Tarleton's reputation as the most hated British officer in America surged. The term "Tarleton's Quarter"—meaning no mercy—became synonymous with the barbarous British officer. Tarleton believed that the terror his reputation wielded would help subdue the rebellion and gain him eternal glory in Britain.

In battle Tarleton's tactics were brutally simple: find the enemy rabble and charge headlong from the line-of-march, attacking with the saber. He didn't care about the odds against him or the disposition of his opponent and counted on the speed and determination of his assault to carry the day. To successfully attack and defeat a defending enemy tactical prudence recommends at least a three-to-one advantage in combat power of the attacker over the defender, but in one battle after another, Tarleton's British Legion charged straight into American lines, even when outnumbered four-to-one, and drove the Americans from the field. The shock action of Tarleton's cavalry, supported by his fast-moving light infantry, overwhelmed the poorly trained American militia units time and again. To the militia Tarleton seemed to be a green devil who was invincible and unstoppable. Invincible, that is, except in the mind of American Brig. Gen. Daniel Morgan.

Morgan was made of different stuff. Morgan was a fighter. He served in the French and Indian War as a civilian wagon-master in support of British troops under General Braddock. In the spring of 1756, while he was moving a wagon laden with supplies, a British lieutenant tried to push Morgan along and slapped him with the flat of his sword. Morgan turned around, pulled the officer from his horse and knocked him out with one punch. He was charged by his British commander with striking a superior officer and was punished with five hundred lashes. That punishment would have killed most men, but not Dan Morgan. He healed, but nurtured a life-long hatred of British injustice. Morgan was fond of telling his men that the drummer had miscounted and he had only been given 499 lashes, so the British still "owed him one more lash."

In 1758 Morgan joined a local company of rangers serving the British Army. They were the ancestors of the 75th Ranger Regiment of today's U.S. Army. His tactical and technical proficiency and skillful leadership soon brought him promotion to ensign, the lowest officer rank in the British Army. During one mission when he was carrying an important message from one commander to another, Morgan proved again how tough he was. He was ambushed by Indians and shot in the back of the neck. The musket ball knocked out all the teeth on the left side of his jaw and exited through his cheek, but Morgan stayed in the saddle and delivered the message.

After the French and Indian War Morgan returned to wagoneering. Always a man who believed in Liberty, Morgan joined the patriot cause in 1775. He served initially at the siege of Boston in 1775 and then fought in the ill-conceived attack on Quebec in December 1775, where he was captured but later exchanged. Promoted to colonel, he organized, formed, trained, and commanded a regiment of backwoodsmen and expert riflemen called the Provisional Rifle Corps, or simply "Morgan's Riflemen." Morgan and his riflemen were largely responsible for the vital American victory at the Battle of Saratoga in September and October 1777. After Saratoga he fought in many other engagements, but he had no political connections and was passed over for promotion. He resigned his commission and went home in 1779 but rejoined the American army after it suffered a series of disastrous defeats. He was promoted to brigadier general and sent south to serve under Nathanael Greene.

In October 1780, American militia won a critical victory against loyalist forces at the Battle of Kings Mountain, but much of the South was still occupied by the British. Washington knew that his forces would have to defeat the British army if he expected to win back the South to the American cause, but with the main British force occupying New York, Washington was obliged to keep most of the Continental Army facing Clinton. After the humiliating defeat of Horatio Gates at Camden, South Carolina, on August 16th, 1780, Alexander Hamilton recommended to Washington, "For God's sake, overcome prejudice and send Greene." Thirty-nine-year-old Nathanael Greene was serving in the critical position of Washington's quartermaster-general, and was younger to many other American generals, but the commander in chief knew his quality and nominated Greene to the position of commander of the American southern army and Congress immediately approved. The appointment made Greene the second-in-command of the entire Continental Army. Washington also sent Daniel Morgan to serve under Greene.

Greene moved south and took command of a force of nearly 2,300 men (with 2307 men on the rosters but only 1482 present for duty), with a core of 949 Continental Army regulars at Charlotte, North Carolina, on December 2, 1781, and Morgan reported for duty the next day. Although Morgan was older than Greene—Morgan was 44—they made a perfect command team, complimenting each others' strengths. Morgan's reputation and personal leadership made him a hero to the troops he commanded. Morgan knew how to inspire men, an uncanny ability to see the ground, deploy his troops and get the most out of them. Greene was Washington's most trusted general and a man of unwavering loyalty, skill and determination. Greene and Morgan respected each other. After a short council of war, Greene and Morgan agreed on a bold strategy to defeat Cornwallis and turn the tide of events in the South against the British. Morgan would entice Tarleton's legion to chase after him, separating Tarleton from Cornwallis's main force. Once the two forces were separated, Morgan would do his best to weaken or destroy Tarleton, while Greene focused on Cornwallis.

Morgan believed he could defeat Tarleton, but first he wanted to study his enemy and set the conditions for success. Morgan believed that Tarleton would jump at the chance gain glory and bag Morgan's small army. He hoped to give Tarleton that chance, but on *his* terms. Morgan talked to militia leaders who had fought Tarleton and learned of Tarleton's inclination for hard driving and swift frontal charges. He also learned that Tarleton didn't think much of American militiamen and considered them poor soldiers. The more Morgan learned about Tarleton the more he felt he could lure this impulsive green-coated dandy into a trap. He moved into South Carolina toward Cornwallis's army and sure enough, Tarleton's force split from the main British force to chase Morgan down.

The chase was on with Morgan planned his withdrawal skillfully. The winter weather in January 1781 was miserable. Cold rain drenched the troops, swelled the creeks, and turned the road to mud. Marching an army in this weather was difficult, but Daniel Morgan, the old wagon-master, knew how to handle any road conditions. Stream and river crossing points became key terrain. Morgan knew it and kept his army on the move, always a few miles ahead of Tarleton's British Legion.

On January 16, 1781, Morgan was in camp when his scouts learned that Tarleton was only a few miles behind him having made a surprise night crossing of the Pacelot River. Morgan immediately put his army on the march. Tarleton's men arrived at Morgan's camp to find warm fires and breakfast still on the spit, but Morgan and his men gone. Tarleton kept up a vigorous pursuit driving his men relentlessly forward, but Morgan eluded his grasp. By nightfall, Morgan arrived at a place called the Cowpens, a place he had reconnoitered before. It was good ground for the trap he had envisioned. He decided to make his stand there.

Morgan briefed his officers on his plan to destroy Tarleton. He would use Tarleton's tendency for hard driving and immediate charges from the line-of-march, against him. He would use the British commander's disdain for American militia against him as well. Accordingly, he formed up his men on an open battlefield dominated by two small rises. The ground looked like perfect cavalry terrain, which was part of Morgan's plan to entice Tarleton to attack him. To Morgan's rear was the swollen Broad River. The river would cut off any chance of escape for Morgan's men.

Morgan planned to place sharpshooters forward to screen his front and deny the enemy an easy view of his deployments. He would place his militia behind these sharpshooters, in front of the first hill, on what soldiers call today the forward slope. A second line of militia would be farther back, near the top of the first rise. Behind them, in the valley between the two rises, Morgan would place his regulars. To defend against Tarleton's cavalry from making a flank attack, Morgan placed Lieutenant Colonel William Washington's cavalry in reserve in a swale that would hide them from Tarleton's view. Washington's cavalry was ready to counterattack on Morgan's signal.

After the riflemen fell back from their screening mission, the first line of militia would be in full view. This line was the bait to lure Tarleton's force into a hasty attack. In past battles, most militia units were unpredictable and could not be depended to hold a firing-line as they would simply fire one or two shots and then run away, often never to be seen again. Morgan knew his men and planned to turn this failing into a virtue. He told his militia that all they had to do was fire two shots, then run back to the next line, fire two more shots then run back again behind the regulars. The regulars would stand and fight and would not pull back. When the militia had reloaded and re-gained their composure they would move forward on both flanks. The militia embraced this simple plan. Morgan's trap was ready.

As the Americans sat by their campfires that night, waiting for morning and the coming battle, Morgan walked among them, encouraging them and explaining what he expected of them. He walked from campfire to campfire, listened to their fears and reassured them that they would lick the Redcoats and win the day if they followed his plan. He showed them the scars on his back from being flogged by the British during the French and Indian War. He explained the battle plan to each group and told the militia that there was no shame in running away, as long as they fired two shots for him and then reformed behind the regulars. He pointed to the Broad River to their back and Tarleton to their front, telling them why they had no choice but to fight like hell. He told them that this was their fight to win, and they believed him.

On the cold, dark morning of January 17 Tarleton's Legion broke camp at 2:00 A.M. and rapidly forced-marched to catch the Americans. Tarleton was not about to let the Americans get away and he drove his men without rest until they arrived near the Cowpens. At 6:45 A.M. Tarleton rode through a clump of trees and saw a thin line of Yankee militiamen on the forward slope of the Cowpens rise.

Tarleton was thrilled. He now had Morgan right where he wanted him, pinned to a hill with a river at his back. Tarleton immediately ordered his men to attack.

A line of British dragoons charged. American skirmishers fired at the British and fifteen of Tarleton's dragoons were hit. The smoke from American rifles masked the American line and made it difficult for Tarleton's men to see the rebel dispositions. Tarleton needed to know exactly where the bulk of the American force was positioned in order to direct his cavalry charge. He was sure that a quick thrust with his cavalry would send the Americans reeling.

Tarleton then ordered his infantry forward to flush out the sharpshooters. The American sharpshooters fell back behind the militia on the forward slope of the first rise. As Tarleton's infantry moved forward, the American militia waited for the British to move into range. As the Redcoats came into the militia's field of fire the militia fired a single, disciplined volley.

Smoke from the musket fire rolled across the field. Red coated figures along the British line fell, but the red line continued to advance. The militia then reloaded and fired another shot in a ragged volley that rippled across the British line. The second volley, ragged as it was, took a heavy toll on Tarleton's infantry as the Redcoats moved closer. British officers shouted orders, the British line stopped with precision and returned fire, but most of their shots went high over the heads of the Americans, as the British were on the high slope of the hill and there is a natural tendency for soldiers to shoot high

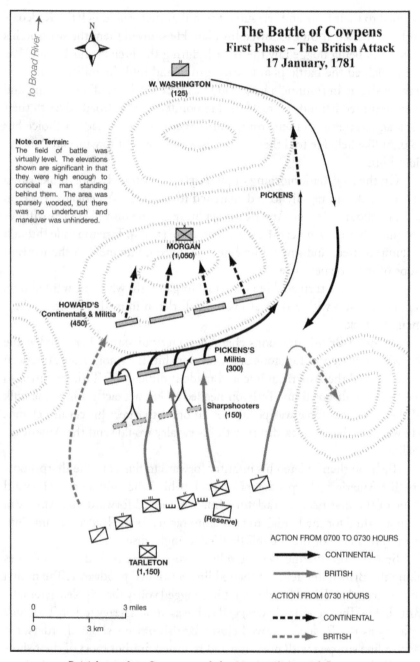

British attack at Cowpens and American militia withdraws: the first phase of the battle.

when on the slope of a hill. The British musket balls hit only a few of the American militiamen. Nevertheless, the American militia broke ranks in apparent disarray, as it had always done in the past, and ran pell-mell toward the safety of the second line of militia on top of the first rise.

The Americans were on the run. In the excitement of the exchange of volleys Tarleton's impulses got the better of him. As he saw the militia routed, he sensed victory. He ordered his dragoons to charge the right flank.

Morgan waited for the British cavalry to close the ground and then, just at the moment they were in range, ordered Washington's cavalry to countercharge the rapidly advancing British dragoons. Washington's cavalry seemed to come out of the trees from nowhere and hit the Tarleton's cavalrymen at full gallop. Surprised by the unexpected attack, the dragoons attempted to wheel to meet the American charge but it was too late; Washington's horsemen were on them and broke up their formation. Panicking, Tarleton's dragoons fled the battlefield.

The cavalry duel had lasted only fifteen minutes when the British dragoons raced away from the field. Tarleton stood high in the saddle as he watched his horsemen ride off. This had never happened to Tarleton before, his cavalry charges had always succeeded, and he was incensed. He cursed and shouted for his Green Jackets to rally, waving his sword in the air, but the dragoons were oblivious to Tarleton's orders and would not reform. Furious beyond measure, but knowing from experience that if pushed hard the Americans would not stand and fight, Tarleton shouted for his infantry to advance and attack the second line of American militia.

The second line of American militia fired a furious volley and then a second volley, just as the first line had done and just as Morgan had instructed them to. The British line staggered and again men dropped. Dense clouds of gray smoke swept across the field from the discharge of hundreds of muskets. Then the entire throng of American militia turned and scampered behind the hill.

Tarleton thought the Americans were running scared again. It finally looked like a retreat . . . no, a rout, as the American militia was fleeing in no ostensible semblance of order. Despite the loss of his dragoons, Tarleton sensed that he only needed to push forward to gain total victory. He ordered a general advance of his entire force. The British infantry marched over the hill in perfect formation to beating drums with regimental colors flapping in the breeze, expecting an easy victory against a disorganized militia that appeared to be in full retreat toward the river.

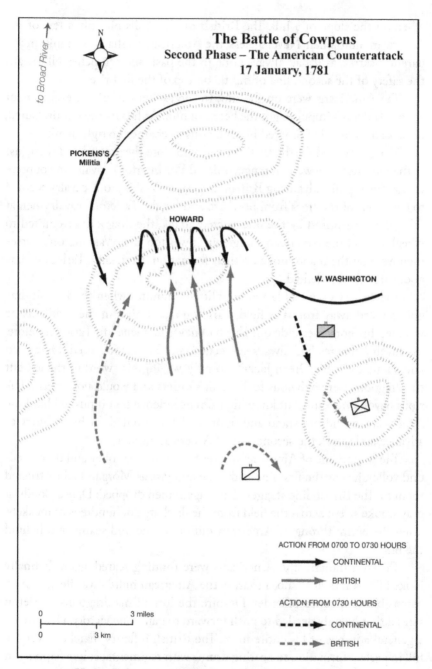

Howard's Continentals stand and counterattack at Cowpens:
the second phase of the battle.

The British line crossed over the rise and suddenly stopped. They couldn't believe their eyes. On the other side of the hill, in the valley below, was a solid wall of Continental Army regulars.

Morgan smiled. The trap was set. He raised his sword and shouted: "Fire!"

The Continental line thundered as the solid line of a thousand American soldiers fired a well-aimed volley of musket fire into the surprised British ranks. Scores of Redcoats fell. The British officers and sergeants screamed to reform ranks. The British regulars recovered quickly, returned fire and smoke thickened in the valley, but to the amazement of the Redcoats the American line held firm. When a gap appeared as a man was hit, another from behind moved forward to fill the gap and hold the line. Blue-clad Continental regulars stepped forward in their ranks and fired another wave of musket fire at the Redcoats. Volley after volley of musket fire was exchanged at close range. Hoping to turn the American line, Tarleton sent in his final infantry reserve to flank the Americans on the right.

Nothing the British had done had moved the American line, but seeing the British movement to their right, a portion of the American line refused the line and pulled back to stop Tarleton's flanking attack. In the confusion and smoke of battle, the rest of Morgan's men thought the order had been given to withdraw and the entire American line turned and headed back.

Morgan saw his army withdrawing. He realized that a mistake had been made. If he didn't take immediate action to stop the withdrawal, there could be a panic. If the line broke, Tarleton could still win the battle and his men might be massacred.

Tarleton saw the American regulars retreating as they had always retreated. He felt vindicated and saw this as the decisive moment in the battle. Now was the time to finish off this rabble and cut them to pieces.

Tarleton's infantry cheered, broke ranks and charged the retreating Americans with their bayonets, advancing through the thick smoke, expecting to slaughter the cowardly rebels fleeing the field.

Morgan ran up to the American line and shouted: "Are you beaten?"

One of his infantry commanders replied. "Do beaten men march in good order like this?"

"Then turn here and fire!" Morgan commanded.

At 7:45 A.M. American officers shouted orders. In unison the line of blue-clad American regulars stopped. On the order of their officers they turned about in perfect discipline. With the British charging not thirty paces

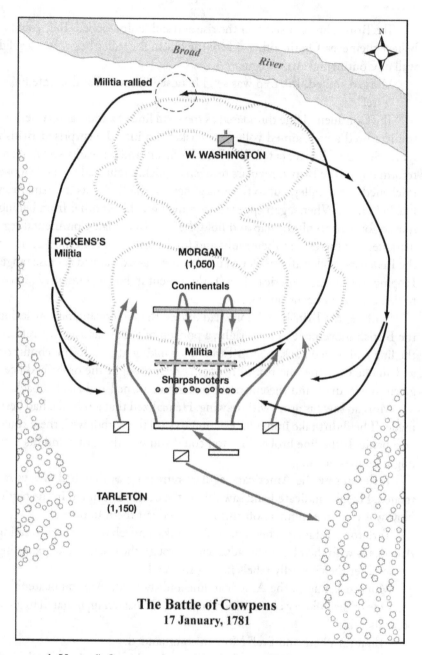

The Battle of Cowpens
17 January, 1781

As Howard's Continentals attack in the center, W. Washington's cavalry counterattack on Tarleton's right flank and Pickens's militia attack Tarleton's left flank in a classic double envelopment in the third phase of the battle.

away, the American regulars leveled their muskets at the enemy and fired!

Redcoats fell in heaps and the British charge collapsed.

"Charge bayonets!" The Americans then cheered and charged with bayonets, raring to smash the Redcoats massed in front of them.

The Redcoats were stunned and fled. In a moment, it was every man for himself as Tarleton's force fled in panic. The militia, who had re-formed behind the regulars, now ran forward on both flanks and attacked. The battle continued as Daniel Morgan's men enveloped the retreating British from the front and both flanks. Washington's cavalry came around from behind the American left to charge the Redcoat right flank and rear. Tarleton's force disintegrated. The Redcoats dropped their muskets and left their wounded on the battlefield; their single thought was to get away from relentless Americans.

Daniel Morgan had achieved what few generals in history had ever achieved: A double envelopment and a crushing, decisive tactical victory.

Tarleton had turned his horse to avoid capture, but it was shot from under him. He grabbed the reins of another horse and rode off the battlefield at a gallop. It was 8:00 A.M. and the battle was over. A few unlucky British artillerymen were left behind and continued to fire their cannons until Lieutenant Colonel Washington's cavalry sabered them off their guns and forced the survivors to surrender. Although there were shouts for "Tarleton's Quarter" along the American lines, Daniel Morgan and his commanders made sure that proper quarter was given and prisoners were taken. There would be no slaughter of prisoners or wounded under Daniel Morgan's command.

The battle had lasted one hour. Daniel Morgan had worked a miracle and defeated Tarleton, commander of General Cornwallis's fastest moving troops. This victory and the subsequent battle of Guilford Courthouse, where Nathanael Greene stopped Cornwallis, causing the British to lose a quarter of their force (over 500 British casualties to about 250 casualties for the Americans), set in motion the final acts of the war in the South. Although technically Guilford Courthouse was a British victory, the fighting character of the Americans so impressed the British that Cornwallis remarked: "I never saw such fighting since God made me. The Americans fought like demons"

The British southern army under Cornwallis was forced to abandon the Carolinas and withdraw to the Virginia coast and the support of the British navy. The vaunted Redcoats been defeated and driven away in no small part because of Daniel Morgan's brilliant and courageous leadership at the Battle of Cowpens.

LEADERSHIP LESSONS LEARNED FROM
DANIEL MORGAN AT THE BATTLE OF COWPENS

There is much that can be learned, for the battlefield or the boardroom, from a study of Daniel Morgan's leadership at the Battle of Cowpens. Most significant are:

• **A true leader sets the conditions for success.** Setting the conditions for victory before the battle took place was the critical skill that Gen. Daniel Morgan displayed at the Battle of Cowpens. Generals who win only because of the courage and stamina of their soldiers are poor commanders. Morgan realized that he could not defeat Tarleton's force on equal terms. He sought an advantage and retreated as Tarleton advanced, looking for a place where he could find a tactical edge over the superior British. By his rapid movement, he tired Tarleton's force. On the day of the battle, the British had been marching for several days and were nearly worn out. Morgan knew his opponent and gambled that Tarleton would push his men ferociously in his quest for glory. Once Morgan found the Cowpens, a suitable spot for the battle he hoped to fight, he turned, enticed Tarleton to attack and in the early hours of the morning set his battle lines to maximize the strengths of his force. At 7:00 A.M., when Tarleton's force rushed into the trap, Morgan had already set in motion a tactical masterpiece that resulted in the defeat of an elite British force.

• **Courage is the vital component of leadership.** Courage is not the absence of fear, but the ability to confront it. Courage is the ability to act correctly under intense pressure. Whether you are on a battlefield or in a boardroom, courage matters. Courage requires that you care more for the team than for your personal safety, comfort or promotion. Daniel Morgan had the courage to stand and fight Tarleton in spite of his reputation. His display of courage in the thick of the battle helped to steady and inspire his men. If "old Dan" could stick it out, his men felt that they must stand as well and vowed not to let him down. Two centuries later, Winston Churchill described courage as "the first of human qualities ... because it is the quality that guarantees all others." Daniel Morgan exemplified courage by acting correctly under intense pressure.

• **Inspire your Team.** Optimism—Cheerfulness—Confidence—Determination in the face of adversity. Soldiers, who are looking defeat in the face, or a business team facing a seemingly insurmountable deadline, need inspired leadership. The leader must communicate by his words, actions, and attitude that the task can be accomplished, that the team will succeed and that the goal of achieving success is worthy of sacrifice. In battle, soldiers sacrifice their blood and lives. In business, the members of a team sacrifice their time, sweat, creativity, and sometimes fortune. A true leader does not waste these valuable resources and takes every opportunity to inspire the team to accomplish the mission and overcome all obstacles. Morgan's leadership on behalf of the American cause was extraordinary and his ability to inspire his men was a crucial ingredient of his remarkable success at Cowpens.

- **Know yourself, know your enemy (or the competition), and know your team members.** The great Chinese strategist on the art of war Sun Tzu said, "if you know your enemies and know yourself, you can win a hundred battles without a single loss. If you only know yourself, but not your opponent, you may win or may lose. If you know neither yourself nor your enemy, you will always endanger yourself." Daniel Morgan had almost assuredly never read Sun Tzu's *Art of War*, but nonetheless he understood and acted upon this main principle. Morgan had to deploy a largely untrained and unreliable force against a better-trained and well-led component of Cornwallis's army. Morgan took the time to study his enemy, learn Tarleton's weaknesses, and understand what made him successful. He used this knowledge against Tarleton and crafted a trap to snare his arrogant, headstrong opponent. Morgan also took the time to get to know his subordinate commanders and his men, and they in turn got to know the mettle of their general. Morgan communicated with his men as equals, shared their campfires and swapped stories with them. He possessed a keen understanding of the psychology of his soldiers and a firm grasp of the tactical principles of eighteenth century warfare. Morgan employed his knowledge of the strengths and weaknesses of his force and those of his enemy to gain a decisive advantage over Tarleton at Cowpens.
- **Articulate your plans and intent.** Daniel Morgan was a rough, hard, uneducated man, but he was a genius at leading men and understood his enemy and his own men. He especially knew that his militia could not hold out long against an assault by a line of British regulars. He articulated his plans to his leaders and his men clearly, asking them to do what was possible— only fire two shots—and not asking them to do more than they were capable of performing. He explained his intent to trap Tarleton in the simplest of terms, so that every soldier in his force knew what was expected, and because his men knew what was expected of them, they acted on their own,

without direct orders. This allowed Morgan's force to orient, observe, decide, and act faster than the British, who waited for nearly every command from Tarleton.

- **Lead by example and be at the right place to make decisions.** Knowing where to be in the thick of the action is a key talent of a true leader. Daniel Morgan could not be everywhere at Cowpens, but he could place himself at the point where he was needed to make decisions. He knew from his experience as a soldier that the vital moment in this battle would come after *all* the militia had fallen behind the regulars. As he surmised, the climax of the battle occurred after the militia had fallen back and when his Continental Army regulars mistook the movement of the right flank as a general order to withdraw. When Morgan observed this mistake, he acted immediately and decisively. He rode his horse to the colonel in charge of the line and ordered him to turn about. This action—when the American line halted, turned and fired—stunned the British to the point that they broke ranks and ran from the field. If Morgan had not acted in time, and had not been at the right place to overcome the confusion and influence the battle, the fight could have been lost. The significance of Daniel Morgan to the cause of American Liberty cannot be overstated, and even though he is not well known today, he is one of America's greatest battlefield leaders and a quintessential example of American leadership in action.

- **When it comes to leadership you bet on people, not strategies.** If you expect to win, select the right leaders. Gen. George Washington picked Gen. Nathanael Greene and Daniel Morgan because he knew the mettle of these leaders. Greene, in turn, bet on the leadership of Daniel Morgan and Morgan never let them down. Former CEO of Honeywell International, Inc. Larry Bossidy put it this way: "At the end of the day, you bet on people, not on strategies." This tenet is as true for picking a little-league baseball coach, to hiring someone to lead a business to selecting a battlefield commander. Selecting the right people to lead teams is one of the most important decisions a leader can make.

General George Washington, the "indispensable man" of the Cause of American Liberty and the "Father of our Country" (portrait by Rembrandt Peale, 1850).

Chapter 7

THE GREAT DUTY I OWE
MY COUNTRY: *Washington at*
Newburgh, New York, 1783

*The moderation and virtue of a single character probably
prevented this Revolution from being closed, as most others
have been, by a subversion of that liberty it was intended
to establish.*
　　　　—Thomas Jefferson on George Washington in 1784

LEADERSHIP REQUIRES *CHARACTER.*

After eight long years of bitter struggle, from 1775 to 1783, the war was
nearly over. After General Morgan's brilliant victory over Tarleton at
Cowpens, South Carolina, on January 17, 1781, British Lt. Gen. Charles
Cornwallis was determined to reverse the situation in the South and revive
the British Southern Strategy. His goal was to defeat the army led by American Gen. Nathanael Greene operating in North Carolina.

Greene, like Morgan before him, continued to withdraw as Cornwallis
approached. To speed up the chase, Cornwallis burned his supply wagons in
order to move as swiftly as Greene's fast-moving force. On March 14, 1781,
Cornwallis discovered that Greene was encamped near the Guilford Court
House with four to five thousand men, mostly militia and within a few miles
march of Cornwallis's army. Although Cornwallis had only nineteen hundred
men, he felt he had finally caught Greene's army, and attacked the American
force on March 15, 1781.

Greene was ready and used similar tactics to those used by Morgan at
Cowpens. Cornwallis, much like Tarleton at Cowpens, rushed into a battle
that the Americans had prepared for. After ninety minutes of hard fighting,
Cornwallis won a pyrrhic victory at Guilford Courthouse, but the Americans

withdrew in good order. Cornwallis had gambled on a decisive victory, and was now out of options. Having burned his supply wagons and with Tarelton's mobile force destroyed, he was unable to continue the chase Greene's elusive army further into the wilds of North Carolina. Reluctantly, Cornwallis was forced to move off the field battered and bloodied, to fall back to resupply. The hard fighting at Guilford Courthouse caused British Whig statesman Charles James Fox to exclaim: "Another such victory would ruin the British Army!"

With the earlier British defeats in South Carolina at Kings Mountain (October 7, 1780) and Cowpens (January 17, 1781) the British Southern Strategy was in shambles and Cornwallis's goal of crushing the American army in the South had evaporated. Accordingly, he moved toward the coast of Virginia in order to draw support from the Royal Navy. Once in Virginia Cornwallis chased around a small force under the Marquis de Lafayette for several weeks then moved to the river port of Yorktown. By late May 1781, Cornwallis's foot-sore and reduced army linked up with reinforcements, dug defensive positions around the village of Yorktown and waited for the navy.

Washington and the French Army were lined up against Gen. Clinton's British forces defending New York. Washington wanted to take New York City, and Clinton knew this, but in August 1781, with Cornwallis ensconced at Yorktown and licking his wounds, George Washington saw a strategic opportunity. Several important events converged to create a perfect storm against the British. First, the French were now open allies of the rebellious Americans and had landed a well-equipped and well-trained fifty-five hundred man army under Gen. Jean-Baptiste Donatien de Vimeur, Comte de Rochambeau, to support Washington against the British in operations around New York. Second, the French fleet, in the fortuitous naval Battle of the Chesapeake on September 5, 1781, defeated the British fleet and forced it to sail back to New York for repairs. This was one of the few times in history that the French Navy bested the British Navy. Fortune was smiling on America and a window of opportunity opened where the Americans and French could deal the British a crushing blow at Yorktown.

As the French fleet controlled the Chesapeake Bay and blocked Cornwallis's escape by sea, Washington and Rochambeau secretly withdrew from their positions in New York. The Americans and French moved south toward Yorktown before British Gen. Henry Clinton, commanding the main British army in New York, knew what was happening. The Americans and French surrounded the British forces at Yorktown, by land and sea, and besieged

Cornwallis's army on September 29, 1781. With Clinton reluctant to move from New York for fear of losing the most important city in America, and with the French fleet controlling the waters around Yorktown, Cornwallis was on his own.

The Americans and French tightened the ring around Cornwallis at Yorktown, moving trench lines closer to British positions and bombarding the British day and night. October 14, 1781, Washington ordered the attack of two critical British defensive positions, redoubts #9 and #10. In a daring night attack the French stormed redoubt #9 and the Americans under Alexander Hamilton used bayonets to capture redoubt #10. The fighting was sharp, short, and bloody and the Americans and French prevailed. With these defenses taken, the Americans and French could move siege guns forward to put a stranglehold on Cornwallis.

Cornwallis had no choice but to surrender or watch his army be hammered into the ground by American and French artillery. On October 19, 1781, Cornwallis surrendered his army to Gen. Washington. At the formal surrender ceremony Cornwallis feigned sickness and a second surrendered for him, but the act was done. The British and Hessian troops marched into American and French lines with their regimental flags cased and their muskets slung over their shoulders reversed, pointing downward, in shame. Although it cannot be verified, as no one listed the songs the band played, the apocryphal record is that the British band played a tune called "The World Turn'd Upside Down" as nearly nine thousand British and Hessian troops were forced to stack arms and became prisoners of war. When Lord North, the prime minister of Great Britain, learned of the surrender of Cornwallis and his army he is reported to have exclaimed, "Oh God, it's all over."

Washington, with the decisive help of the French army and navy, won a decisive victory at Yorktown, but the war was not yet over. The British agreed to meet with the Americans in peace talks that dragged on throughout 1782. In the meantime, the British army remained in New York City. In case the British decided to do mischief during the peace talks, Washington encamped his army nearby at Newburgh, New York, eight miles north of the fortifications at West Point.

As 1782 turned to 1783, the American army was restless. Peace negotiations were moving slowly and except for some small patrol actions major fighting was over. Washington's soldiers wanted to go home, but Washington had to maintain the army intact until the official surrender in case the British changed their minds and decided to continue the war. During this time the

American army grumbled about wages that had long been promised but remained unpaid. For most of the war the soldiers had been promised pay for their service but received little or nothing from Congress. They were frustrated with a Congress they viewed as uncaring and unengaged. While soldiers had suffered and sacrificed in the field for the cause of Liberty, Congress had been unable to properly support the troops. The soldiers wanted Congress to fulfill its promise of back-pay and pensions for the men who had fought so long and courageously in the long eight years they had been fighting for independence.

Congress, however, had almost no money to pay anyone. In 1783, Congress was operating under the "Articles of Confederation and Perpetual Union," initiated in 1776 but not formally ratified by all thirteen states until 1781. The Articles of Confederation bound the states in a loose union, but gave little power to the Congress and specifically denied Congress the right to levy taxes from the states. In fact, Congress was at the mercy of the states for *all* revenue and the states were unwilling to pay. With nearly no money, Congress could not pay the army, let alone the pensions they had promised. A group of army officers, hoping to bring their troubles to the attention of the American government, asked Gen. Henry Knox to take their grievances to Congress. The petition was received by Congress, but was answered with more promises of payment sometime in the future when Congress solved its financial problems. This answer was not well received by the men garrisoned at Newburgh.

Gen. Washington sympathized with his officers and men over Congress's unfulfilled promises. He understood their sacrifice, but he maintained a steady resolve to obey the orders of the civilian government. He had argued vigorously with Congress over the past eight years to keep its commitments to the men. He did not underestimate the passion of his officers and men concerning the promises that Congress had made. He loved his soldiers and knew firsthand how courageously they had fought against terrible odds for so many hard, difficult years. He knew that his men felt betrayed. They had persevered through eight long years of conflict while others, safe in their homes with family and fires, had not served or sacrificed for the Glorious Cause. But Washington believed in the American Liberty. He saw the new nation as a nation of laws, ruled by the people. He believed wholeheartedly in the ideals of the Revolution and Congress's right to direct the army. He would not tolerate any thoughts that his men would violate the rule of Congress or usurp power.

With the army idle the soldiers grumbled and the officers grew more frustrated with Congress every day. Many good men, some of them in Congress, felt the soldiers were right to feel that way. Several officers openly talked about their right to force Congress to pay the army what had been promised to them and of "the injuries the troops have received" from lack of Congressional support. One officer, Lewis Nicola, even hinted that America would be better off if the army declared Washington as king. Washington replied in writing to Nicola's proposal: "No incident in the course of the war in me triggers painful feelings as your message, that such ideas are circulating in the army, as you expressed it."

Passions flared and the crisis in civil-military control came to a head when a group of officers led by Major John Armstrong published anonymous letters, which are now called the "Newburgh Addresses," demanding a meeting to discuss the payment issue and possibly the replacement of Washington with Gen. Horatio Gates. The letters urged the use of whatever means necessary to secure the army's just recompenses and declared that if they were not paid as the Congress had promised, the army would refuse to fight to protect the Congress if the British attacked. Furthermore, the army would not disband until Congress's promises were kept.

In the extreme case these letters supported bypassing Congress and establishing a military dictatorship.

The officers organizing the effort articulated in the "Newburgh Addresses" called for an open meeting on March 12. As soon as Washington learned of the scheduling of this meeting he cancelled it. Undeterred, the conspirators scheduled another meeting. On March 15, 1783, the unauthorized meeting formed in the "New Building," a wooden hall in the Newburgh Camp. General Gates presided over the opening of the meeting and nearly all the army's officers were present. Washington had not been invited as the organizers of the meeting felt that Washington would not act against Congress on the their behalf. In essence, the army was in mutiny and acting without the consent of its commanding general.

The meeting had just begun when to everyone's surprise Washington entered the New Building and asked to address the assembly of officers. Washington's demeanor visibly demonstrated that he understood the challenge that was occurring to his authority. Gates quietly relinquished the floor.

Washington stood in front of his officers. He paused, gazed at them carefully and saw the frustration and anger on their faces.

It would have been easy for Washington to agree with the crowd, denounce Congress for their lies, and promise to march on Philadelphia and demand what was due them at the point of a bayonet. Many another general in history would have done just that and declared himself dictator or king. Maybe a Caesar or a Napoleon would have led a revolt against Congress but Washington was made of finer stuff. Washington believed in the Glorious Cause and in Liberty.

He addressed them saying:

> Gentlemen: By an anonymous summons, an attempt has been made to convene you together; how inconsistent with the rules of propriety! how unmilitary! and how subversive of all order and discipline, let the good sense of the Army decide. In the moment of this Summons, another anonymous production was sent into circulation, addressed more to the feelings and passions, than to the reason and judgment of the Army. The author of the piece, is entitled to much credit for the goodness of his Pen and I could wish he had as much credit for the rectitude of his Heart, for, as Men see thro' different Optics, and are induced by the reflecting faculties of the Mind, to use different means, to attain the same end, the Author of the Address, should have had more charity, than to mark for Suspicion, the Man who should recommend moderation and longer forbearance, or, in other words, who should not think as he thinks, and act as he advises. But he had another plan in view, in which candor and liberality of Sentiment, regard to justice, and love of Country, have no part; and he was right, to insinuate the darkest suspicion, to effect the blackest designs.

These were harsh words and Washington was not pulling any punches.

Washington continued speaking as his officers stood in silence. "My God! What can this writer have in view, by recommending such measures? Can he be a friend to the Army? Can he be a friend to this Country? Rather, is he not an insidious Foe?"

He went on to tell them that they must trust Congress and that he would continue to press for their just payments, but would never threaten Congress or use the military in any way to overturn civilian rule. He then said about the army that:

> I have so long had the honor to Command, will oblige me to declare,

in this public and solemn manner, that, in the attainment of complete justice for all your toils and dangers, and in the gratification of every wish, so far as may be done consistently with the great duty I owe my Country, and those powers we are bound to respect, you may freely command my Services to the utmost of my abilities. While I give you these assurances, and pledge myself in the most unequivocal manner, to exert whatever ability I am possessed of, in your favor, let me entreat you, Gentlemen, on your part, not to take any measures, which viewed in the calm light of reason, will lessen the dignity, and sully the glory you have hitherto maintained; let me request you to rely on the plighted faith of your Country, and place a full confidence in the purity of the intentions of Congress .... By thus determining, and thus acting, you will pursue the plain and direct road to the attainment of your wishes. You will defeat the insidious designs of our Enemies, who are compelled to resort from open force to secret Artifice. You will give one more distinguished proof of unexampled patriotism and patient virtue, rising superior to the pressure of the most complicated sufferings; And you will, by the dignity of your Conduct, afford occasion of Posterity to say, when speaking of the glorious example you have exhibited to Mankind, "had this day been wanting, the World had never seen the last stage of perfection to which human nature is capable of attaining."

Washington stopped speaking and the room was silent. He placed his prepared comments on a table. After a moment, he reached into his pocket and pulled out another letter, written by Congress to explain their financial problems and express Congress' efforts on the part of the Army. The letter was handwritten in small script and difficult for Washington to read.

In the dim light Washington fumbled in his breast pocket for a set of reading glasses. His men had seen their tireless, gallant general lead them in dozens of battles and always braving the enemy's fire. Washington had always been at the front. He had never left his men during the entire war. He served for no pay and expected Congress only to reimburse him for reasonable expenses. Washington's character was above reproach and he was the hero of the army.

His officers had never witnessed Washington wearing reading glasses before.

As Washington put on the glasses he announced: "Gentlemen, you will permit me to put on my spectacles, for I have not only grown gray but almost blind in the service of my country."

This act was the defining moment. The personal strength and esteem of one man, George Washington, saved the Republic. Instantly, the officers gathered in the New Building were reminded of how much they, and Washington, had sacrificed for the Glorious Cause of Liberty and the independence of the United States. The conspiracy collapsed in that shining moment. Washington was so respected and loved by his officers and his men that it was inconceivable that he should first admonish them and now allow them to see him reduced to wearing spectacles.

A simple pair of reading glasses played an important part in American history. There would be no coup by the army in America.

Tears flowed in the eyes of many of those officers present as Washington put on his spectacles. Washington's inspiration had turned their hearts and restored republican values. Every man there realized the personal sacrifice that General Washington had made and was willing to continue to make for freedom. Washington's sterling character, and his reading glasses, saved the country!

The officers voted overwhelmingly to reject the "Newburgh Addresses" and wholeheartedly followed Washington's wishes to obey the Congress. From this point on the army would work on their grievances with Congress and not work against the government. A precedent, uncommon in the history of man, had been set. In America, the bayonet would not rule; Liberty would survive.

Congress was not able to keep its original promises, but over time, at Washington's urgings and persistence, Congress found a way to pay army officers a lump-sum for five-year's service in the form of government issued bonds. Although the bonds were not considered legal tender, they were a promise of payment and were eventually redeemed at full value in 1790. Congress promised each soldier who served three months pay, but since Congress had no funds, patriot financier Robert Morris stepped forward and issued a total $800 thousand in personal notes to the soldiers.

On November 23, 1783, the British troops left New York and the American army took possession of the city. The War for Independence concluded on September 3, 1783, when the American delegation consisting of John Jay, John Adams, Benjamin Franklin, Henry Laurens, and William Temple Franklin, signed the Treaty of Paris. The treaty was signed in the Hotel d'York, which today is the Hotel du Danube at 56 Rue Jacob in Paris. Later, on January14, 1784, the American Congress ratified the Treaty of Paris and officially ended the war between the United States of America and Great Britain.

With the treaty signed, Congress issued a proclamation declaring that the vast majority of the soldiers as well as noncommissioned and commissioned officers were to be discharged by December 3, 1783. On November 2, 1783, at Rocky Hill, near Princeton, New Jersey, George Washington believed he had completed his duty to the nation and issued an order to the army voluntarily surrendering his power as commander in chief of America's military forces. In this order Washington noted "the unparalleled perseverance of the Armies of the United States, through almost every possible suffering and discouragement, for the space of eight long years was little short of a standing Miracle." He disbanded the army, called them a "patriotic band of brothers," thanked them for their "extraordinary patience in suffering, as well as their invincible fortitude in action," and asked them to "prove themselves not less virtuous and useful as Citizens, than they have been persevering and victorious as Soldiers." In short, in his actions at Newburgh and in the proclamation of his last public order as General of the Army, Washington reaffirmed the tenets of civilian control of the military and set the example for generations of Americans to come.

———

LEADERSHIP LESSONS LEARNED FROM GEORGE WASHINGTON AT NEWBURGH

There are many lessons to be garnered from George Washington's leadership of the American Army at Newburgh in 1783. Some of the most significant are:

- **Leadership requires character.** Today's news is filled with sad tales of the dramatic character failures of senior leaders in government and business. The truth is that these failures are a failure of values. You can improve your character every day by changing your behavior to follow a set of guiding values. Leaders of character, like George Washington, displayed an unswerving pattern of conduct that had a positive influence on others. Washington understood the need to set the example. He wanted his officers to imitate him and act according to the principles of Liberty and the ideals of the American Revolution in all things. Washington realized that in the ultimate crucible of leadership, the example that he set would decide the fate of Liberty and the Revolution. Washington exemplified the notion of setting the example for others to follow. Philosopher and humanitarian Albert Schweitzer (January 14, 1875–September 4, 1965), said: "Example is not the main thing in influencing others, *it is the only thing*," and this, more than anything else, defines Washington's leadership.

- **Make principled leadership your leadership compass.** Washington's core beliefs drove him to support the ideals of Liberty as exemplified by the Declaration of Independence: "We hold these truths to be self evident, that all men are created equal, that they are endowed by their Creator with certain inalienable Rights, that among these are Life, Liberty and the pursuit of Happiness.— That to secure these rights, Governments are instituted among Men, deriving their just powers from the consent of the governed." Washington embraced these principles. They guided his actions and, like a compass, kept him on course. At his farewell, rather than acting to retain power, he set the example of the American patriotic ideal for generations to come by abdicating his eminent position and becoming a plain citizen. It is interesting to contrast Washington with Napoleon Bonaparte. Both men lived at nearly the same time, Washington from February 22, 1732, to December 14, 1799, and Napoleon from August 15, 1769, to May 5, 1821). Both men were leaders of their respective revolutions and both were generals, leading armies against difficult odds. Napoleon was arguably the better military man and possessed a genius for war, but Washington's character shines though the ages and marks him as the superior human being. Washington's leadership was selfless, while Napoleon's leadership was self-aggrandizing. Napoleon's ego created a great empire in which he became emperor, brought about the death of millions and ended in disaster. Washington's leadership birthed a nation that offers the greatest degree of individual freedom the world has ever seen. Washington did not seek personal power, riches or glory. Instead, Washington viewed his leadership as a "great duty that he owed his country" and a necessary sacrifice. It was Washington's response to power, not his military skill that made him the most respected and revered leader in America and, many say, in the world. Napoleon overpowered his opponents and held on to power until he was dethroned. Washington always respected the civil government, handing over the command of the army in 1783 and later, after his second term as president, voluntarily giving up power to set an example for the continuation of elected government in the United States. Upon learning this, his former enemy, King George III, said, "if Washington went back to his farm after his public career he would be the greatest character of the age." Washington returned to Mount Vernon upon leaving the army and hoped to retire to a quiet life at home. Six years later his country would call him again to be sworn in as the nation's first president. Many Americans wanted Washington to be president for a third term, but he refused. If you had a choice of leaders to follow, who would you prefer, Washington or Napoleon?

- **Leaders must inspire.** Ralph Waldo Emerson once said, "Our chief want is someone who will inspire us to be what we know we could be." Washington was that kind of man. He was not the most brilliant speaker or the greatest philosopher of his time, but he was a man whose character inspired those he led. Washington's personal life goal was to discipline himself, to develop his character, and to gain the respect of those around him. Washington inspired a generation of leaders by this selfless dedication to self-development. By disciplining himself, he inspired others to act according to his example. At Newburgh, he established the shining principle of supremacy of Congress over the American military. In his farewell address to his soldiers he revealed his central attitude about the importance of character and personal honor and the necessity of a strong federal government to preserve the freedoms they had all fought for. By the dignity of his conduct at Newburgh, Washington provided "one more distinguished proof of unexampled patriotism and patient virtue."

- **Effective leaders build personal bonds of trust.** At the meeting at Newburgh, Washington was able to tap into a deep personal bond with his officers and, through this connection, change their hearts. Washington didn't try to manipulate the situation; he approached the situation honestly. He recognized the significance of people, treated them with respect and tapped into the strong relationships of trust and loyalty that he had worked to build during eight years of war. The ability of the leader to build mutual trust is vital for any team: military, business, or social. Mutual trust is a shared belief, that you can depend on each other to achieve a common purpose. Effective leadership requires trust; it is like money saved away for a time of need. Building trust develops a competitive advantage for your team. Build trust and when your defining test arrives, you will succeed, and your team will help carry you over the top.

- **Leadership requires loyalty.** Washington strongly believed in the principle of civilian control over the military. One of Washington's most admirable qualities was the care he gave to relations with Congress. He constantly kept Congress informed and tirelessly wrote volumes of correspondence to ensure they understood the state of the army and the requirements for success. Congress' support of the army during the war was often wanting, but Washington never faltered in his unwavering support for the civil authority. He respected Congress and would not stand for his officers blaming Congress for the lack of supplies, recruits, or pay. His years of experience in the Virginia legislature had provided a valuable education in the purpose of government and those lessons were invaluable during the darkest days of the war and during the Newburgh Conspiracy. He was loyal to the Congress and the Glorious Cause and understood that if Liberty was to survive, the people had to rule.

DONT TREAD ON ME

The Gadsden Flag is considered one of the first flags of the United States during the American Revolution and the motto "Don't Tread on Me" represented the mood of the patriot cause. The flag was designed by Brig. Gen. Christopher Gadsden (February 16, 1724 to September 15, 1805) of South Carolina. Gadsden was a patriot who opposed the overbearing power of the British Crown, fought for independence and was a member of the First and Second Continental Congress. In 1776 he left Congress to serve with the Continental Army. In 1780, after the fall of Charleston, he became a prisoner of war, refused special pardon from the British, and was held in solitary confinement for 42 weeks until his release in 1781 after the defeat of Tarleton at Cowpens and the withdrawal of British forces under General Cornwallis to Yorktown. Gadsden later was elected governor of South Carolina, but declined due to poor health stemming from his captivity. He was a member of the state convention of 1788 called to ratify the Constitution of the United States.

Chapter 8

EXCEPTIONALISM, LIBERTY, AND LEADERSHIP

A Definition of Leadership: Leadership is a sacred trust and the art of influence. It is the ability to motivate, inspire and impel people to accomplish a mission.

Moments define us. Moments of adversity reveal character. Moments of challenge disclose courage or cowardice. Moments of action uncover decision or irresolution. Defining moments reveal leadership. Your leadership ability is a critical skill that can be improved through study and experience. Your personal leadership ability matters to everyone you come in contact with. *Everything you do in life is impacted by your ability to lead. In every aspect of life, you will only rise to the level of your leadership.* Unless you are the lone occupant of a deserted island, leadership matters.

Leadership is a sacred trust. It is an agreement between the leader and those he leads, that the leader will do everything in his power to respect the life, liberty, and honor of the led. It is a sacred trust because the leader has power over another person; his time, money, and dignity in the case of employment, or his life in the case of the government or the military. It is a *sacred trust* because leadership is a promise from the leader to the led that the leader will not waste his most valuable team asset: people.

Leadership is the art of influence. It is an art, not a science. There is no equation that leaders can input to determine how to act. Leadership takes knowledge and experience to know how to successfully lead people. The combination of the right knowledge and the right experience can generate the wisdom to influence people to get something done even when the situation is difficult, dire or deadly.

Leadership is the ability to motivate, inspire, and impel people to accomplish a mission. This definition emphasizes that the leader take positive action to motivate and inspire people to act. Notice this definition uses the word *impel*, not *compel*. Impel is a word that is very similar in meaning to compel but suggests even more strongly an inner drive to do something and often a greater urgency in the desire to act. In this definition, *impel* means to urge or encourage while *compel* means to take action as a result of pressure or coercion. Impel implies that the leader act in a manner to obtain the loyal obedience, confidence, respect, and loyal cooperation of the led. The difference is decisive. In every case, leaders should strive to impel, rather than compel. The act of compelling someone to follow instructions may be necessary at times, but should be the method of last resort.

LEADERSHIP LESSONS

The leaders discussed in the previous chapters are from a very different time than ours. These leadership lessons, however, are timeless. The seven leadership moments recounted in this book provide insights that you can use to raise your leadership ability in your home, work, community, state, and nation. These stories explained the leadership challenges of real people facing real challenges, who overcame what reasonable people believed were insurmountable odds. In each of the previous chapters, key leaders provided the vital ingredient for success. They accomplished the mission, often overcoming unbelievable hardships, challenges, and personal sacrifices. These stories of leadership describe a uniquely American style of leadership that helped form the American character. The synthesis of these seven stories generates seven unambiguous themes:

A leader chooses courage:
Fear is a reaction; courage is a decision, a choice: Samuel Adams, Patrick Henry, Henry Knox, Benjamin Franklin, John Adams, Thomas Jefferson, George Washington, and Daniel Morgan chose courage. They placed themselves in dangerous situations, felt the fear, but chose to be courageous. They realized that without courage, nothing else mattered. No one would follow them if they showed fear, cowered and failed to act. Leaders must choose courage. Courage is the first prerequisite of leadership. Courage does not mean fearlessness; it means acting in spite of your fears.

A leader must learn to follow to learn to lead:
All of the leaders described in these stories first learned to be successful followers before they became leaders. They became the kind of follower

you want to have on your team, enthusiastic, can-do, and ready to work hard and sacrifice to get the job done. By learning how to follow, they learned selflessness, for they had to give up their time, livelihood, and safety for the greater cause. By learning selflessness, they learned how to be selfless in their leadership. The leaders described in these chapters risked their "lives, liberty and sacred honor," for a greater good—to motivate people to win the independence of the United States.

A leader must be determined to succeed:
Determination is a common thread in all these stories as it is essential for successful leadership. Leaders must see things as they are, not as they wish them to be, as Washington did at the Battle of Trenton and as Morgan persevered during the Battle of Cowpens. Determination to continue the effort often generates unforeseen opportunities, whereas quitting closes off all options. During the Battle of Trenton, when Washington was told that the powder in his soldier's muskets was wet and might not fire, he did not flinch and ordered the attack to continue and to use the bayonet. Had he hesitated or turned around, the battle might have been lost. Washington knew then that there was no alternative but "victory or death." He knew that there were no other options. Knowing when to abandon a failed course of action and take another option is a skill that every leader must learn. The difference between determination and stubbornness is a fine line that each leader must weigh, but without determination to succeed the game is over.

A leader must teach, coach, and mentor:
In every case, but especially in the example of George Washington, the leader was also a teacher, a coach, and a mentor. Washington took every opportunity to spend time with his officers and men to get to know them and to use every opportunity to grow the leadership of his team. Whenever possible he dined with his officers early in the afternoon in order to get to know them and to engage them in conversation. Washington's mere example was enough to show his people how to lead. Washington strove to treat all people with dignity and respect, to lead by example and to never forget that character provides a leader with a moral compass that will provide direction when times are tough. On the battlefield Washington's personal example of courage under fire provided tangible instruction to his officers and men of what was expected of them in battle.

A leader must delegate authority:
Leaders who train subordinate leaders and prepare them for leadership multiply their own effectiveness. Knowing when and how to delegate authority is a vital leadership skill. In each of these stories, the leader succeeded when he delegated authority to trusted subordinate and ready subordinate leaders. In each case, the leader provided the subordinate leader with the *authority* and the *responsibility* to accomplish the mission. If a leader has authority but no responsibility, that leader is a tyrant. If a leader has responsibility but no authority, that leader is a victim. Tyrants and victims usually make poor leaders. To empower subordinate leaders, the leader must give him the right mix of responsibility and authority.

A leader pulls and a boss pushes:
The leadership of Benjamin Franklin during the writing of the Declaration of Independence is the quintessential example of a leader pulling verses pushing. The delegates of the Second Continental Congress were the elected leaders of each of their respective states and all accomplished men. Pushing them would only have created resistance. Instead, Franklin used his extensive knowledge and experience of human nature to win over those who hesitated to support the vote for independence. His leadership, and the persuasion of John Adams, made a difference during those hot summer days before the signing of the Declaration. Likewise, the ability of George Washington to convince his officers not to take action against Congress for legitimate grievances during the Newburgh Conspiracy, and to obey the superiority of the civilian authority, was a gleaming example of pulling verses pushing. Had Washington ordered them to desist, without convincing them by a personal address, the outcome might have been dramatically different.

A leader doesn't shine, but reflects:
This idea is the essence of selfless leadership, allowing your team and subordinate leaders to receive the accolades, rather than taking credit as the leader for a team effort. Leaders cannot accomplish missions without a team. When a leader asks the team to sacrifice time, effort, money, sweat, or more, the leader has entered into an agreement with the team that their efforts will be recognized. Daniel Morgan understood this at the Battle of Cowpens. Around their campfires on the night before the

fight, Morgan talked to his men, reinforcing the plan for the battle and emphasizing that the victory would be theirs. After the battle he consistently told people that it was his men, not Daniel Morgan, who won that fight. His men loved him for this—his ability to reflect rather than shine—and would do anything for him.

LIBERTY AND THE AMERICAN REVOLUTION

Thankfully, these leaders were unreasonable for the cause of Liberty. Through their leadership, the United States took the exceptional act to declare independence, fight for eight long years, and secure Liberty. Their efforts created an exceptional nation.

Let there be no mistake, the United States of America *is* an exceptional nation. The Liberty won by the bold leadership of the men and women who fought and served during the American Revolution was the seed for this exceptionalism. The leadership of the patriots who won our Liberty is the focus of this book. The patriots of 1776 felt that America was not just an extension of Europe but something new. They saw America as a place of unlimited possibilities and opportunity and, as Ronald Reagan would later say, a "shining city on a hill."

Americans have many firsts to be proud of, most of which were generated at the birth of our nation. Americans were the *first* people to rebel against the awesome power of the British Empire and win independence. Unlike other successful revolutions, America was the *first* nation born of revolution that did not eventually succumb to military dictatorship or a despotic autocratic government. Americans were the *first* to craft their independence and government based on the notion of individual merit and individual liberty. Americans were the *first* to establish a government on the belief that the rights of man were inalienable and came not from the benevolence of royalty, but from the grace of "nature and nature's God."

Americans were the *first* to declare formally that the powers of government derive from the consent of the people, not the other way around, and Americans were the *first* to recognize that the best government was limited government. Americans were the *first* to create a system of government that balanced the power of government among executive, legislative, and judicial branches, sharing authority between federal and state governments. Americans were the *first* to demonstrate and institutionalize the subordination of military power to civilian control.

An important example of the understanding of American exceptionalism stems from the understanding of the word liberty. You may have noticed that "Liberty" is capitalized throughout this book when the word represents the *cause* of liberty. In common English grammar, proper nouns are capitalized. Proper nouns refer to specific, named people, places, and things. Writers of English capitalize proper nouns such as Texas, Pearl Harbor, or The United States of America. In 1776, many of the delegates of the Second Continental Congress capitalized the word Liberty. They wanted to distinguish American Liberty, set it apart from mere freedom, and separate it from the common usage of the word. Here, in text, is the one of the most important sentences in the English language, shown in the capitalization format of the actual Declaration of Independence:

> We hold these truths to be self-evident, that all men are created equal, that they are endowed by their Creator with certain unalienable Rights, that among these are Life, Liberty and the pursuit of Happiness.

Thomas Jefferson and the editors of the Declaration of Independence specifically capitalized Life, Liberty, and Happiness for the purpose of defining those terms to the world. The capitalization of Liberty gives the word a precisely defined, exact meaning and was designed to exemplify the inalienable rights of all human beings, bestowed on them by their creator, and the protection of these rights is the reason the people institute government.

Lastly, America has always been a nation of immigrants. Assimilation is often not an easy process, but the successful assimilation of immigrants since the birth of the Republic is a key factor in our Republic's longevity.

If anyone makes the argument to you that America is not an exceptional nation, that its evils and faults mark it unworthy of the title, don't you believe them. America is not a perfect nation, but it is the last best place on earth where free people, inspired by a vision of exceptionalism, can hope to secure "Life, Liberty and the pursuit of Happiness."

AMERICAN EXCEPTIONALISM

What is American exceptionalism? It is a uniquely American belief that Americans are entitled by their inalienable rights as citizens of their country to individual liberty, to equality, to opportunity, to a free market, to a limited government, and to the right to defend all of this by force, if required. The United States is a martial nation when attacked, but Americans prefer peace to war. Underpinning it all is the unshakable dictum that governing power is derived from the *consent of the people.*

Some scoff at the concept that America is exceptional, pointing to our failings and errors. Even President Barak Obama stated that America is no more exceptional than any other nation: "I believe in American exceptionalism, just as I suspect that the Brits believe in British exceptionalism and the Greeks believe in Greek exceptionalism." This statement declares that the concept of exceptionalism is a relative term and therefore American exceptionalism is irrelevant.

Most Europeans and many American liberals would agree with Mr. Obama, as they long for the day when America is less exceptional and more like Europe. Many Americans, however, reject the liberal Eurocentric view.

One American who believed that his country was truly exceptional was the fortieth President of the United States, Ronald Reagan. During President Reagan's First Inaugural Address on January 20, 1981, he explained it this way:

> In this present crisis, government is not the solution to our problem; government is the problem. From time to time we've been tempted to believe that society has become too complex to be managed by self-rule, that government by an elite group is superior to government for, by, and of the people. Well, if no one among us is capable of governing himself, then who among us has the capacity to govern someone else? . . . It does require, however, our best effort and our willingness to believe in ourselves and to believe in our capacity to perform great deeds, to believe that together with God's help we can and will resolve the problems which now confront us. And after all, why shouldn't we believe that? We are Americans.

Cynics will tell you that Americans have nothing special to be proud of, that our blessings are the result of chance or luck. These critics have the luxury to mock the notion of American exceptionalism as they live comfortably in a society that was built on the blood and sacrifice of those who believed that America was special and worth advancing, even at the risk of their "lives, fortunes and sacred honor." We need leaders today who see things differently from the cynics and detractors.

American exceptionalism is not a blank check to do as we wish in the world. It does not give the United States the right to do anything it wants.

American exceptionalism does not place America above the law. No nation is perfect and the United States is not perfect. American exceptionalism is an ideal that should act as a force to hold this country and its leaders to a higher level of scrutiny. When the United States of America misses the mark in actions foreign or domestic, when we fall short of our belief in the exceptional character of our democratic-republic, we err against our most important principles: we err against Liberty.

The more you study the lessons of leadership, the more you will learn from the great leaders of history, and the greater your chances of leading well will ensue. Leaders like Gen. George Washington knew that free men and women must be inspired, not driven; impelled, not compelled. The leadership required to inspire free people is the highest order of leadership and cannot be gained by harsh or tyrannical treatment. Were he alive today General Washington would be the first to tell you that Americans resent authority more than anything else. Bowing to authority is anathema to the American character. General Washington's inspector general and drillmaster, Baron von Steuben, an immigrant who came to America to join the Continental Army to fight for Liberty, recognized this when training the Continental Army at Valley Forge. In a letter to a German soldier he wrote, "You say to your soldier, 'Do this' and he does it. But I am obliged to say to the American, 'This is why you ought to do this,' and then he does it."

When Americans fought during the Revolution to create for the first time in history a government that was a servant of the people and not its master, we were onto something. Since then, America has come a long way and has become the most powerful and free nation on earth. Yet in our success we seem to have lost our way. The system of government that the patriots of 1776 created hasn't failed us, but it seems that today we may be failing it.

If ideas can change people's hearts and minds, then leadership imbued with knowledge, passion and a belief in the best ideals of America can change the world for the better. We need the courage of the convictions of the heroes of 1776 along with a deep passion for the concept of Liberty and self-government. In short, we need a rebirth in the belief of American exceptionalism.

Ronald Reagan summed it up very well:

> My fellow citizens, our Nation is poised for greatness. We must do what we know is right and do it with all our might. Let history say of us, these were golden years—when the American Revolution was reborn, when freedom gained new life, when America reached for

her best. . . . Now we hear again the echoes of our past: a general falls to his knees in the hard snow of Valley Forge; a lonely President paces the darkened halls, and ponders his struggle to preserve the Union; the men of the Alamo call out encouragement to each other; a settler pushes west and sings a song, and the song echoes out forever and fills the unknowing air. It is the American sound. It is hopeful, big-hearted, idealistic, daring, decent, and fair. That's our heritage; that is our song. We sing it still.

If the United States of America is to endure as it was conceived, we must rebuild the pillars of American exceptionalism. Americans should know their history and learn that their nation *is* exceptional: it will remain the most free, most democratic, most individualistic and most vigorous country on earth as long as it holds Liberty at its core. Americans should be told that maintaining Liberty requires a steadfast style of leadership, leadership that is willing to stand and say "Don't Tread on Me!" to tyranny in all its forms.

To communicate a vision to others that inspires, leaders must reinforce courage, self-reliance, and passion for a task in them. Leaders understand that the sacrifice of our forebears must be appreciated and honored with courage. You should root in others the unshakable belief that America is *the* indispensable nation in the world.

For most of our history America has been exceptionally free. Today, the heart and soul of America's national character is at stake. We are in danger of surrendering our liberty. The challenge is fundamental: What kind of government do we wish to have? One that is everywhere or limited? Forces within our country are attempting to transform and change the United States into a welfare society run by an omnipresent centralized government, a mirror image of Europe.

Our ancestors didn't fight a revolution against European rule for nothing. The Founding Fathers embraced Liberty and individual freedom and rejected big-government. Did the heroes of the American Revolution bleed and sacrifice against the rule of a heavy-handed British monarchy only to have their posterity hand over their hard-won liberties to the soft-despotism of today's bureaucrats?

"No country upon earth ever had it more in its power to attain these blessings than United America," George Washington wrote in a letter to Benjamin Lincoln on June 29, 1788. "Wondrously strange, then, and much to be regretted indeed would it be, were we to neglect the means and to depart from the road which Providence has pointed us to so plainly; I cannot believe it will ever come to pass."

Americans face a time of choosing, where leadership at all levels is required. Our gravest danger is not external, but internal. The ability to rule ourselves, guided by the wisdom written in the documents set down by our forefathers, is at risk. Will we muster our leadership and fight for Liberty or will we surrender it for promises of security? Will we continue to be an exceptional nation where the individual is supreme and the federal government has limited powers? Or will we reject the new challenge of leadership, abrogate Liberty, and allow the government to grow so large and so powerful that it touches nearly every aspect of our lives through high taxation, burdensome regulation, and omnipotent bureaucracy?

In 1964 Ronald Reagan stated clearly what is at stake for us today:

> Whether we believe in our capacity for self-government or whether we abandon the American revolution and confess that a little intellectual elite in a far-distant capitol can plan our lives for us better than we can plan them ourselves. You and I are told increasingly we have to choose between a left or right. Well I'd like to suggest there is no such thing as a left or right. There is only an up or down. Up to man's age-old dream—the maximum of individual freedom consistent with order—or down to the ant heap of totalitarianism. And regardless of their sincerity, their humanitarian motives, those who would trade our freedom for security have embarked on this downward course.

Never underestimate the value of leadership or the fact that leadership is learned. In countless pursuits in life—in families, businesses, governments, and war—when the situation is dire and all looks lost, leadership makes the difference. The events recounted in this book can help increase your understanding of what it takes to be a successful leader. At every level of life, the exercise of leadership drives results. Without leaders, nothing happens. Leaders like Samuel Adams, Patrick Henry, Thomas Paine, Henry Knox, Daniel Morgan, and George Washington won the American Revolution against tremendous odds that a reasonable person would consider impossible. But these men were not reasonable. They were unreasonable for the cause of Liberty, willing to risk all for the prize of self-government. Although many other Americans fought in the war, it took exceptional leaders of character to inspire the people, lead the troops, sustain the cause, and win the fight.

A second American Revolution is happening today, but this one is fought with ballots, ideas, and leadership, not guns. The only thing standing between limited and unlimited government is the individual citizen casting his vote, standing up for Liberty and saying "enough already!" We owe the patriots of 1776 a great debt, the least of which is to know and understand their struggle and in so doing, to carry on the fight for Liberty. *Their* story is *our* story and we should learn it and embrace it. The Liberty they won is ours to lose; it is the sure possession of those alone who have the courage to defend it. Americans must not trade Liberty for security. We must not embark on a downward course. What say you?

The seven leadership stories contained in the chapters of this book describe a leadership that is as relevant today as it was essential at the birth of the United States. The leadership described in these stories is the leadership that forged Americans into a nation. They define the leadership that hammered out the standard for how Americans are expected to lead. In 1775 this leadership created the flame of Liberty that lit the world, and offered a beacon of freedom and human progress to all people. Learn from these stories and raise your leadership abilities to new heights. If you do, and remain *unreasonable* to the cause of Liberty, our Nation's future will be bright.

COMMON SENSE;

ADDRESSED TO THE

INHABITANTS

OF

AMERICA,

On the following interesting

SUBJECTS.

I. Of the Origin and Design of Government in general, with concise Remarks on the English Constitution.

II. Of Monarchy and Hereditary Succession.

III. Thoughts on the present State of American Affairs.

IV. Of the present Ability of America, with some miscellaneous Reflections.

Man knows no Master save creating Heaven,
Or those whom choice and common good ordain.

THOMSON.

PHILADELPHIA;
Printed, and Sold, by R. BELL, in Third-Street.

MDCCLXXVI.

Title page from Thomas Paine's Common Sense.
Library of Congress

Appendix A
Common Sense *by Thomas Paine*

INTRODUCTION

PERHAPS THE SENTIMENTS contained in the following pages, are not yet sufficiently fashionable to procure them general favor; a long habit of not thinking a thing wrong, gives it a superficial appearance of being right, and raises at first a formidable outcry in defence of custom. But tumult soon subsides. Time makes more converts than reason.

As a long and violent abuse of power is generally the means of calling the right of it in question, (and in matters too which might never have been thought of, had not the sufferers been aggravated into the inquiry,) and as the king of England hath undertaken in his own right, to support the parliament in what he calls theirs, and as the good people of this country are grievously oppressed by the combination, they have an undoubted privilege to inquire into the pretensions of both, and equally to reject the usurpations of either.

In the following sheets, the author hath studiously avoided every thing which is personal among ourselves. Compliments as well as censure to individuals make no part thereof. The wise and the worthy need not the triumph of a pamphlet; and those whose sentiments are injudicious or unfriendly, will cease of themselves, unless too much pains is bestowed upon their conversion.

The cause of America is, in a great measure, the cause of all mankind. Many circumstances have, and will arise, which are not local, but universal, and through which the principles of all lovers of mankind are affected, and in the event of which, their affections are interested. The laying a country desolate with fire and sword, declaring war against the natural rights of all mankind, and extirpating the defenders thereof from the face of the earth, is the concern of every man to whom nature hath given the power of feeling; of which class, regardless of party censure, is

THE AUTHOR
Philadelphia, Feb. 14, 1776.

Of the Origin and Design of Government in General.
With Concise Remarks on the English Constitution

SOME WRITERS HAVE so confounded society with government, as to leave little or no distinction between them; whereas they are not only different, but have different origins. Society is produced by our wants, and government by our wickedness; the former promotes our happiness positively by uniting our affections, the latter negatively by restraining our vices. The one encourages intercourse, the other creates distinctions. The first is a patron, the last a punisher.

Society in every state is a blessing, but government even in its best state is but a necessary evil in its worst state an intolerable one; for when we suffer, or are exposed to the same miseries by a government, which we might expect in a country without government, our calamities is heightened by reflecting that we furnish the means by which we suffer! Government, like dress, is the badge of lost innocence; the palaces of kings are built on the ruins of the bowers of paradise. For were the impulses of conscience clear, uniform, and irresistibly obeyed, man would need no other lawgiver; but that not being the case, he finds it necessary to surrender up a part of his property to furnish means for the protection of the rest; and this he is induced to do by the same prudence which in every other case advises him out of two evils to choose the least. Wherefore, security being the true design and end of government, it unanswerably follows that whatever form thereof appears most likely to ensure it to us, with the least expense and greatest benefit, is preferable to all others.

In order to gain a clear and just idea of the design and end of government, let us suppose a small number of persons settled in some sequestered part of the earth, unconnected with the rest, they will then represent the first peopling of any country, or of the world. In this state of natural liberty, society will be their first thought. A thousand motives will excite them thereto, the strength of one man is so unequal to his wants, and his mind so unfitted for perpetual solitude, that he is soon obliged to seek assistance and relief of another, who in his turn requires the same. Four or five united would be able to raise a tolerable dwelling in the midst of a wilderness, but one man might labor out the common period of life without accomplishing any thing; when he had felled his timber he could not remove it, nor erect it after it was removed; hunger in the mean time would urge him from his work, and every different want call him a different way. Disease, nay even misfortune would be death, for though neither might be mortal, yet either would disable him from living, and reduce him to a state in which he might rather be said to perish than to die.

Thus necessity, like a gravitating power, would soon form our newly arrived emigrants into society, the reciprocal blessings of which, would supersede, and render the obligations of law and government unnecessary while they remained perfectly just to each other; but as nothing but heaven is impregnable to vice, it will unavoidably happen, that in proportion as they surmount the first difficulties of emigration, which bound them together in a common cause, they will begin to relax in their duty and attachment to each other; and this remissness, will point out the necessity, of establishing some form of government to supply the defect of moral virtue.

Some convenient tree will afford them a State-House, under the branches of which, the whole colony may assemble to deliberate on public matters. It is more than probable that their first laws will have the title only of Regulations, and be enforced by no other penalty than public disesteem. In this first parliament every man, by natural right will have a seat.

But as the colony increases, the public concerns will increase likewise, and the distance at which the members may be separated, will render it too inconvenient for all of them to meet on every occasion as at first, when their number was small, their habitations near, and the public concerns few and trifling. This will point out the convenience of their consenting to leave the legislative part to be managed by a select number chosen from the whole body, who are supposed to have the same concerns at stake which those have who appointed them, and who will act in the same manner as the whole body would act were they present. If the colony continue increasing, it will become necessary to augment the number of the representatives, and that the interest of every part of the colony may be attended to, it will be found best to divide the whole into convenient parts, each part sending its proper number; and that the elected might never form to themselves an interest separate from the electors, prudence will point out the propriety of having elections often; because as the elected might by that means return and mix again with the general body of the electors in a few months, their fidelity to the public will be secured by the prudent reflection of not making a rod for themselves. And as this frequent interchange will establish a common interest with every part of the community, they will mutually and naturally support each other, and on this (not on the unmeaning name of king) depends the strength of government, and the happiness of the governed.

Here then is the origin and rise of government; namely, a mode rendered necessary by the inability of moral virtue to govern the world; here too is the design and end of government, viz., freedom and security. And however our eyes may be dazzled with snow, or our ears deceived by sound; however prejudice may warp our wills, or interest darken our understanding, the simple voice of nature and of reason will say, it is right.

I draw my idea of the form of government from a principle in nature, which no art can overturn, viz., that the more simple any thing is, the less liable it is to be disordered, and the easier repaired when disordered; and with this maxim in view, I offer a few remarks on the so much boasted constitution of England. That it was noble for the dark and slavish times in which it was erected is granted. When the world was overrun with tyranny the least therefrom was a glorious rescue. But that it is imperfect, subject to convulsions, and incapable of producing what it seems to promise, is easily demonstrated.

Absolute governments (though the disgrace of human nature) have this advantage with them, that they are simple; if the people suffer, they know the head from which their suffering springs, know likewise the remedy, and are not bewildered by a variety of causes and cures. But the constitution of England is so exceedingly complex, that the nation may suffer for years together without being able to discover in which part the fault lies, some will say in one and some in another, and every political physician will advise a different medicine.

I know it is difficult to get over local or long standing prejudices, yet if we will suffer ourselves to examine the component parts of the English constitution, we shall find them to be the base remains of two ancient tyrannies, compounded with some new republican materials.

First.—The remains of monarchical tyranny in the person of the king. Secondly.—The remains of aristocratical tyranny in the persons of the peers. Thirdly.—The new republican materials, in the persons of the commons, on whose virtue depends the freedom of England.

The two first, by being hereditary, are independent of the people; wherefore in a constitutional sense they contribute nothing towards the freedom of the state.

To say that the constitution of England is a union of three powers reciprocally checking each other, is farcical, either the words have no meaning, or they are flat contradictions.

To say that the commons is a check upon the king, presupposes two things.

First.—That the king is not to be trusted without being looked after, or in other words, that a thirst for absolute power is the natural disease of monarchy. Secondly.—That the commons, by being appointed for that purpose, are either wiser or more worthy of confidence than the crown.

But as the same constitution which gives the commons a power to check the king by withholding the supplies, gives afterwards the king a power to check the commons, by empowering him to reject their other bills; it again supposes that the king is wiser than those whom it has already supposed to be wiser than him. A mere absurdity!

There is something exceedingly ridiculous in the composition of monarchy; it first excludes a man from the means of information, yet empowers him to act in cases where the highest judgment is required. The state of a king shuts him from the world, yet the business of a king requires him to know it thoroughly; wherefore the different parts, unnaturally opposing and destroying each other, prove the whole character to be absurd and useless.

Some writers have explained the English constitution thus; the king, say they, is one, the people another; the peers are an house in behalf of the king; the commons in behalf of the people; but this hath all the distinctions of an house divided against itself; and though the expressions be pleasantly arranged, yet when examined they appear idle and ambiguous; and it will always happen, that the nicest construction that words are capable of, when applied to the description of something which either cannot exist, or is too incomprehensible to be within the compass of description, will be words of sound only, and though they may amuse the ear, they cannot inform the mind, for this explanation includes a previous question, viz. How came the king by a power which the people are afraid to trust, and always obliged to check? Such a power could not be the gift of a wise people, neither can any power, which needs checking, be from God; yet the provision, which the constitution makes, supposes such a power to exist.

But the provision is unequal to the task; the means either cannot or will not accomplish the end, and the whole affair is a felo de se; for as the greater weight will always carry up the less, and as all the wheels of a machine are put in motion by one, it only remains to know which power in the constitution has the most weight, for that will govern; and though the others, or a part of them, may clog, or, as the phrase is, check the rapidity of its motion, yet so long as they cannot stop it, their endeavors will be ineffectual; the first moving power will at last have its way, and what it wants in speed is supplied by time.

That the crown is this overbearing part in the English constitution needs not be mentioned, and that it derives its whole consequence merely from being the giver of places pensions is self evident, wherefore, though we have and wise enough to shut and lock a door against absolute monarchy, we at the same time have been foolish enough to put the crown in possession of the key.

The prejudice of Englishmen, in favor of their own government by king, lords, and commons, arises as much or more from national pride than reason. Individuals are undoubtedly safer in England than in some other countries, but the will of the king is as much the law of the land in Britain as in France, with this difference, that instead of proceeding directly from his mouth, it is handed to the people under the most formidable shape of an act of parliament. For the fate of Charles the First, hath only made kings more subtle not—more just.

Wherefore, laying aside all national pride and prejudice in favor of modes and forms, the plain truth is, that it is wholly owing to the constitution of the people, and not to the constitution of the government that the crown is not as oppressive in England as in Turkey.

An inquiry into the constitutional errors in the English form of government is at this time highly necessary; for as we are never in a proper condition of doing justice to others, while we continue under the influence of some leading partiality, so neither are we capable of doing it to ourselves while we remain fettered by any obstinate prejudice. And as a man, who is attached to a prostitute, is unfitted to choose or judge of a wife, so any prepossession in favor of a rotten constitution of government will disable us from discerning a good one.

Of Monarchy and Hereditary Succession

MANKIND BEING ORIGINALLY equals in the order of creation, the equality could only be destroyed by some subsequent circumstance; the distinctions of rich, and poor, may in a great measure be accounted for, and that without having recourse to the harsh, ill-sounding names of oppression and avarice. Oppression is often the consequence, but seldom or never the means of riches; and though avarice will preserve a man from being necessitously poor, it generally makes him too timorous to be wealthy. But there is another and greater distinction for which no truly natural or religious reason can be assigned, and that is, the distinction of men into KINGS and SUBJECTS. Male and female are the distinctions of nature, good and bad the distinctions of heaven; but how a race of men came into the world so exalted above the rest, and distinguished like some new species, is worth enquiring into, and whether they are the means of happiness or of misery to mankind.

In the early ages of the world, according to the scripture chronology, there were no kings; the consequence of which was there were no wars; it is the pride of kings which throw mankind into confusion. Holland without a king hath enjoyed more peace for this last century than any of the monarchial governments in Europe. Antiquity favors the same remark; for the quiet and rural lives of the first patriarchs hath a happy something in them, which vanishes away when we come to the history of Jewish royalty.

Government by kings was first introduced into the world by the Heathens, from whom the children of Israel copied the custom. It was the most prosperous invention the Devil ever set on foot for the promotion of idolatry. The Heathens paid divine honors to their deceased kings, and the Christian world hath improved on the plan by doing the same to their living ones. How impious is the title of sacred majesty applied to a worm, who in the midst of his splendor is crumbling into dust!

As the exalting one man so greatly above the rest cannot be justified on the equal rights of nature, so neither can it be defended on the authority of scripture; for the will of the Almighty, as declared by Gideon and the prophet Samuel, expressly disapproves of government by kings. All anti-monarchial parts of scripture have been very smoothly glossed over in monarchial governments, but they undoubtedly merit the attention of countries which have their governments yet to form. Render unto Caesar the things which are Caesar's is the scriptural doctrine of courts, yet it is no support of monarchial government, for the Jews at that time were without a king, and in a state of vassalage to the Romans.

Near three thousand years passed away from the Mosaic account of the creation, till the Jews under a national delusion requested a king. Till then their form of government (except in extraordinary cases, where the Almighty interposed) was a kind of republic administered by a judge and the elders of the tribes. Kings they had none, and it was held sinful to acknowledge any being under that title but the Lords of Hosts. And when a man seriously reflects on the idolatrous homage which is paid to the persons of kings he need not wonder, that the Almighty, ever jealous of his honor, should disapprove of a form of government which so impiously invades the prerogative of heaven.

Monarchy is ranked in scripture as one of the sins of the Jews, for which a curse in reserve is denounced against them. The history of that transaction is worth attending to.

The children of Israel being oppressed by the Midianites, Gideon marched against them with a small army, and victory, through the divine interposition, decided in his favor. The Jews elate with success, and attributing it to the generalship of Gideon, proposed making him a king, saying, Rule thou over us, thou and thy son and thy son's son. Here was temptation in its fullest extent; not a kingdom only, but an hereditary one, but Gideon in the piety of his soul replied, I will not rule over you, neither shall my son rule over you, THE LORD SHALL RULE OVER YOU. Words need not be more explicit; Gideon doth not decline the honor but denieth their right to give it; neither doth be compliment them with invented declarations of his thanks, but in the positive stile of a prophet charges them with disaffection to their proper sovereign, the King of Heaven.

About one hundred and thirty years after this, they fell again into the same error. The hankering which the Jews had for the idolatrous customs of the Heathens, is something exceedingly unaccountable; but so it was, that laying hold of the misconduct of Samuel's two sons, who were entrusted with some secular concerns, they came in an abrupt and clamorous manner to Samuel, saying, Behold thou art old and thy sons walk not in thy ways, now make us a king to judge us like all the other nations. And here we cannot but observe that their motives were bad, viz., that they might be like unto other nations, i.e., the Heathen, whereas their true glory laid in being as much unlike them as possible. But the thing displeased Samuel when they said, give us a king to judge us; and Samuel prayed unto the Lord, and the Lord said unto Samuel, Hearken unto the voice of the people in all that they say unto thee, for they have not rejected thee, but they have rejected me, THEN I SHOULD NOT REIGN OVER THEM.

According to all the works which have done since the day; wherewith they brought them up out of Egypt, even unto this day; wherewith they have forsaken me and served other Gods; so do they also unto thee. Now therefore hearken unto their voice, howbeit, protest solemnly unto them and show them the manner of the king that shall reign over them, i.e., not of any particular king, but the general manner of the kings of the earth, whom Israel was so eagerly copying after. And notwithstanding the great distance of time and difference of manners, the character is still in fashion. And Samuel told all the words of the Lord unto the people, that asked of him a king. And he said, This shall be the manner of the king that shall reign over you; he will take your sons and appoint them for himself for his chariots, and to be his horsemen, and some shall run before his chariots (this description agrees with the present mode of impressing men) and he will appoint him captains over thousands and captains over fifties, and will set them to ear his ground and to read his harvest, and to make his instruments of war, and instruments of his chariots; and he will take your daughters to be confectionaries and to be cooks and to be bakers (this describes the expense and luxury as well as the oppression of kings) and he will take your fields and your olive yards, even the best of them, and give them to his servants; and he will take the tenth of your seed, and of your vineyards, and give them to his officers and to his servants (by which we see that bribery, corruption, and favoritism are the standing vices of kings) and he will take the tenth of your men servants, and your maid servants, and your goodliest young men and your asses, and put them to his work; and he will take the tenth of your sheep, and ye shall be his servants, and ye shall cry out in that day because of your king which ye shall have chosen, AND THE LORD WILL NOT HEAR YOU IN THAT DAY. This accounts for the continuation of monarchy; neither do the characters of the few good kings which have lived since, either sanctify the title, or blot out the sinfulness of the origin; the high encomium given of David takes no notice of him officially as a king, but only as a man after God's own heart. Nevertheless the People refused to obey the voice of Samuel, and they said, Nay, but we will have a king over us, that we may be like all the nations, and that our king may judge us, and go out before us and fight our battles. Samuel continued to reason with them, but to no purpose; he set before them their ingratitude, but all would not avail; and seeing them fully bent on their folly, he cried out, I will call unto the Lord, and he shall sent thunder and rain (which then was a punishment, being the time of wheat harvest) that ye may perceive and see that your wickedness is great which ye have done in the sight of the Lord, IN ASKING YOU A KING. So Samuel called unto the Lord, and the Lord sent thunder and rain that day, and all the people greatly feared the Lord and Samuel And all the people said unto Samuel, Pray for thy servants unto the Lord thy God that we die not, for WE HAVE ADDED UNTO OUR SINS THIS EVIL, TO ASK A KING. These portions of scripture are direct and positive. They admit of no equivocal construction. That the Almighty hath here entered his protest against monarchial government is true, or the scripture is false. And a man hath good reason to believe that there is as much of kingcraft, as priestcraft in withholding the scripture from the public in Popish countries. For monarchy in every instance is the Popery of government.

To the evil of monarchy we have added that of hereditary succession;

and as the first is a degradation and lessening of ourselves, so the second, claimed as a matter of right, is an insult and an imposition on posterity. For all men being originally equals, no one by birth could have a right to set up his own family in perpetual preference to all others for ever, and though himself might deserve some decent degree of honors of his contemporaries, yet his descendants might be far too unworthy to inherit them. One of the strongest natural proofs of the folly of hereditary right in kings, is, that nature disapproves it, otherwise she would not so frequently turn it into ridicule by giving mankind an ass for a lion.

Secondly, as no man at first could possess any other public honors than were bestowed upon him, so the givers of those honors could have no power to give away the right of posterity, and though they might say, "We choose you for our head," they could not, without manifest injustice to their children, say, "that your children and your children's children shall reign over ours for ever." Because such an unwise, unjust, unnatural compact might (perhaps) in the next succession put them under the government of a rogue or a fool. Most wise men, in their private sentiments, have ever treated hereditary right with contempt; yet it is one of those evils, which when once established is not easily removed; many submit from fear, others from superstition, and the more powerful part shares with the king the plunder of the rest.

This is supposing the present race of kings in the world to have had an honorable origin; whereas it is more than probable, that could we take off the dark covering of antiquity, and trace them to their first rise, that we should find the first of them nothing better than the principal ruffian of some restless gang, whose savage manners of preeminence in subtlety obtained him the title of chief among plunderers; and who by increasing in power, and extending his depredations, overawed the quiet and defenseless to purchase their safety by frequent contributions. Yet his electors could have no idea of giving hereditary right to his descendants, because such a perpetual exclusion of themselves was incompatible with the free and unrestrained principles they professed to live by. Wherefore, hereditary succession in the early ages of monarchy could not take place as a matter of claim, but as something casual or complemental; but as few or no records were extant in those days, and traditionary history stuffed with fables, it was very easy, after the lapse of a few generations, to trump up some superstitious tale, conveniently timed, Mahomet like, to cram hereditary right down the throats of the vulgar. Perhaps the disorders which threatened, or seemed to threaten on the decease of a leader and the choice of a new one (for elections among ruffians could not be very orderly) induced many at first to favor hereditary pretensions; by which means it happened, as it hath happened since, that what at first was submitted to as a convenience, was afterwards claimed as a right.

England, since the conquest, hath known some few good monarchs, but groaned beneath a much larger number of bad ones, yet no man in his senses can say that their claim under William the Conqueror is a very honorable one. A French bastard landing with an armed banditti, and establishing himself king of England against the consent of the natives, is in plain terms a very paltry rascally original. It certainly hath no divinity in it. However, it is needless to spend much time in exposing the folly of hereditary right, if there are any so weak as to believe it, let them promiscuously worship the ass and lion, and welcome. I shall neither copy their humility, nor disturb their devotion.

Yet I should be glad to ask how they suppose kings came at first? The question admits but of three answers, viz., either by lot, by election, or by usurpation. If the first king was taken by lot, it establishes a precedent for the next, which excludes hereditary succession. Saul was by lot, yet the succession was not hereditary, neither does it appear from that transaction there was any intention it ever should. If the first king of any country was by election, that likewise establishes a precedent for the next; for to say, that the right of all future generations is taken away, by the act of the first electors, in their choice not only of a king, but of a family of kings for ever, hath no parallel in or out of scripture but the doctrine of original sin, which supposes the free will of all men lost in Adam; and from such comparison, and it will admit of no other, hereditary succession can derive no glory. For as in Adam all sinned, and as in the first electors all men obeyed; as in the one all mankind were subjected to Satan, and in the other to Sovereignty; as our innocence was lost in the first, and our authority in the last; and as both disable us from reassuming some former state and privilege, it unanswerably follows that original sin and hereditary succession are parallels. Dishonorable rank! Inglorious connection! Yet the most subtle sophist cannot produce a juster simile.

As to usurpation, no man will be so hardy as to defend it; and that William the Conqueror was an usurper is a fact not to be contradicted. The plain truth is, that the antiquity of English monarchy will not bear looking into.

But it is not so much the absurdity as the evil of hereditary succession which concerns mankind. Did it ensure a race of good and wise men it would have the seal of divine authority, but as it opens a door to the foolish, the wicked; and the improper, it hath in it the nature of oppression. Men who look upon themselves born to reign, and others to obey, soon grow insolent; selected from the rest of mankind their minds are early poisoned by importance; and the world they act in differs so materially from the world at large, that they have but little opportunity of knowing its true interests, and when they succeed to the government are frequently the most ignorant and unfit of any throughout the dominions.

Another evil which attends hereditary succession is, that the throne is subject to be possessed by a minor at any age; all which time the regency, acting under the cover of a king, have every opportunity and inducement to betray their trust. The same national misfortune happens, when a king worn out with age and infirmity, enters the last stage of human weakness. In both these cases the public becomes a prey to every miscreant, who can tamper successfully with the follies either of age or infancy.

The most plausible plea, which hath ever been offered in favor of hereditary succession, is, that it preserves a nation from civil wars; and were this true, it would be weighty; whereas, it is the most barefaced falsity ever imposed upon mankind. The whole history of England disowns the fact. Thirty kings and two minors have reigned in that distracted kingdom since the conquest, in which time there have been (including the Revolution) no less than eight civil wars and nineteen rebellions. Wherefore instead of making for peace, it makes against it, and destroys the very foundation it seems to stand on.

The contest for monarchy and succession, between the houses of York and Lancaster, laid England in a scene of blood for many years. Twelve pitched battles, besides skirmishes and sieges, were fought between Henry and Edward. Twice was Henry prisoner to Edward, who in his turn was prisoner to Henry. And so uncertain is the fate of war and the temper of a nation, when nothing but personal matters are the ground of a quarrel, that Henry was taken in triumph from a prison to a palace, and Edward obliged to fly from a palace to a foreign land; yet, as sudden transitions of temper are seldom lasting, Henry in his turn was driven from the throne, and Edward recalled to succeed him. The parliament always following the strongest side.

This contest began in the reign of Henry the Sixth, and was not entirely extinguished till Henry the Seventh, in whom the families were united. Including a period of 67 years, viz., from 1422 to 1489.

In short, monarchy and succession have laid (not this or that kingdom only) but the world in blood and ashes. 'Tis a form of government which the word of God bears testimony against, and blood will attend it.

If we inquire into the business of a king, we shall find that (in some countries they have none) and after sauntering away their lives without pleasure to themselves or advantage to the nation, withdraw from the scene, and leave their successors to tread the same idle round. In absolute monarchies the whole weight of business civil and military, lies on the king; the children of Israel in their request for a king, urged this plea "that he may judge us, and go out before us and fight our battles." But in countries where he is neither a judge nor a general, as in England, a man would be puzzled to know what is his business.

The nearer any government approaches to a republic, the less business there is for a king. It is somewhat difficult to find a proper name for the government of England. Sir William Meredith calls it a republic; but in its present state it is unworthy of the name, because the corrupt influence of the crown, by having all the places in its disposal, hath so effectually swallowed up the power, and eaten out the virtue of the house of commons (the republican part in the constitution) that the government of England is nearly as monarchical as that of France or Spain. Men fall out with names without understanding them. For it is the republican and not the monarchical part of the constitution of England which Englishmen glory in, viz., the liberty of choosing a house of commons from out of their own body—and it is easy to see that when the republican virtue fails, slavery ensues. My is the constitution of England sickly, but because monarchy hath poisoned the republic, the crown hath engrossed the commons?

In England a king hath little more to do than to make war and give away places; which in plain terms, is to impoverish the nation and set it together by the ears. A pretty business indeed for a man to be allowed eight hundred thousand sterling a year for, and worshipped into the bargain! Of more worth is one honest man to society, and in the sight of God, than all the crowned ruffians that ever lived.

Thoughts of the Present State of American Affairs

IN THE FOLLOWING pages I offer nothing more than simple facts, plain arguments, and common sense; and have no other preliminaries to settle with the reader, than that he will divest himself of prejudice and prepossession, and suffer his reason and his feelings to determine for themselves; that he will put on, or rather that he will not put off the true character of a man, and generously enlarge his views beyond the present day.

Volumes have been written on the subject of the struggle between England and America. Men of all ranks have embarked in the controversy, from different motives, and with various designs; but all have been ineffectual, and the period of debate is closed. Arms, as the last resource, decide the contest; the appeal was the choice of the king, and the continent hath accepted the challenge.

It hath been reported of the late Mr. Pelham (who tho' an able minister was not without his faults) that on his being attacked in the house of commons, on the score, that his measures were only of a temporary kind, replied, "they will fast my time." Should a thought so fatal and unmanly possess the colonies in the present contest, the name of ancestors will be remembered by future generations with detestation.

The sun never shined on a cause of greater worth. 'Tis not the affair of a city, a country, a province, or a kingdom, but of a continent—of at least one eighth part of the habitable globe. 'Tis not the concern of a day, a year, or an age; posterity are virtually involved in the contest, and will be more or less affected, even to the end of time, by the proceedings now. Now is the seed time of continental union, faith and honor. The least fracture now will be like a name engraved with the point of a pin on the tender rind of a young oak; The wound will enlarge with the tree, and posterity read it in full grown characters.

By referring the matter from argument to arms, a new area for politics is struck; a new method of thinking hath arisen. All plans, proposals, &c. prior to the nineteenth of April, i.e., to the commencement of hostilities, are like the almanacs of the last year; which, though proper then, are superseded and useless now. Whatever was advanced by the advocates on either side of the question then, terminated in one and the same point, viz., a union with Great Britain; the only difference between the parties was the method of effecting it; the one proposing force, the other friendship; but it hath so far happened that the first hath failed, and the second hath withdrawn her influence.

As much hath been said of the advantages of reconciliation, which, like an agreeable dream, hath passed away and left us as we were, it is but right, that we should examine the contrary side of the argument, and inquire into some of the many material injuries which these colonies sustain, and always will sustain, by being connected with, and dependant on Great Britain. To examine that connection and dependance, on the principles of nature and common sense, to see what we have to trust to, if separated, and what we are to expect, if dependant.

I have heard it asserted by some, that as America hath flourished under her former connection with Great Britain, that the same connection is necessary towards her future happiness, and will always have the same effect. Nothing can be more fallacious than this kind of argument. We may as well assert, that because a child has thrived upon milk, that it is never to have meat; or that the first twenty years of our lives is to become a precedent for the next twenty. But even this is admitting more than is true, for I answer roundly, that America would have flourished as much, and probably much more, had no European power had any thing to do with her. The commerce by which she hath enriched herself are the necessaries of life, and will always have a market while eating is the custom of Europe.

But she has protected us, say some. That she hath engrossed us is true, and defended the continent at our expense as well as her own is admitted, and she would have defended Turkey from the same motive, viz., the sake of trade and dominion.

Alas! we have been long led away by ancient prejudices and made large sacrifices to superstition. We have boasted the protection of Great Britain, without considering, that her motive was interest not attachment; that she did not protect us from our enemies on our account, but from her enemies on her own account, from those who had no quarrel with us on any other account, and who will always be our enemies on the same account. Let Britain wave her pretensions to the continent, or the continent throw off the dependance, and we should be at peace with France and Spain were they at war with Britain. The miseries of Hanover last war, ought to warn us against connections.

It hath lately been asserted in parliament, that the colonies have no relation to each other but through the parent country, i.e., that Pennsylvania and the Jerseys, and so on for the rest, are sister colonies by the way of England; this is certainly a very roundabout way of proving relation ship, but it is the nearest and only true way of proving enemyship, if I may so call it. France and Spain never were, nor perhaps ever will be our enemies as Americans, but as our being the subjects of Great Britain.

But Britain is the parent country, say some. Then the more shame upon her conduct. Even brutes do not devour their young; nor savages make war upon their families; wherefore the assertion, if true, turns to her reproach; but it happens not to be true, or only partly so, and the phrase parent or mother country hath been jesuitically adopted by the king and his parasites, with a low papistical design of gaining an unfair bias on the credulous weakness of our minds. Europe, and not England, is the parent country of America. This new world hath been the asylum for the persecuted lovers off civil and religious liberty from every Part of Europe. Hither have they fled, not from the tender embraces of the mother, but from the cruelty of the monster; and it is so far true of England, that the same tyranny which drove the first emigrants from home pursues their descendants still.

In this extensive quarter of the globe, we forget the narrow limits of three hundred and sixty miles (the extent of England) and carry our friendship on a larger scale; we claim brotherhood with every European Christian, and triumph in the generosity of the sentiment.

It is pleasant to observe by what regular gradations we surmount the force of local prejudice, as we enlarge our acquaintance with the world. A man born in any town in England divided into parishes, will naturally associate most with his fellow parishioners (because their interests in many cases will be common) and distinguish him by the name of neighbor; if he meet him but a few miles from home, he drops the narrow idea of a street, and salutes him by the name of townsman; if he travels out of the county, and meet him in any other, he forgets the minor divisions of street and town, and calls him countryman; i.e., countyman; but if in their foreign excursions they should associate in France or any other part of Europe, their local remembrance would be enlarged into that of Englishmen. And by a just parity of reasoning, all Europeans meeting in America, or any other quarter of the globe, are countrymen; for England, Holland, Germany, or Sweden, when compared with the whole, stand in the same places on the larger scale, which the divisions of street, town, and county do on the smaller ones; distinctions too limited for continental minds. Not one third of the inhabitants, even of this province, are of English descent. Wherefore, I reprobate the phrase of parent or mother country applied to England only, as being false, selfish, narrow and ungenerous.

But admitting that we were all of English descent, what does it amount to? Nothing. Britain, being now an open enemy, extinguishes every other name and title: And to say that reconciliation is our duty, is truly farcical. The first king of England, of the present line (William the Conqueror) was a Frenchman, and half the peers of England are descendants from the same country; wherefore by the same method of reasoning, England ought to be governed by France.

Much hath been said of the united strength of Britain and the colonies, that in conjunction they might bid defiance to the world. But this is mere presumption; the fate of war is uncertain, neither do the expressions mean anything; for this continent would never suffer itself to be drained of inhabitants to support the British arms in either Asia, Africa, or Europe.

Besides, what have we to do with setting the world at defiance? Our plan is commerce, and that, well attended to, will secure us the peace and friendship of all Europe; because it is the interest of all Europe to have America a free port. Her trade will always be a protection, and her barrenness of gold and silver secure her from invaders.

I challenge the warmest advocate for reconciliation, to show, a single advantage that this continent can reap, by being connected with Great Britain. I repeat the challenge, not a single advantage is derived. Our corn will fetch its price in any market in Europe, and our imported goods must be paid for buy them where we will.

But the injuries and disadvantages we sustain by that connection, are without number; and our duty to mankind I at large, as well as to ourselves, instruct us to renounce the alliance: Because, any submission to, or dependance on Great Britain, tends directly to involve this continent in European wars and quarrels; and sets us at variance with nations, who would otherwise seek our friendship, and against whom, we have neither anger nor complaint. As Europe is our market for trade, we ought to form no partial connection with any part of it. It is the true interest of America to steer clear of European contentions, which she never can do, while by her dependance on Britain, she is made the make-weight in the scale of British politics.

Europe is too thickly planted with kingdoms to be long at peace, and whenever a war breaks out between England and any foreign power, the trade of America goes to ruin, because of her connection with Britain. The next war may not turn out like the Past, and should it not, the advocates for reconciliation now will be wishing for separation then, because, neutrality in that case, would be a safer convoy than a man of war. Every thing that is right or natural pleads for separation. The blood of the slain, the weeping voice of nature cries, 'tis time to part. Even the distance at which the Almighty hath placed England and America, is a strong and natural proof, that the authority of the one, over the other, was never the design of Heaven. The time likewise at which the continent was discovered, adds weight to the argument, and the manner in which it was peopled increases the force of it. The reformation was preceded by the discovery of America, as if the Almighty graciously meant to open a sanctuary to the persecuted in future years, when home should afford neither friendship nor safety.

The authority of Great Britain over this continent, is a form of government, which sooner or later must have an end: And a serious mind can draw no true pleasure by looking forward, under the painful and positive conviction, that what he calls "the present constitution" is merely temporary. As parents, we can have no joy, knowing that this government is not sufficiently lasting to ensure any thing which we may bequeath to posterity: And by a plain method of argument, as we are running the next generation into debt, we ought to do the work of it, otherwise we use them meanly and pitifully. In order to discover the line of our duty rightly, we should take our children in our hand, and fix our station a few years farther into life; that eminence will present a prospect, which a few present fears and prejudices conceal from our sight.

Though I would carefully avoid giving unnecessary offence, yet I am inclined to believe, that all those who espouse the doctrine of reconciliation, may be included within the following descriptions:

Interested men, who are not to be trusted; weak men who cannot see; prejudiced men who will not see; and a certain set of moderate men, who think better of the European world than it deserves; and this last class by an ill-judged deliberation, will be the cause of more calamities to this continent than all the other three.

It is the good fortune of many to live distant from the scene of sorrow; the evil is not sufficiently brought to their doors to make them feel the precariousness with which all American property is possessed. But let our imaginations transport us for a few moments to Boston, that seat of wretchedness will teach us wisdom, and instruct us for ever to renounce a power in whom we can have no trust. The inhabitants of that unfortunate city, who but a few months ago were in ease and affluence, have now no other alternative than to stay and starve, or turn out to beg. Endangered by the fire of their friends if they continue within the city, and plundered by the soldiery if they leave it. In their present condition they are prisoners without the hope of redemption, and in a general attack for their relief, they would be exposed to the fury of both armies.

Men of passive tempers look somewhat lightly over the offenses of Britain, and, still hoping for the best, are apt to call out, Come we shall be friends again for all this. But examine the passions and feelings of mankind. Bring the doctrine of reconciliation to the touchstone of nature, and then tell me, whether you can hereafter love, honor, and faithfully serve the power that hath carried fire and sword into your land? If you cannot do all these, then are you only deceiving yourselves, and by your delay bringing ruin upon posterity. Your future connection with Britain, whom you can neither love nor honor, will be forced and unnatural, and being formed only on the plan of present convenience, will in a little time fall into a relapse more wretched than the first. But if you say, you can still pass the violations over, then I ask, Hath your house been burnt? Hath you property been destroyed before your face? Are your wife and children destitute of a bed to lie on, or bread to live on? Have you lost a parent or a child by their hands, and yourself the ruined and wretched survivor? If you have not, then are you not a judge of those who have. But if you have, and can still shake hands with the murderers, then are you unworthy the name of husband, father, friend, or lover, and whatever may be your rank or title in life, you have the heart of a coward, and the spirit of a sycophant.

This is not inflaming or exaggerating matters, but trying them by those feelings and affections which nature justifies, and without which, we should be incapable of discharging the social duties of life, or enjoying the felicities of it. I mean not to exhibit horror for the purpose of provoking revenge, but to awaken us from fatal and unmanly slumbers, that we may pursue determinately some fixed object. It is not in the power of Britain or of Europe to conquer America, if she do not conquer herself by delay and timidity. The present winter is worth an age if rightly employed, but if lost or neglected, the whole continent will partake of the misfortune; and there is no punishment which that man will not deserve, be he who, or what, or where he will, that may be the means of sacrificing a season so precious and useful.

It is repugnant to reason, to the universal order of things, to all examples from the former ages, to suppose, that this continent can longer remain subject to any external power. The most sanguine in Britain does not think so. The utmost stretch of human wisdom cannot, at this time compass a plan short of separation, which can promise the continent even a year's security. Reconciliation is was a fallacious dream. Nature hath deserted the connection, and Art cannot supply her place. For, as Milton wisely expresses, "never can true reconcilement grow where wounds of deadly hate have pierced so deep."

Every quiet method for peace hath been ineffectual. Our prayers have been rejected with disdain; and only tended to convince us, that nothing flatters vanity, or confirms obstinacy in kings more than repeated petitioning— and nothing hath contributed more than that very measure to make the kings of Europe absolute: Witness Denmark and Sweden. Wherefore since nothing but blows will do, for God's sake, let us come to a final separation, and not leave the next generation to be cutting throats, under the violated unmeaning names of parent and child.

To say, they will never attempt it again is idle and visionary, we thought so at the repeal of the stamp act, yet a year or two undeceived us; as well me we may suppose that nations, which have been once defeated, will never renew the quarrel.

As to government matters, it is not in the powers of Britain to do this continent justice: The business of it will soon be too weighty, and intricate, to be managed with any tolerable degree of convenience, by a power, so distant from us, and so very ignorant of us; for if they cannot conquer us, they cannot govern us. To be always running three or four thousand miles with a tale or a petition, waiting four or five months for an answer, which when obtained requires five or six more to explain it in, will in a few years be looked upon as folly and childishness—there was a time when it was proper, and there is a proper time for it to cease.

Small islands not capable of protecting themselves, are the proper objects for kingdoms to take under their care; but there is something very absurd, in supposing a continent to be perpetually governed by an island. In no instance hath nature made the satellite larger than its primary planet, and as England and America, with respect to each Other, reverses the common order of nature, it is evident they belong to different systems: England to Europe—America to itself.

I am not induced by motives of pride, party, or resentment to espouse the doctrine of separation and independence; I am clearly, positively, and conscientiously persuaded that it is the true interest of this continent to be so; that every thing short of that is mere patchwork, that it can afford no lasting felicity,—that it is leaving the sword to our children, and shrinking back at a time, when, a little more, a little farther, would have rendered this continent the glory of the earth.

As Britain hath not manifested the least inclination towards a compromise, we may be assured that no terms can be obtained worthy the acceptance of the continent, or any ways equal to the expense of blood and treasure we have been already put to.

The object contended for, ought always to bear some just proportion to the expense. The removal of the North, or the whole detestable junto, is a matter unworthy the millions we have expended. A temporary stoppage of trade, was an inconvenience, which would have sufficiently balanced the repeal of all the acts complained of, had such repeals been obtained; but if the whole continent must take up arms, if every man must be a soldier, it is scarcely worth our while to fight against a contemptible ministry only. Dearly,

dearly, do we pay for the repeal of the acts, if that is all we fight for; for in a just estimation, it is as great a folly to pay a Bunker Hill price for law, as for land. As I have always considered the independency of this continent, as an event, which sooner or later must arrive, so from the late rapid progress of the continent to maturity, the event could not be far off. Wherefore, on the breaking out of hostilities, it was not worth the while to have disputed a matter, which time would have finally redressed, unless we meant to be in earnest; otherwise, it is like wasting an estate of a suit at law, to regulate the trespasses of a tenant, whose lease is just expiring. No man was a warmer wisher for reconciliation than myself, before the fatal nineteenth of April, 1775 (Massacre at Lexington), but the moment the event of that day was made known, I rejected the hardened, sullen tempered Pharaoh of England for ever; and disdain the wretch, that with the pretended title of Father of his people, can unfeelingly hear of their slaughter, and composedly sleep with their blood upon his soul.

But admitting that matters were now made up, what would be the event? I answer, the ruin of the continent. And that for several reasons:

First. The powers of governing still remaining in the hands of the king, he will have a negative over the whole legislation of this continent. And as he hath shown himself such an inveterate enemy to liberty, and discovered such a thirst for arbitrary power, is he, or is he not, a proper man to say to these colonies, "You shall make no laws but what I please?" And is there any inhabitants in America so ignorant, as not to know, that according to what is called the present constitution, that this continent can make no laws but what the king gives leave to? and is there any man so unwise, as not to see, that (considering what has happened) he will suffer no Law to be made here, but such as suit his purpose? We may be as effectually enslaved by the want of laws in America, as by submitting to laws made for us in England. After matters are make up (as it is called) can there be any doubt but the whole power of the crown will be exerted, to keep this continent as low and humble as possible? Instead of going forward we shall go backward, or be perpetually quarrelling or ridiculously petitioning. We are already greater than the king wishes us to be, and will he not hereafter endeavor to make us less? To bring the matter to one point. Is the power who is jealous of our prosperity, a proper power to govern us? Whoever says No to this question is an independent, for independency means no more, than, whether we shall make our own laws, or whether the king, the greatest enemy this continent hath, or can have, shall tell us, "there shall be now laws but such as I like."

But the king you will say has a negative in England; the people there can make no laws without his consent. in point of right and good order, there is something very ridiculous, that a youth of twenty-one (which hath often happened) shall say to several millions of people, older and wiser than himself, I forbid this or that act of yours to be law. But in this place I decline this sort of reply, though I will never cease to expose the absurdity of it, and only answer, that England being the king's residence, and America not so, make quite another case. The king's negative here is ten times more dangerous and fatal than it can be in England, for there he will scarcely refuse his consent to a bill for putting England into as strong a state of defence as possible, and in America he would never suffer such a bill to be passed.

America is only a secondary object in the system of British politics— England consults the good of this country, no farther than it answers her own purpose. Wherefore, her own interest leads her to suppress the growth of ours in every case which doth not promote her advantage, or in the least interfere with it. A pretty state we should soon be in under such a second-hand government, considering what has happened! Men do not change from enemies to friends by the alteration of a name; and in order to show that reconciliation now is a dangerous doctrine, I affirm, that it would be policy in the kingdom at this time, to repeal the acts for the sake of reinstating himself in the government of the provinces; in order, that he may accomplish by craft and subtlety, in the long run, what he cannot do by force and violence in the short one. Reconciliation and ruin are nearly related.

Secondly. That as even the best terms, which we can expect to obtain, can amount to no more than a temporary expedient, or a kind of government by guardianship, which can last no longer than till the colonies come of age, so the general face and state of things, in the interim, will be unsettled and unpromising. Emigrants of property will not choose to come to a country whose form of government hangs but by a thread, and who is every day tottering on the brink of commotion and disturbance; and numbers of the present inhabitant would lay hold of the interval, to dispose of their effects, and quit the continent.

But the most powerful of all arguments, is, that nothing but independence, i.e., a continental form of government, can keep the peace of the continent and preserve it inviolate from civil wars. I dread the event of a reconciliation with Britain now, as it is more than probable, that it will be followed by a revolt somewhere or other, the consequences of which may be far more fatal than all the malice of Britain.

Thousands are already ruined by British barbarity; (thousands more will probably suffer the same fate.) Those men have other feelings than us who have nothing suffered. All they now possess is liberty, what they before enjoyed is sacrificed to its service, and having nothing more to lose, they disdain submission. Besides, the general temper of the colonies, towards a British government, will be like that of a youth, who is nearly out of his time, they will care very little about her. And a government which cannot preserve the peace, is no government at all, and in that case we pay our money for nothing; and pray what is it that Britain can do, whose power will be wholly on paper, should a civil tumult break out the very day after reconciliation? I have heard some men say, many of whom I believe spoke without thinking, that they dreaded independence, fearing that it would produce civil wars. It is but seldom that our first thoughts are truly correct, and that is the case here; for there are ten times more to dread from a patched up connection than from independence. I make the sufferers case my own, and I protest, that were I driven from house and home, my property destroyed, and my circumstances ruined, that as man, sensible of injuries, I could never relish the doctrine of reconciliation, or consider myself bound thereby.

The colonies have manifested such a spirit of good order and obedience to continental government, as is sufficient to make every reasonable person easy and happy on that head. No man can assign the least pretence for his fears, on any other grounds, that such as are truly childish and ridiculous, viz., that one colony will be striving for superiority over another.

Where there are no distinctions there can be no superiority, perfect equality affords no temptation. The republics of Europe are all (and we may say always) in peace. Holland and Switzerland are without wars, foreign or domestic; monarchical governments, it is true, are never long at rest: the crown itself is a temptation to enterprising ruffians at home; and that degree of pride and insolence ever attendant on regal authority swells into a rupture with foreign powers, in instances where a republican government, by being formed on more natural principles, would negotiate the mistake.

If there is any true cause of fear respecting independence it is because no plan is yet laid down. Men do not see their way out; wherefore, as an opening into that business I offer the following hints; at the same time modestly affirming, that I have no other opinion of them myself, than that they may be the means of giving rise to something better. Could the straggling thoughts of individuals be collected, they would frequently form materials for wise and able men to improve to useful matter.

Let the assemblies be annual, with a President only. The representation more equal. Their business wholly domestic, and subject to the authority of a continental congress.

Let each colony be divided into six, eight, or ten, convenient districts, each district to send a proper number of delegates to congress, so that each colony send at least thirty. The whole number in congress will be at least three hundred ninety. Each congress to sit ... and to choose a president by the following method. When the delegates are met, let a colony be taken from the whole thirteen colonies by lot, after which let the whole congress choose (by ballot) a president from out of the delegates of that province. I the next Congress, let a colony be taken by lot from twelve only, omitting that colony from which the president was taken in the former congress, and so proceeding on till the whole thirteen shall have had their proper rotation. And in order that nothing may pass into a law but what is satisfactorily just, not less than three fifths of the congress to be called a majority. He that will promote discord, under a government so equally formed as this, would join Lucifer in his revolt.

But as there is a peculiar delicacy, from whom, or in what manner, this business must first arise, and as it seems most agreeable and consistent, that it should come from some intermediate body between the governed and the governors, that is between the Congress and the people, let a Continental Conference be held, in the following manner, and for the following purpose:

A committee of twenty-six members of Congress, viz., two for each colony. Two members for each house of assembly, or provincial convention; and five representatives of the people at large, to be chosen in the capital city or town of each province, for, and in behalf of the whole province, by as many qualified voters as shall think proper to attend from all parts of the province for that purpose; or, if more convenient, the representatives may be chosen in two or three of the most populous parts thereof. In this conference, thus assembled, will be united, the two grand principles of business, knowledge and power. The members of Congress, Assemblies, or Conventions, by having had experience in national concerns, will be able and useful counsellors, and the whole, being empowered by the people will have a truly legal authority.

The conferring members being met, let their business be to frame a Continental Charter, or Charter of the United Colonies; (answering to what is called the Magna Charta of England) fixing the number and manner of choosing members of Congress, members of Assembly, with their date of sitting, and drawing the line of business and jurisdiction between them: always remembering, that our strength is continental, not provincial: Securing freedom and property to all men, and above all things the free exercise of religion, according to the dictates of conscience; with such other matter as is necessary for a charter to contain. Immediately after which, the said conference to dissolve, and the bodies which shall be chosen conformable to the said charter, to be the legislators and governors of this continent for the time being: Whose peace and happiness, may God preserve, Amen.

Should any body of men be hereafter delegated for this or some similar purpose, I offer them the following extracts from that wise observer on governments Dragonetti. "The science" says he, "of the politician consists in fixing the true point of happiness and freedom. Those men would deserve the gratitude of ages, who should discover a mode of government that contained the greatest sum of individual happiness, with the least national expense."— Dragonetti on Virtue and Rewards.

But where says some is the king of America? I'll tell you Friend, he reigns above, and doth not make havoc of mankind like the Royal of Britain. Yet that we may not appear to be defective even in earthly honors, let a day be solemnly set apart for proclaiming the charter; let it be brought forth placed on the divine law, the word of God; let a crown be placed thereon, by which the world may know, that so far as we approve of monarchy, that in America the law is king. For as in absolute governments the king is law, so in free countries the law ought to be king; and there ought to be no other. But lest any ill use should afterwards arise, let the crown at the conclusion of the ceremony be demolished, and scattered among the people whose right it is.

A government of our own is our natural right: And when a man seriously reflects on the precariousness of human affairs, he will become convinced, that it is in finitely wiser and safer, to form a constitution of our own in a cool deliberate manner, while we have it in our power, than to trust such an interesting event to time and chance. If we omit it now, some Massenello* may hereafter arise, who laying hold of popular disquietudes, may collect together the desperate and the discontented, and by assuming to themselves the powers of government, may sweep away the liberties of the continent like a deluge. Should the government of America return again into the hands of Britain, the tottering situation of things, will be a temptation for some desperate adventurer to try his fortune; and in such a case, what relief can Britain

---

* Thomas Anello, otherwise Massenello, a fisherman of Naples, who after spiriting up his countrymen in the public market place, against the oppression of the Spaniards, to whom the place was then subject, prompted them to revolt, and in the space of a day became king.

give? Ere she could hear the news the fatal business might be done, and ourselves suffering like the wretched Britons under the oppression of the Conqueror. Ye that oppose independence now, ye know not what ye do; ye are opening a door to eternal tyranny, by keeping vacant the seat of government.

There are thousands and tens of thousands; who would think it glorious to expel from the continent, that barbarous and hellish power, which hath stirred up the Indians and Negroes to destroy us; the cruelty hath a double guilt, it is dealing brutally by us, and treacherously by them. To talk of friendship with those in whom our reason forbids us to have faith, and our affections, (wounded through a thousand pores) instruct us to detest, is madness and folly. Every day wears out the little remains of kindred between us and them, and can there be any reason to hope, that as the relationship expires, the affection will increase, or that we shall agree better, when we have ten times more and greater concerns to quarrel over than ever?

Ye that tell us of harmony and reconciliation, can ye restore to us the time that is past? Can ye give to prostitution its former innocence? Neither can ye reconcile Britain and America. The last cord now is broken, the people of England are presenting addresses against us. There are injuries which nature cannot forgive; she would cease to be nature if she did. As well can the lover forgive the ravisher of his mistress, as the continent forgive the murders of Britain. The Almighty hath implanted in us these inextinguishable feelings for good and wise purposes. They are the guardians of his image in our hearts. They distinguish us from the herd of common animals. The social compact would dissolve, and justice be extirpated the earth, of have only a casual existence were we callous to the touches of affection. The robber and the murderer, would often escape unpunished, did not the injuries which our tempers sustain, provoke us into justice.

O ye that love mankind! Ye that dare oppose, not only the tyranny, but the tyrant, stand forth! Every spot of the old world is overrun with oppression. Freedom hath been hunted round the globe. Asia, and Africa, have long expelled her. Europe regards her like a stranger, and England hath given her warning to depart. O! receive the fugitive, and prepare in time an asylum for mankind.

Of the Present Ability of America with Some Miscellaneous Reflections
I HAVE NEVER met with a man, either in England or America, who hath not confessed his opinion, that a separation between the countries, would take place one time or other. And there is no instance in which we have

shown less judgment, than in endeavoring to describe, what we call, the ripeness or fitness of the Continent for independence.

As all men allow the measure, and vary only in their opinion of the time, let us, in order to remove mistakes, take a general survey of things and endeavor if possible, to find out the very time. But we need not go far, the inquiry ceases at once, for the time hath found us. The general concurrence, the glorious union of all things prove the fact.

It is not in numbers but in unity, that our great strength lies; yet our present numbers are sufficient to repel the force of all the world. The Continent hath, at this time, the largest body of armed and disciplined men of any power under Heaven; and is just arrived at that pitch of strength, in which no single colony is able to support itself, and the whole, who united can accomplish the matter, and either more, or, less than this, might be fatal in its effects. Our land force is already sufficient, and as to naval affairs, we cannot be insensible, that Britain would never suffer an American man of war to be built while the continent remained in her hands. Wherefore we should be no forwarder an hundred years hence in that branch, than we are now; but the truth is, we should be less so, because the timber of the country is every day diminishing, and that which will remain at last, will be far off and difficult to procure.

Were the continent crowded with inhabitants, her sufferings under the present circumstances would be intolerable. The more sea port towns we had, the more should we have both to defend and to loose. Our present numbers are so happily proportioned to our wants, that no man need be idle. The diminution of trade affords an army, and the necessities of an army create a new trade. Debts we have none; and whatever we may contract on this account will serve as a glorious memento of our virtue. Can we but leave posterity with a settled form of government, an independent constitution of its own, the purchase at any price will be cheap. But to expend millions for the sake of getting a few we acts repealed, and routing the present ministry only, is unworthy the charge, and is using posterity with the utmost cruelty; because it is leaving them the great work to do, and a debt upon their backs, from which they derive no advantage. Such a thought is unworthy a man of honor, and is the true characteristic of a narrow heart and a peddling politician.

The debt we may contract doth not deserve our regard if the work be but accomplished. No nation ought to be without a debt. A national debt is a national bond; and when it bears no interest, is in no case a grievance. Britain is oppressed with a debt of upwards of one hundred and forty millions sterling, for which she pays upwards of four millions interest. And as a compensation for her debt, she has a large navy; America is without a debt, and without a navy; yet for the twentieth part of the English national debt, could have a navy as large again. The navy of England is not worth, at this time, more than three millions and a half sterling.

The first and second editions of this pamphlet were published without the following calculations, which are now given as a proof that the above estimation of the navy is a just one. (See Entick's naval history, intro. page 56.)

The charge of building a ship of each rate, and furnishing her with masts, yards, sails and rigging, together with a proportion of eight months boatswain's and carpenter's sea-stores, as calculated by Mr. Burchett, Secretary to the navy, is as follows:

For a ship of 100 guns	£35,553
90	£29,886
80	£23,638
70	£17,785
60	£14,197
50	£10,606
40	£7,558
30	£5,846
20	£3,710

And from hence it is easy to sum up the value, or cost rather, of the whole British navy, which in the year 1757, when it was as its greatest glory consisted of the following ships and guns:

Ships	Guns	Cost of one	Cost of all
6	100	£35,533	£213,318
12	90	£29,886	£358,632
12	80	£23,638	£283,656
43	70	£17,785	£746,755
35	60	£14,197	£496,895
40	50	£10,606	£424,240
45	40	£7,758	£344,110
58	20	£3,710	£215,180
85 Sloops, bombs, and fireships, one another		£2,000	£170,000

Cost	£3,266,786
Remains for guns	£229,214
TOTAL	£3,500,000

No country on the globe is so happily situated, so internally capable of raising a fleet as America. Tar, timber, iron, and cordage are her natural produce. We need go abroad for nothing. Whereas the Dutch, who make large profits by hiring out their ships of war to the Spaniards and Portuguese, are obliged to import most of the materials they use. We ought to view the building a fleet as an article of commerce, it being the natural manufactory of this country. It is the best money we can lay out. A navy when finished is worth more than it cost. And is that nice point in national policy, in which commerce and protection are united. Let us build; if we want them not, we can sell; and by that means replace our paper currency with ready gold and silver.

In point of manning a fleet, people in general run into great errors; it is not necessary that one-fourth part should be sailors. The privateer Terrible, Captain Death, stood the hottest engagement of any ship last war, yet had not twenty sailors on board, though her complement of men was upwards of two hundred. A few able and social sailors will soon instruct a sufficient number of active landsmen in the common work of a ship. Wherefore, we never can be more capable to begin on maritime matters than now, while our timber is standing, our fisheries blocked up, and our sailors and shipwrights out of employ. Men of war of seventy and eighty guns were built forty years ago in New England, and why not the same now? Ship building is America's greatest pride, and in which, she will in time excel the whole world. The great empires of the east are mostly inland, and consequently excluded from the possibility of rivalling her. Africa is in a state of barbarism; and no power in Europe, hath either such an extent or coast, or such an internal supply of materials. Where nature hath given the one, she has withheld the other; to America only hath she been liberal of both. The vast empire of Russia is almost shut out from the sea; wherefore, her boundless forests, her tar, iron, and cordage are only articles of commerce.

In point of safety, ought we to be without a fleet? We are not the little people now, which we were sixty years ago; at that time we might have trusted our property in the streets, or fields rather; and slept securely without locks or bolts to our doors or windows. The case now is altered, and our methods of defence ought to improve with our increase of property. A common pirate, twelve months ago, might have come up the Delaware, and laid the city of Philadelphia under instant contribution, for what sum he pleased; and the same might have happened to other places. Nay, any daring fellow, in a brig of fourteen or sixteen guns, might have robbed the whole Continent, and carried off half a million of money. These are circumstances which demand our attention, and point out the necessity of naval protection.

Some, perhaps, will say, that after we have made it up with Britain, she will protect us. Can we be so unwise as to mean, that she shall keep a navy in our harbors for that purpose? Common sense will tell us, that the power which hath endeavored to subdue us, is of all others the most improper to defend us. Conquest may be effected under the pretence of friendship; and ourselves, after a long and brave resistance, be at last cheated into slavery. And if her ships are not to be admitted into our harbors, I would ask, how is she to protect us? A navy three or four thousand miles off can be of little use, and on sudden emergencies, none at all. Wherefore, if we must hereafter protect ourselves, why not do it for ourselves? Why do it for another.

The English list of ships of war is long and formidable, but not a tenth part of them are at any one time fit for service, numbers of them not in being; yet their names are pompously continued in the list, if only a plank be left of the ship: and not a fifth part, of such as are fit for service, can be spared on any one station at one time. The East, and West Indies, Mediterranean, Africa, and other parts over which Britain extends her claim, make large demands upon her navy. From a mixture of prejudice and inattention, we have contracted a false notion respecting the navy of England, and have talked as if we should have the whole of it to encounter at once, and for that reason, supposed that we must have one as large; which not being instantly practicable, have been made use of by a set of disguised tories to discourage our beginning thereon. Nothing can be farther from truth than this; for if America had only a twentieth part of the naval force of Britain, she would be by far an over match for her; because, as we neither have, nor claim any foreign dominion, our whole force would be employed on our own coast, where we should, in the long run, have two to one the advantage of those who had three or four thousand miles to sail over, before they could attack us, and the same distance to return in order to refit and recruit. And although Britain by her fleet, hath a check over our trade to Europe, we have as large a one over her trade to the West Indies, which, by laying in the neighborhood of the Continent, is entirely at its mercy.

Some method might be fallen on to keep up a naval force in time of peace, if we should not judge it necessary to support a constant navy. If premiums were to be given to merchants, to build and employ in their service, ships mounted with twenty, thirty, forty, or fifty guns, (the premiums to be in proportion to the loss of bulk to the merchants) fifty or sixty of those ships, with a few guard ships on constant duty, would keep up a sufficient navy, and that without burdening ourselves with the evil so loudly complained of in England, of suffering their fleet, in time of peace to lie rotting in the docks. To unite the sinews of commerce and defence is sound policy; for when our strength and our riches, play into each other's hand, we need fear no external enemy.

In almost every article of defence we abound. Hemp flourishes even to rankness, so that we need not want cordage. Our iron is superior to that of other countries. Our small arms equal to any in the world. Cannon we can cast at pleasure. Saltpetre and gunpowder we are every day producing. Our knowledge is hourly improving. Resolution is our inherent character, and courage hath never yet forsaken us. Wherefore, what is it that we want? Why is it that we hesitate? From Britain we can expect nothing but ruin. If she is once admitted to the government of America again, this Continent will not be worth living in. Jealousies will be always arising; insurrections will be constantly happening; and who will go forth to quell them? Who will venture his life to reduce his own countrymen to a foreign obedience? The difference between Pennsylvania and Connecticut, respecting some unlocated lands, shows the insignificance of a British government, and fully proves, that nothing but Continental authority can regulate Continental matters.

Another reason why the present time is preferable to all others, is, that the fewer our numbers are, the more land there is yet unoccupied, which instead of being lavished by the king on his worthless dependents, may be hereafter applied, not only to the discharge of the present debt, but to the constant support of government. No nation under heaven hath such an advantage as this.

The infant state of the Colonies, as it is called, so far from being against, is an argument in favor of independence. We are sufficiently numerous, and were we more so, we might be less united. It is a matter worthy of observation, that the more a country is peopled, the smaller their armies are. In military numbers, the ancients far exceeded the moderns: and the reason is evident, for trade being the consequence of population, men become too much absorbed thereby to attend to anything else. Commerce diminishes the spirit, both of patriotism and military defence. And history sufficiently informs us, that the bravest achievements were always accomplished in the non-age of a nation. With the increase of commerce England hath lost its spirit. The city of London, notwithstanding its numbers, submits to continued insults with the patience of a coward. The more men have to lose, the less willing are they to venture. The rich are in general slaves to fear, and submit to courtly power with the trembling duplicity of a spaniel.

Youth is the seed-time of good habits, as well in nations as in individuals. It might be difficult, if not impossible, to form the Continent into one government half a century hence. The vast variety of interests, occasioned by an increase of trade and population, would create confusion. Colony would be against colony. Each being able might scorn each other's assistance: and while the proud and foolish gloried in their little distinctions, the wise would lament that the union had not been formed before. Wherefore, the present time is the true time for establishing it. The intimacy which is contracted in infancy, and the friendship which is formed in misfortune, are, of all others, the most lasting and unalterable. Our present union is marked with both these characters: we are young, and we have been distressed; but our concord hath withstood our troubles, and fixes a memorable area for posterity to glory in.

The present time, likewise, is that peculiar time, which never happens to a nation but once, viz., the time of forming itself into a government. Most nations have let slip the opportunity, and by that means have been compelled to receive laws from their conquerors, instead of making laws for themselves. First, they had a king, and then a form of government; whereas, the articles or charter of government, should be formed first, and men delegated to execute them afterwards: but from the errors of other nations, let us learn wisdom, and lay hold of the present opportunity—to begin government at the right end.

When William the Conqueror subdued England he gave them law at the point of the sword; and until we consent that the seat of government in America, be legally and authoritatively occupied, we shall be in danger of having it filled by some fortunate ruffian, who may treat us in the same manner, and then, where will be our freedom? where our property?

As to religion, I hold it to be the indispensable duty of all government, to protect all conscientious professors thereof, and I know of no other business which government hath to do therewith. Let a man throw aside that narrowness of soul, that selfishness of principle, which the niggards of all professions are so unwilling to part with, and he will be at once delivered of his fears on that head. Suspicion is the companion of mean souls, and the bane of all good society. For myself I fully and conscientiously believe, that it is the will of the Almighty, that there should be diversity of religious opinions among us: It affords a larger field for our Christian kindness. Were we all of one way of thinking, our religious dispositions would want matter for probation; and on this liberal principle, I look on the various denominations among us, to be like children of the same family, differing only, in what is called their Christian names.

Earlier in this work, I threw out a few thoughts on the propriety of a Continental Charter, (for I only presume to offer hints, not plans) and in this place, I take the liberty of rementioning the subject, by observing, that a charter is to be understood as a bond of solemn obligation, which the whole enters into, to support the right of every separate part, whether of religion, personal freedom, or property, A firm bargain and a right reckoning make long friends.

In a former page I likewise mentioned the necessity of a large and equal representation; and there is no political matter which more deserves our attention. A small number of electors, or a small number of representatives, are equally dangerous. But if the number of the representatives be not only small, but unequal, the danger is increased. As an instance of this, I mention the following; when the Associators petition was before the House of Assembly of Pennsylvania; twenty-eight members only were present, all the Bucks County members, being eight, voted against it, and had seven of the Chester members done the same, this whole province had been governed by two counties only, and this danger it is always exposed to. The unwarrantable stretch likewise, which that house made in their last sitting, to gain an undue authority over the delegates of that province, ought to warn the people at large, how they trust power out of their own hands. A set of instructions for the Delegates were put together, which in point of sense and business would have dishonored a school-boy, and after being approved by a few, a very few without doors, were carried into the house, and there passed in behalf of the whole colony; whereas, did the whole colony know, with what ill-will that House hath entered on some necessary public measures, they would not hesitate a moment to think them unworthy of such a trust.

Immediate necessity makes many things convenient, which if continued would grow into oppressions. Expedience and right are different things. When the calamities of America required a consultation, there was no method so ready, or at that time so proper, as to appoint persons from the several Houses of Assembly for that purpose and the wisdom with which they have proceeded hath preserved this continent from ruin. But as it is more than probable that we shall never be without a Congress, every well-wisher to good order, must own, that the mode for choosing members of that body, deserves consideration. And I put it as a question to those, who make a study of mankind, whether representation and election is not too great a power for one and the same body of men to possess? When we are planning for posterity, we ought to remember that virtue is not hereditary.

It is from our enemies that we often gain excellent maxims, and are frequently surprised into reason by their mistakes. Mr. Cornwall (one of the Lords of the Treasury) treated the petition of the New York Assembly with contempt, because that House, he said, consisted but of twenty-six members, which trifling number, he argued, could not with decency be put for the whole. We thank him for his involuntary honesty.*

To conclude: However strange it may appear to some, or however unwilling they may be to think so, matters not, but many strong and striking reasons may be given, to show, that nothing can settle our affairs so expeditiously as an open and determined declaration for independence. Some of which are:

First. It is the custom of nations, when any two are at war, for some other powers, not engaged in the quarrel, to step in as mediators, and bring about the preliminaries of a peace: but while America calls herself the subject of Great Britain, no power, however well disposed she may be, can offer her mediation. Wherefore, in our present state we may quarrel on for ever.

Secondly. It is unreasonable to suppose, that France or Spain will give us any kind of assistance, if we mean only to make use of that assistance for the purpose of repairing the breach, and strengthening the connection between Britain and America; because, those powers would be sufferers by the consequences.

Thirdly. While we profess ourselves the subjects of Britain, we must, in the eye of foreign nations, be considered as rebels. The precedent is somewhat dangerous to their peace, for men to be in arms under the name of subjects; we on the spot, can solve the paradox: but to unite resistance and subjection, requires an idea much too refined for common understanding.

Fourthly. Were a manifesto to be published, and despatched to foreign courts, setting forth the miseries we have endured, and the peaceable methods we have ineffectually used for redress; declaring, at the same time, that not being able, any longer to live happily or safely under the cruel disposition of the British court, we had been driven to the necessity of breaking off all connection with her; at the same time assuring all such courts of our peaceable

---

* Those who would fully understand of what great consequence a large and equal representation is to a state, should read Burgh's political Disquisitions.

disposition towards them, and of our desire of entering into trade with them. Such a memorial would produce more good effects to this Continent, than if a ship were freighted with petitions to Britain.

Under our present denomination of British subjects we can neither be received nor heard abroad: The custom of all courts is against us, and will be so, until, by an independence, we take rank with other nations.

These proceedings may at first appear strange and difficult; but, like all other steps which we have already passed over, will in a little time become familiar and agreeable; and, until an independence is declared, the continent will feel itself like a man who continues putting off some unpleasant business from day to day, yet knows it must be done, hates to set about it, wishes it over, and is continually haunted with the thoughts of its necessity.

Appendix

SINCE THE PUBLICATION of the first edition of this pamphlet, or rather, on the same day on which it came out, the king's speech made its appearance in this city. Had the spirit of prophecy directed the birth of this production, it could not have brought it forth, at a more seasonable juncture, or a more necessary time. The bloody-mindedness of the one, show the necessity of pursuing the doctrine of the other. Men read by way of revenge. And the speech instead of terrifying, prepared a way for the manly principles of independence.

Ceremony, and even, silence, from whatever motive they may arise, have a hurtful tendency, when they give the least degree of countenance to base and wicked performances; wherefore, if this maxim be admitted, it naturally follows, that the king's speech, as being a piece of finished villainy, deserved, and still deserves, a general execration both by the congress and the people. Yet as the domestic tranquility of a nation, depends greatly on the chastity of what may properly be called national manners, it is often better, to pass some things over in silent disdain, than to make use of such new methods of dislike, as might introduce the least innovation, on that guardian of our peace and safety. And perhaps, it is chiefly owing to this prudent delicacy, that the king's speech, hath not before now, suffered a public execution. The speech if it may be called one, is nothing better than a wilful audacious libel against the truth, the common good, and the existence of mankind; and is a formal and pompous method of offering up human sacrifices to the pride of tyrants. But this general massacre of mankind, is one of the privileges, and the certain consequences of kings; for as nature knows them not, they know not her, and although they are beings of our own creating, they know not us, and are become the gods of their creators. The speech hath one good quality, which is, that it is not calculated to deceive, neither can we, even if we would, be deceived by it. Brutality and tyranny appear on the face of it. It leaves us at no loss: And every line convinces, even in the moment of reading, that He, who hunts the woods for prey, the naked and untutored Indian, is less a savage than the king of Britain.

Sir John Dalrymple, the putative father of a whining jesuitical piece, fallaciously called, The address of the people of ENGLAND to the inhabitants of America, hath, perhaps from a vain supposition, that the people here were to be frightened at the pomp and description of a king, given, (though very unwisely on his part) the real character of the present one: "But," says this writer, "if you are inclined to pay compliments to an administration, which we do not complain of," (meaning the Marquis of Rockingham's at the repeal of the Stamp Act) "it is very unfair in you to withhold them from that prince, by whose NOD ALONE they were permitted to do anything." This is toryism with a witness! Here is idolatry even without a mask: And he who can calmly hear, and digest such doctrine, hath forfeited his claim to rationality an apostate from the order of manhood; and ought to be considered—as one, who hath, not only given up the proper dignity of a man, but sunk himself beneath the rank of animals, and contemptibly crawl through the world like a worm.

However, it matters very little now, what the king of England either says or does; he hath wickedly broken through every moral and human obligation, trampled nature and conscience beneath his feet; and by a steady and constitutional spirit of insolence and cruelty, procured for himself an universal hatred. It is now the interest of America to provide for herself. She hath already a large and young family, whom it is more her duty to take care of, than to be granting away her property, to support a power who is become a reproach to the names of men and Christians. Ye, whose office it is to watch over the morals of a nation, of whatsoever sect or denomination ye are of, as well as ye, who are more immediately the guardians of the public liberty, if ye wish to preserve your native country uncontaminated by European corruption, ye must in secret wish a separation But leaving the moral part to private reflection, I shall chiefly confine my farther remarks to the following heads:

First. That it is the interest of America to be separated from Britain. Secondly. Which is the easiest and most practicable plan, reconciliation or independence? with some occasional remarks.

In support of the first, I could, if I judged it proper, produce the opinion of some of the ablest and most experienced men on this continent; and whose sentiments, on that head, are not yet publicly known. It is in reality a self-evident position: For no nation in a state of foreign dependance, limited in its commerce, and cramped and fettered in its legislative powers, can ever arrive at any material eminence. America doth not yet know what opulence is; and although the progress which she hath made stands unparalleled in the history of other nations, it is but childhood, compared with what she would be capable of arriving at, had she, as she ought to have, the legislative powers in her own hands. England is, at this time, proudly coveting what would do her no good, were she to accomplish it; and the Continent hesitating on a matter, which will be her final ruin if neglected. It is the commerce and not the conquest of America, by which England is to be benefited, and that would in a great measure continue, were the countries as independent of each other as France and Spain; because in many articles, neither can go to a better market. But it is the independence of this country on Britain or any other which is now the main and only object worthy of contention, and which, like all other truths discovered by necessity, will appear clearer and stronger every day.

First. Because it will come to that one time or other. Secondly. Because the longer it is delayed the harder it will be to accomplish.

I have frequently amused myself both in public and private companies, with silently remarking the spacious errors of those who speak without reflecting. And among the many which I have heard, the following seems the most general, viz., that had this rupture happened forty or fifty years hence, instead of now, the Continent would have been more able to have shaken off the dependance. To which I reply, that our military ability at this time, arises from the experience gained in the last war, and which in forty or fifty years time, would have been totally extinct. The Continent, would not, by that time, have had a General, or even a military officer left; and we, or those who may succeed us, would have been as ignorant of martial matters as the ancient Indians: And this single position, closely attended to, will unanswerably prove, that the present time is preferable to all others: The argument turns thus— at the conclusion of the last war, we had experience, but wanted numbers; and forty or fifty years hence, we should have numbers, without experience; wherefore, the proper point of time, must be some particular point between the two extremes, in which a sufficiency of the former remains, and a proper increase of the latter is obtained: And that point of time is the present time.

The reader will pardon this digression, as it does not properly come under the head I first set out with, and to which I again return by the following position, viz.:

Should affairs be patched up with Britain, and she to remain the governing and sovereign power of America, (which as matters are now circumstanced, is giving up the point entirely) we shall deprive ourselves of the very means of sinking the debt we have or may contract. The value of the back lands which some of the provinces are clandestinely deprived of, by the unjust extension of the limits of Canada, valued only at five pounds sterling per hundred acres, amount to upwards of twenty-five millions, Pennsylvania currency; and the quit-rents at one penny sterling per acre, to two millions yearly.

It is by the sale of those lands that the debt may be sunk, without burden to any, and the quit-rent reserved thereon, will always lessen, and in time, will wholly support the yearly expense of government. It matters not how long the debt is in paying, so that the lands when sold be applied to the discharge of it, and for the execution of which, the Congress for the time being, will be the continental trustees.

I proceed now to the second head, viz. Which is the earliest and most practicable plan, reconciliation or independence? with some occasional remarks.

He who takes nature for his guide is not easily beaten out of his argument, and on that ground, I answer generally—That INDEPENDENCE being a SINGLE SIMPLE LINE, contained within ourselves; and reconciliation, a matter exceedingly perplexed and complicated, and in which, a treacherous capricious court is to interfere, gives the answer without a doubt.

The present state of America is truly alarming to every man who is capable of reflection. Without law, without government, without any other mode of power than what is founded on, and granted by courtesy. Held together by an unexampled concurrence of sentiment, which is nevertheless subject to change, and which every secret enemy is endeavoring to dissolve. Our present condition, is, legislation without law; wisdom without a plan; a constitution without a name; and, what is strangely astonishing, perfect Independence contending for dependance. The instance is without a precedent; the case never existed before; and who can tell what may be the event? The property of no man is secure in the present unbraced system of things. The mind of the multitude is left at random, and feeling no fixed object before them, they pursue such as fancy or opinion starts. Nothing is criminal; there is no such thing as treason; wherefore, every one thinks himself at liberty to act as he pleases. The tories dared not to have assembled offensively, had they known that their lives, by that act were forfeited to the laws of the state. A line of distinction should be drawn, between English soldiers taken in battle, and inhabitants of America taken in arms. The first are prisoners, but the latter traitors. The one forfeits his liberty the other his head.

Notwithstanding our wisdom, there is a visible feebleness in some of our proceedings which gives encouragement to dissensions. The Continental Belt is too loosely buckled. And if something is not done in time, it will be too late to do any thing, and we shall fall into a state, in which, neither reconciliation nor independence will be practicable. The king and his worthless adherents are got at their old game of dividing the continent, and there are not wanting among us printers, who will be busy spreading specious falsehoods. The artful and hypocritical letter which appeared a few months ago in two of the New York papers, and likewise in two others, is an evidence that there are men who want either judgment or honesty. It is easy getting into holes and corners and talking of reconciliation: But do such men seriously consider, how difficult the task is, and how dangerous it may prove, should the Continent divide thereon. Do they take within their view, all the various orders of men whose situation and circumstances, as well as their own, are to be considered therein. Do they put themselves in the place of the sufferer whose all is already gone, and of the soldier, who hath quitted all for the defence of his country. If their ill judged moderation be suited to their own private situations only, regardless of others, the event will convince them, that "they are reckoning without their Host."

Put us, says some, on the footing we were in the year 1763: To which I answer, the request is not now in the power of Britain to comply with, neither will she propose it; but if it were, and even should be granted, I ask, as a reasonable question, By what means is such a corrupt and faithless court to be kept to its engagements? Another parliament, nay, even the present, may hereafter repeal the obligation, on the pretence of its being violently obtained, or unwisely granted; and in that case, Where is our redress? No going to law with nations; cannon are the barristers of crowns; and the sword, not of justice, but of war, decides the suit. To be on the footing of 1763, it is not sufficient, that the laws only be put on the same state, but, that our circumstances, likewise, be put on the same state; our burnt and destroyed towns repaired or built up, our private losses made good, our public debts (contracted for defence) discharged; otherwise, we shall be millions worse than we were at that enviable period. Such a request had it been complied with a year ago, would have won the heart and soul of the continent—but now it is too late, "the Rubicon is passed."

Besides the taking up arms, merely to enforce the repeal of a pecuniary law, seems as unwarrantable by the divine law, and as repugnant to human feelings, as the taking up arms to enforce obedience thereto. The object, on either side, doth not justify the ways and means; for the lives of men are too valuable to be cast away on such trifles. It is the violence which is done and threatened to our persons; the destruction of our property by an armed force; the invasion of our country by fire and sword, which conscientiously qualifies the use of arms: And the instant, in which such a mode of defence became necessary, all subjection to Britain ought to have ceased; and the independency of America should have been considered, as dating its area from, and published by, the first musket that was fired against her. This line is a line of consistency; neither drawn by caprice, nor extended by ambition; but produced by a chain of events, of which the colonies were not the authors.

I shall conclude these remarks, with the following timely and well intended hints, We ought to reflect, that there are three different ways by which an independency may hereafter be effected; and that one of those three, will one day or other, be the fate of America, viz. By the legal voice of the people in congress; by a military power; or by a mob: It may not always happen that our soldiers are citizens, and the multitude a body of reasonable men; virtue, as I have already remarked, is not hereditary, neither is it perpetual. Should an independency be brought about by the first of those means, we have every opportunity and every encouragement before us, to form the noblest, purest constitution on the face of the earth. We have it in our power to begin the world over again. A situation, similar to the present, hath not happened since the days of Noah until now. The birthday of a new world is at hand, and a race of men perhaps as numerous as all Europe contains, are to receive their portion of freedom from the event of a few months. The reflection is awful—and in this point of view, how trifling, how ridiculous, do the little, paltry cavillings, of a few weak or interested men appear, when weighed against the business of a world.

Should we neglect the present favorable and inviting period, and an independence be hereafter effected by any other means, we must charge the consequence to ourselves, or to those rather, whose narrow and prejudiced souls, are habitually opposing the measure, without either inquiring or reflecting. There are reasons to be given in support of Independence, which men should rather privately think of, than be publicly told of. We ought not now to be debating whether we shall be independent or not, but, anxious to accomplish it on a firm, secure, and honorable basis, and uneasy rather that it is not yet began upon. Every day convinces us of its necessity. Even the tories (if such beings yet remain among us) should, of all men, be the most solicitous to promote it; for, as the appointment of committees at first, protected them from popular rage, so, a wise and well established form of government, will be the only certain means of continuing it securely to them. Wherefore, if they have not virtue enough to be Whigs, they ought to have prudence enough to wish for independence.

In short, independence is the only bond that can tie and keep us together. We shall then see our object, and our ears will be legally shut against the schemes of an intriguing, as well as a cruel enemy. We shall then too, be on a proper footing, to treat with Britain; for there is reason to conclude, that the pride of that court, will be less hurt by treating with the American states for terms of peace, than with those, whom she denominates, "rebellious subjects," for terms of accommodation. It is our delaying it that encourages her to hope for conquest, and our backwardness tends only to prolong the war. As we have, without any good effect therefrom, withheld our trade to obtain a redress of our grievances, let us now try the alternative, by independently redressing them ourselves, and then offering to open the trade. The mercantile and reasonable part of England will be still with us; because, peace with trade, is preferable to war without it. And if this offer be not accepted, other courts may be applied to.

On these grounds I rest the matter. And as no offer hath yet been made to refute the doctrine contained in the former editions of this pamphlet, it is a negative proof, that either the doctrine cannot be refuted, or, that the party in favor of it are too numerous to be opposed. Wherefore, instead of gazing at each other with suspicious or doubtful curiosity, let each of us, hold out to his neighbor the hearty hand of friendship, and unite in drawing a line, which, like an act of oblivion, shall bury in forgetfulness every former dissention. Let the names of Whig and Tory be extinct; and let none other be heard among us, than those of a good citizen, an open and resolute friend, and a virtuous supporter of the RIGHTS of MANKIND and of the FREE AND INDEPENDENT STATES OF AMERICA.

Epistle to Quakers
TO THE REPRESENTATIVES of the Religious Society of the People called Quakers, or to so many of them as were concerned in publishing a late piece,

entitled "THE ANCIENT TESTIMONY and PRINCIPLES of the people called QUAKERS renewed with respect to the KING and GOVERNMENT, and Touching the COMMOTIONS now prevailing in these and other parts of AMERICA, addressed to the PEOPLE IN GENERAL."

THE writer of this is one of those few, who never dishonors religion either by ridiculing, or cavilling at any denomination whatsoever. To God, and not to man, are all men accountable on the score of religion. Wherefore, this epistle is not so properly addressed to you as a religious, but as a political body, dabbling in matters, which the professed quietude of your Principles instruct you not to meddle with.

As you have, without a proper authority for so doing, put yourselves in the place of the whole body of the Quakers, so, the writer of this, in order to be on an equal rank with yourselves, is under the necessity, of putting himself in the place of all those who approve the very writings and principles, against which your testimony is directed: And he hath chosen their singular situation, in order that you might discover in him, that presumption of character which you cannot see in yourselves. For neither he nor you have any claim or title to Political Representation.

When men have departed from the right way, it is no wonder that they stumble and fall. And it is evident from the manner in which ye have managed your testimony, that politics, (as a religious body of men) is not your proper walk; for however well adapted it might appear to you, it is, nevertheless, a jumble of good and bad put unwisely together, and the conclusion drawn therefrom, both unnatural and unjust.

The two first pages, (and the whole doth not make four) we give you credit for, and expect the same civility from you, because the love and desire of peace is not confined to Quakerism, it is the natural, as well as the religious wish of all denominations of men. And on this ground, as men laboring to establish an Independent Constitution of our own, do we exceed all others in our hope, end, and aim. Our plan is peace for ever. We are tired of contention with Britain, and can see no real end to it but in a final separation. We act consistently, because for the sake of introducing an endless and uninterrupted peace, do we bear the evils and burdens of the present day. We are endeavoring, and will steadily continue to endeavor, to separate and dissolve a connection which hath already filled our land with blood; and which, while the name of it remains, will be the fatal cause of future mischiefs to both countries.

We fight neither for revenge nor conquest; neither from pride nor passion; we are not insulting the world with our fleets and armies, nor ravaging the globe for plunder. Beneath the shade of our own vines are we attacked; in our own houses, and on our own lands, is the violence committed against us. We view our enemies in the characters of highwaymen and housebreakers, and having no defence for ourselves in the civil law; are obliged to punish them by the military one, and apply the sword, in the very case, where you have before now, applied the halter. Perhaps we feel for the ruined and in-sulted sufferers in all and every part of the continent, and with a degree of tenderness which hath not yet made its way into some of your bosoms. But be ye sure that ye mistake not the cause and ground of your Testimony. Call not coldness of soul, religion; nor put the bigot in the place of the Christian.

O ye partial ministers of your own acknowledged principles! If the bear-ing arms be sinful, the first going to war must be more so, by all the difference between wilful attack and unavoidable defence.

Wherefore, if ye really preach from conscience, and mean not to make a political hobby-horse of your religion, convince the world thereof, by pro-claiming your doctrine to our enemies, for they likewise bear ARMS. Give us proof of your sincerity by publishing it at St. James's, to the commanders in chief at Boston, to the admirals and captains who are practically ravaging our coasts, and to all the murdering miscreants who are acting in authority under HIM whom ye profess to serve. Had ye the honest soul of Barclay* ye would preach repentance to your king; Ye would tell the royal tyrant of his sins, and warn him of eternal ruin. Ye would not spend your partial invectives against the injured and the insulted only, but like faithful ministers, would cry aloud and spare none. Say not that ye are persecuted, neither endeavor to make us the authors of that reproach, which, ye are bringing upon yourselves; for we testify unto all men, that we do not complain against you because ye are Quakers, but because ye pretend to be and are NOT Quakers.

---

* "Thou hast tasted of prosperity and adversity; thou knowest what it is to be banished thy native country, to be overruled as well as to rule, and set upon the throne; and being op-pressed thou hast reason to know now hateful the oppressor is both to God and man. If after all these warnings and advertisements, thou dost not turn unto the Lord with all thy heart, but forget him who remembered thee in thy distress, and give up thyself to follow lust and vanity, surely great will be thy condemnation. Against which snare, as well as the temptation of those who may or do feed thee, and prompt thee to evil, the most excellent and prevalent remedy will be, to apply thyself to that light of Christ which shineth in thy conscience and which neither can, nor will flatter thee, nor suffer thee to be at ease in thy sins."—Barclay's Address to Charles II.

Alas! it seems by the particular tendency of some part of your Testimony, and other parts of your conduct, as if all sin was reduced to, and comprehended in the act of bearing arms, and that by the people only. Ye appear to us, to have mistaken party for conscience, because the general tenor of your actions wants uniformity: And it is exceedingly difficult to us to give credit to many of your pretended scruples; because we see them made by the same men, who, in the very instant that they are exclaiming against the mammon of this world, are nevertheless, hunting after it with a step as steady as Time, and an appetite as keen as Death.

The quotation which ye have made from Proverbs, in the third page of your testimony, that, "when a man's ways please the Lord, he maketh even his enemies to be at peace with him;" is very unwisely chosen on your part; because it amounts to a proof, that the king's ways (whom ye are so desirous of supporting) do not please the Lord, otherwise, his reign would be in peace.

I now proceed to the latter part of your testimony, and that, for which all the foregoing seems only an introduction, viz:

"It hath ever been our judgment and principle, since we were called to profess the light of Christ Jesus, manifested in our consciences unto this day, that the setting up and putting down kings and governments, is God's peculiar prerogative; for causes best known to himself: And that it is not our business to have any hand or contrivance therein; nor to be busy-bodies above our station, much less to plot and contrive the ruin, or overturn any of them, but to pray for the king, and safety of our nation, and good of all men: that we may live a peaceable and quiet life, in all goodliness and honesty; under the government which God is pleased to set over us." If these are really your principles why do ye not abide by them? Why do ye not leave that, which ye call God's work, to be managed by himself? These very principles instruct you to wait with patience and humility, for the event of all public measures, and to receive that event as the divine will towards you. Wherefore, what occasion is there for your political Testimony if you fully believe what it contains? And the very publishing it proves, that either, ye do not believe what ye profess, or have not virtue enough to practice what ye believe.

The principles of Quakerism have a direct tendency to make a man the quiet and inoffensive subject of any, and every government which is set over him. And if the setting up and putting down of kings and governments is God's peculiar prerogative, he most certainly will not be robbed thereof by us; wherefore, the principle itself leads you to approve of every thing, which ever happened, or may happen to kings as being his work. Oliver Cromwell thanks you. Charles, then, died not by the hands of man; and should the present proud imitator of him, come to the same untimely end, the writers and publishers of the Testimony, are bound by the doctrine it contains, to applaud the fact. Kings are not taken away by miracles, neither are changes in governments brought about by any other means than such as are common and human; and such as we are now using. Even the dispersing of the Jews, though foretold by our Savior, was effected by arms. Wherefore, as ye refuse to be the means on one side, ye ought not to be meddlers on the other; but to wait the issue in silence; and unless you can produce divine authority, to prove, that the Almighty who hath created and placed this new world, at the greatest distance it could possibly stand, east and west, from every part of the old, doth, nevertheless, disapprove of its being independent of the corrupt and abandoned court of Britain; unless I say, ye can show this, how can ye, on the ground of your principles, justify the exciting and stirring up of the people "firmly to unite in the abhorrence of all such writings, and measures, as evidence a desire and design to break off the happy connection we have hitherto enjoyed, with the kingdom of Great Britain, and our just and necessary subordination to the king, and those who are lawfully placed in authority under him." What a slap in the face is here! the men, who, in the very paragraph before, have quietly and passively resigned up the ordering, altering, and disposal of kings and governments, into the hands of God, are now recalling their principles, and putting in for a share of the business. Is it possible, that the conclusion, which is here justly quoted, can any ways follow from the doctrine laid down? The inconsistency is too glaring not to be seen; the absurdity too great not to be laughed at; and such as could only have been made by those, whose understandings were darkened by the narrow and crabby spirit of a despairing political party; for ye are not to be considered as the whole body of the Quakers but only as a factional and fractional part thereof.

Here ends the examination of your testimony; (which I call upon no man to abhor, as ye have done, but only to read and judge of fairly;) to which I subjoin the following remark; "That the setting up and putting down of kings," most certainly mean, the making him a king, who is yet not so, and the making him no king who is already one. And pray what hath this to do in the present case? We neither mean to set up nor to put down, neither to make nor to unmake, but to have nothing to do with them. Wherefore your testimony in whatever light it is viewed serves only to dishonor your judgment, and for many other reasons had better have been let alone than published.

First. Because it tends to the decrease and reproach of religion whatever, and is of the utmost danger to society, to make it a party in political disputes. Secondly. Because it exhibits a body of men, numbers of whom disavow the publishing political testimonies, as being concerned therein and approvers thereof. Thirdly. Because it hath a tendency to undo that continental harmony and friendship which yourselves by your late liberal and charitable donations hath lent a hand to establish; and the preservation of which, is of the utmost consequence to us all.

And here, without anger or resentment I bid you farewell. Sincerely wishing, that as men and Christians, ye may always fully and uninterruptedly enjoy every civil and religious right; and be, in your turn, the means of securing it to others; but that the example which ye have unwisely set, of mingling religion with politics, may be disavowed and reprobated by every inhabitant of America.

— THE END —

Source: Common Sense, by Thomas Paine, printed by W. and T. Bradford, Philadelphia, 1791.

Appendix B

The Declaration of Independence

IN CONGRESS, JULY 4, 1776.

The unanimous Declaration of the thirteen united States of America,

When in the Course of human events, it becomes necessary for one people to dissolve the political bands which have connected them with another, and to assume among the powers of the earth, the separate and equal station to which the Laws of Nature and of Nature's God entitle them, a decent respect to the opinions of mankind requires that they should declare the causes which impel them to the separation.

We hold these truths to be self-evident, that all men are created equal, that they are endowed by their Creator with certain unalienable Rights, that among these are Life, Liberty and the pursuit of Happiness.—That to secure these rights, Governments are instituted among Men, deriving their just powers from the consent of the governed,—That whenever any Form of Government becomes destructive of these ends, it is the Right of the People to alter or to abolish it, and to institute new Government, laying its foundation on such principles and organizing its powers in such form, as to them shall seem most likely to effect their Safety and Happiness. Prudence, indeed, will dictate that Governments long established should not be changed for light and transient causes; and accordingly all experience hath shewn, that mankind are more disposed to suffer, while evils are sufferable, than to right themselves by abolishing the forms to which they are accustomed. But when a long train of abuses and usurpations, pursuing invariably the same Object evinces a design to reduce them under absolute Despotism, it is their right, it is their duty, to throw off such Government, and to provide new Guards for their future security.—Such has been the patient sufferance of these Colonies; and such is now the necessity which constrains them to alter their former Systems of Government. The history of the present King of Great Britain is a history of repeated injuries and usurpations, all having in direct object the establishment of an absolute Tyranny over these States. To prove this, let Facts be submitted to a candid world.

He has refused his Assent to Laws, the most wholesome and necessary for the public good.

He has forbidden his Governors to pass Laws of immediate and pressing importance, unless suspended in their operation till his Assent should be obtained; and when so suspended, he has utterly neglected to attend to them.

He has refused to pass other Laws for the accommodation of large districts of people, unless those people would relinquish the right of Representation in the Legislature, a right inestimable to them and formidable to tyrants only.

He has called together legislative bodies at places unusual, uncomfortable, and distant from the depository of their public Records, for the sole purpose of fatiguing them into compliance with his measures.

He has dissolved Representative Houses repeatedly, for opposing with manly firmness his invasions on the rights of the people.

He has refused for a long time, after such dissolutions, to cause others to be elected; whereby the Legislative powers, incapable of Annihilation, have returned to the People at large for their exercise; the State remaining in the mean time exposed to all the dangers of invasion from without, and convulsions within.

He has endeavoured to prevent the population of these States; for that purpose obstructing the Laws for Naturalization of Foreigners; refusing to pass others to encourage their migrations hither, and raising the conditions of new Appropriations of Lands.

He has obstructed the Administration of Justice, by refusing his Assent to Laws for establishing Judiciary powers.

He has made Judges dependent on his Will alone, for the tenure of their offices, and the amount and payment of their salaries.

He has erected a multitude of New Offices, and sent hither swarms of Officers to harrass our people, and eat out their substance.

He has kept among us, in times of peace, Standing Armies without the Consent of our legislatures.

He has affected to render the Military independent of and superior to the Civil power.

He has combined with others to subject us to a jurisdiction foreign to our constitution, and unacknowledged by our laws; giving his Assent to their Acts of pretended Legislation:

For Quartering large bodies of armed troops among us:

For protecting them, by a mock Trial, from punishment for any Murders which they should commit on the Inhabitants of these States:

For cutting off our Trade with all parts of the world:

For imposing Taxes on us without our Consent:

For depriving us in many cases, of the benefits of Trial by Jury:

For transporting us beyond Seas to be tried for pretended offenses

For abolishing the free System of English Laws in a neighboring Province, establishing therein an Arbitrary government, and enlarging its Boundaries so as to render it at once an example and fit instrument for introducing the same absolute rule into these Colonies:

For taking away our Charters, abolishing our most valuable Laws, and altering fundamentally the Forms of our Governments:

For suspending our own Legislatures, and declaring themselves invested with power to legislate for us in all cases whatsoever.

He has abdicated Government here, by declaring us out of his Protection and waging War against us.

He has plundered our seas, ravaged our Coasts, burnt our towns, and destroyed the lives of our people.

He is at this time transporting large Armies of foreign Mercenaries to compleat the works of death, desolation and tyranny, already begun with circumstances of Cruelty & perfidy scarcely paralleled in the most barbarous ages, and totally unworthy the Head of a civilized nation.

He has constrained our fellow Citizens taken Captive on the high Seas to bear Arms against their Country, to become the executioners of their friends and Brethren, or to fall themselves by their Hands.

He has excited domestic insurrections amongst us, and has endeavored to bring on the inhabitants of our frontiers, the merciless Indian Savages, whose known rule of warfare, is an undistinguished destruction of all ages, sexes and conditions.

In every stage of these Oppressions We have Petitioned for Redress in the most humble terms: Our repeated Petitions have been answered only by repeated injury. A Prince whose character is thus marked by every act which may define a Tyrant, is unfit to be the ruler of a free people.

Nor have We been wanting in attentions to our British brethren. We have warned them from time to time of attempts by their legislature to extend an unwarrantable jurisdiction over us. We have reminded them of the circumstances of our emigration and settlement here. We have appealed to their native justice and magnanimity, and we have conjured them by the ties of our common kindred to disavow these usurpations, which, would inevitably interrupt our connections and correspondence. They too have been deaf to the voice of justice and of consanguinity. We must, therefore, acquiesce in the necessity, which denounces our Separation, and hold them, as we hold the rest of mankind, Enemies in War, in Peace Friends.

We, therefore, the Representatives of the united States of America, in General Congress, Assembled, appealing to the Supreme Judge of the world for the rectitude of our intentions, do, in the Name, and by Authority of the good People of these Colonies, solemnly publish and declare, That these United Colonies are, and of Right ought to be Free and Independent States; that they are Absolved from all Allegiance to the British Crown, and that all political connection between them and the State of Great Britain, is and ought to be totally dissolved; and that as Free and Independent States, they have full Power to levy War, conclude Peace, contract Alliances, establish Commerce, and to do all other Acts and Things which Independent States may of right do. And for the support of this Declaration, with a firm reliance on the protection of divine Providence, we mutually pledge to each other our Lives, our Fortunes and our sacred Honor.

The 56 signatures on the Declaration appear in the positions indicated:

> *Column 1*
> ### GEORGIA:
> Button Gwinnett
> Lyman Hall
> George Walton
>
> *Column 2*
> ### NORTH CAROLINA:
> William Hooper
> Joseph Hewes
> John Penn
> ### SOUTH CAROLINA:
> Edward Rutledge
> Thomas Heyward, Jr.
> Thomas Lynch, Jr.
> Arthur Middleton

Column 3

MASSACHUSETTS:
John Hancock

MARYLAND:
Samuel Chase
William Paca
Thomas Stone
Charles Carroll of
  Carrollton

VIRGINIA:
George Wythe
Richard Henry Lee
Thomas Jefferson
Benjamin Harrison
Thomas Nelson, Jr.
Francis Lightfoot Lee
Carter Braxton

Column 4

PENNSYLVANIA:
Robert Morris
Benjamin Rush
Benjamin Franklin
John Morton
George Clymer
James Smith
George Taylor
James Wilson
George Ross

DELAWARE:
Caesar Rodney
George Read
Thomas McKean

Column 5

NEW YORK:
William Floyd
Philip Livingston
Francis Lewis
Lewis Morris

NEW JERSEY:
Richard Stockton
John Witherspoon
Francis Hopkinson
John Hart
Abraham Clark

Column 6

NEW HAMPSHIRE:
Josiah Bartlett
William Whipple

MASSACHUSETTS:
Samuel Adams
John Adams
Robert Treat Paine
Elbridge Gerry

RHODE ISLAND:
Stephen Hopkins
William Ellery

CONNECTICUT:
Roger Sherman
Samuel Huntington
William Williams
Oliver Wolcott

NEW HAMPSHIRE:
Matthew Thornton

Source: http://www.archives.gov/exhibits/charters/declaration_transcript.html
U.S. National Archives & Records Administration

The American Crisis *by Thomas Paine.*
Library of Congress

Appendix C

THE CRISIS *by Thomas Paine*

DECEMBER 23, 1776

THESE ARE THE times that try men's souls. The summer soldier and the sunshine patriot will, in this crisis, shrink from the service of their country; but he that stands by it now, deserves the love and thanks of man and woman. Tyranny, like hell, is not easily conquered; yet we have this consolation with us, that the harder the conflict, the more glorious the triumph. What we obtain too cheap, we esteem too lightly: it is dearness only that gives every thing its value. Heaven knows how to put a proper price upon its goods; and it would be strange indeed if so celestial an article as FREEDOM should not be highly rated. Britain, with an army to enforce her tyranny, has declared that she has a right (not only to TAX) but "to BIND us in ALL CASES WHATSOEVER" and if being bound in that manner, is not slavery, then is there not such a thing as slavery upon earth. Even the expression is impious; for so unlimited a power can belong only to God.

Whether the independence of the continent was declared too soon, or delayed too long, I will not now enter into as an argument; my own simple opinion is, that had it been eight months earlier, it would have been much better. We did not make a proper use of last winter, neither could we, while we were in a dependent state. However, the fault, if it were one, was all our own (Note: The present winter is worth an age, if rightly employed; but, if lost or neglected, the whole continent will partake of the evil; and there is no punishment that man does not deserve, be he who, or what, or where he will, that may be the means of sacrificing a season so precious and useful.); we have none to blame but ourselves. But no great deal is lost yet. All that Howe has been doing for this month past, is rather a ravage than a conquest, which the spirit of the Jerseys, a year ago, would have quickly repulsed, and which time and a little resolution will soon recover.

I have as little superstition in me as any man living, but my secret opinion has ever been, and still is, that God Almighty will not give up a people to military destruction, or leave them unsupportedly to perish, who have so earnestly and so repeatedly sought to avoid the calamities of war, by every decent method which wisdom could invent. Neither have I so much of the infidel in me, as to suppose that He has relinquished the government of the world, and given us up to the care of devils; and as I do not, I cannot see on what grounds the king of Britain can look up to heaven for help against us: a common murderer, a highwayman, or a house-breaker, has as good a pretense as he.

'Tis surprising to see how rapidly a panic will sometimes run through a country. All nations and ages have been subject to them. Britain has trembled like an ague at the report of a French fleet of flat-bottomed boats; and in the fourteenth [fifteenth] century the whole English army, after ravaging the kingdom of France, was driven back like men petrified with fear; and this brave exploit was performed by a few broken forces collected and headed by a woman, Joan of Arc. Would that heaven might inspire some Jersey maid to spirit up her countrymen, and save her fair fellow sufferers from ravage and ravishment! Yet panics, in some cases, have their uses; they produce as much good as hurt. Their duration is always short; the mind soon grows through them, and acquires a firmer habit than before. But their peculiar advantage is, that they are the touchstones of sincerity and hypocrisy, and bring things and men to light, which might otherwise have lain forever undiscovered. In fact, they have the same effect on secret traitors, which an imaginary apparition would have upon a private murderer. They sift out the hidden thoughts of man, and hold them up in public to the world. Many a disguised Tory has lately shown his head, that shall penitentially solemnize with curses the day on which Howe arrived upon the Delaware.

As I was with the troops at Fort Lee, and marched with them to the edge of Pennsylvania, I am well acquainted with many circumstances, which those who live at a distance know but little or nothing of. Our situation there was exceedingly cramped, the place being a narrow neck of land between the North River and the Hackensack. Our force was inconsiderable, being not one-fourth so great as Howe could bring against us. We had no army at hand to have relieved the garrison, had we shut ourselves up and stood on our defence. Our ammunition, light artillery, and the best part of our stores, had been removed, on the apprehension that Howe would endeavor to penetrate the Jerseys, in which case Fort Lee could be of no use to us; for it must occur to every thinking man, whether in the army or not, that these kind of field forts are only for temporary purposes, and last in use no longer than the enemy directs his force against the particular object which such forts are raised to defend. Such was our situation and condition at Fort Lee on the morning of the 20th of November, when an officer arrived with information that the enemy with 200 boats had landed about seven miles above; Major General [Nathaniel] Green, who commanded the garrison, immediately ordered them under arms, and sent express to General Washington at the town of Hackensack, distant by the way of the ferry—six miles. Our first object was to secure the bridge over the Hackensack, which laid up the river between the enemy and us, about six miles from us, and three from them. General Washington arrived in about three-quarters of an hour, and marched at the head of the troops towards the bridge, which place I expected we should have a brush for; however, they did not choose to dispute it with us, and the greatest part of our troops went over the bridge, the rest over the ferry, except some which passed at a mill on a small creek, between the bridge and the ferry, and made their way through some marshy grounds up to the town of Hackensack, and there passed the river. We brought off as much baggage as the wagons could contain, the rest was lost. The simple object was to bring off the garrison, and march them on till they could be strengthened by the Jersey or Pennsylvania militia, so as to be enabled to make a stand. We staid four days at Newark, collected our out-posts with some of the Jersey militia, and marched out twice to meet the enemy, on being informed that they were advancing, though our numbers were greatly inferior to theirs. Howe, in my little opinion, committed a great error in generalship in not throwing a body of forces off from Staten Island through Amboy, by which means he might have seized all our stores at Brunswick, and intercepted our march into Pennsylvania; but if we believe the power of hell to be limited, we must likewise believe that their agents are under some providential control.

I shall not now attempt to give all the particulars of our retreat to the Delaware; suffice it for the present to say, that both officers and men, though greatly harassed and fatigued, frequently without rest, covering, or provision, the inevitable consequences of a long retreat, bore it with a manly and martial spirit. All their wishes centred in one, which was, that the country would turn out and help them to drive the enemy back. Voltaire has remarked that King William never appeared to full advantage but in difficulties and in action; the same remark may be made on General Washington, for the character fits him. There is a natural firmness in some minds which cannot be unlocked by trifles, but which, when unlocked, discovers a cabinet of fortitude; and I reckon it among those kind of public blessings, which we do not immediately see, that God hath blessed him with uninterrupted health, and given him a mind that can even flourish upon care.

I shall conclude this paper with some miscellaneous remarks on the state of our affairs; and shall begin with asking the following question, Why is it that the enemy have left the New England provinces, and made these middle ones the seat of war? The answer is easy: New England is not infested with Tories, and we are. I have been tender in raising the cry against these men, and used numberless arguments to show them their danger, but it will not do to sacrifice a world either to their folly or their baseness. The period is now arrived, in which either they or we must change our sentiments, or one or both must fall. And what is a Tory? Good God! What is he? I should not be afraid to go with a hundred Whigs against a thousand Tories, were they to attempt to get into arms. Every Tory is a coward; for servile, slavish, self-interested fear is the foundation of Toryism; and a man under such influence, though he may be cruel, never can be brave.

But, before the line of irrecoverable separation be drawn between us, let us reason the matter together: Your conduct is an invitation to the enemy, yet not one in a thousand of you has heart enough to join him. Howe is as much deceived by you as the American cause is injured by you. He expects you will all take up arms, and flock to his standard, with muskets on your shoulders. Your opinions are of no use to him, unless you support him personally, for 'tis soldiers, and not Tories, that he wants.

I once felt all that kind of anger, which a man ought to feel, against the mean principles that are held by the Tories: a noted one, who kept a tavern at Amboy, was standing at his door, with as pretty a child in his hand, about eight or nine years old, as I ever saw, and after speaking his mind as freely as he thought was prudent, finished with this unfatherly expression, "Well! give me peace in my day." Not a man lives on the continent but fully believes that a separation must some time or other finally take place, and a generous parent should have said, "If there must be trouble, let it be in my day, that my child may have peace;" and this single reflection, well applied, is sufficient to awaken every man to duty. Not a place upon earth might be so happy as America. Her situation is remote from all the wrangling world, and she has nothing to do but to trade with them. A man can distinguish himself between temper and principle, and I am as confident, as I am that God governs the world, that America will never be happy till she gets clear of foreign dominion. Wars, without ceasing, will break out till that period arrives, and the continent must in the end be conqueror; for though the flame of liberty may sometimes cease to shine, the coal can never expire.

America did not, nor does not want force; but she wanted a proper application of that force. Wisdom is not the purchase of a day, and it is no wonder that we should err at the first setting off. From an excess of tenderness, we were unwilling to raise an army, and trusted our cause to the temporary defence of a well-meaning militia. A summer's experience has now taught us better; yet with those troops, while they were collected, we were able to set bounds to the progress of the enemy, and, thank God! they are again assembling. I always considered militia as the best troops in the world for a sudden exertion, but they will not do for a long campaign. Howe, it is probable, will make an attempt on this city [Philadelphia]; should he fail on this side the Delaware, he is ruined. If he succeeds, our cause is not ruined. He stakes all on his side against a part on ours; admitting he succeeds, the consequence will be, that armies from both ends of the continent will march to assist their suffering friends in the middle states; for he cannot go everywhere, it is impossible. I consider Howe as the greatest enemy the Tories have; he is bringing a war into their country, which, had it not been for him and partly for themselves, they had been clear of. Should he now be expelled, I wish with all the devotion of a Christian, that the names of Whig and Tory may never more be mentioned; but should the Tories give him encouragement to come, or assistance if he come, I as sincerely wish that our next year's arms may expel them from the continent, and the Congress appropriate their possessions to the relief of those who have suffered in well-doing. A single successful battle next year will settle the whole. America could carry on a two years' war by the confiscation of the property of disaffected persons, and be made happy by their expulsion. Say not that this is revenge, call it rather the soft resentment of a suffering people, who, having no object in view but the good of all, have staked their own all upon a seemingly doubtful event. Yet it is folly to argue against determined hardness; eloquence may strike the ear, and the language of sorrow draw forth the tear of compassion, but nothing can reach the heart that is steeled with prejudice.

Quitting this class of men, I turn with the warm ardor of a friend to those who have nobly stood, and are yet determined to stand the matter out: I call not upon a few, but upon all: not on this state or that state, but on every state: up and help us; lay your shoulders to the wheel; better have too much force than too little, when so great an object is at stake. Let it be told to the future world, that in the depth of winter, when nothing but hope and virtue could survive, that the city and the country, alarmed at one common danger, came forth to meet and to repulse it. Say not that thousands are gone, turn out your tens of thousands; throw not the burden of the day upon Providence, but "show your faith by your works," that God may bless you. It matters not where you live, or what rank of life you hold, the evil or the blessing will reach you all. The far and the near, the home counties and the back, the rich and the poor, will suffer or rejoice alike. The heart that feels not now is dead; the blood of his children will curse his cowardice, who shrinks back at a time when a little might have saved the whole, and made them happy. I love the man that can smile in trouble, that can gather strength from distress, and grow brave by reflection. 'Tis the business of little minds to shrink; but he whose heart is firm, and whose conscience approves his conduct, will pursue his principles unto death. My own line of reasoning is to myself as straight and clear as a ray of light. Not all the treasures of the world, so far as I believe, could have induced me to support an offensive war, for I think it murder; but if a thief breaks into my house, burns and destroys my property, and kills or threatens to kill me, or those that are in it, and to "bind me in all cases whatsoever" to his absolute will, am I to suffer it? What signifies it to me, whether he who does it is a king or a common man; my countryman or not my countryman; whether it be done by an individual villain, or an army of them? If we reason to the root of things we shall find no difference; neither can any just cause be assigned why we should punish in the one case and pardon in the other. Let them call me rebel and welcome, I feel no concern from it; but I should suffer the misery of devils, were I to make a whore of my soul by swearing allegiance to one whose character is that of a sottish, stupid, stubborn, worthless, brutish man. I conceive likewise a horrid idea in receiving mercy from a being, who at the last day shall be shrieking to the rocks and mountains to cover him, and fleeing with terror from the orphan, the widow, and the slain of America.

There are cases which cannot be overdone by language, and this is one. There are persons, too, who see not the full extent of the evil which threatens them; they solace themselves with hopes that the enemy, if he succeed, will be merciful. It is the madness of folly, to expect mercy from those who have refused to do justice; and even mercy, where conquest is the object, is only a trick of war; the cunning of the fox is as murderous as the violence of the wolf, and we ought to guard equally against both. Howe's first object is, partly by threats and partly by promises, to terrify or seduce the people to deliver up their arms and receive mercy. The ministry recommended the same plan to Gage, and this is what the tories call making their peace, "a peace which passeth all understanding" indeed! A peace which would be the immediate forerunner of a worse ruin than any we have yet thought of. Ye men of Pennsylvania, do reason upon these things! Were the back counties to give up their arms, they would fall an easy prey to the Indians, who are all armed: this perhaps is what some Tories would not be sorry for. Were the home counties to deliver up their arms, they would be exposed to the resentment of the back counties who would then have it in their power to chastise their defection at pleasure. And were any one state to give up its arms, that state must be garrisoned by all Howe's army of Britons and Hessians to preserve it from the anger of the rest. Mutual fear is the principal link in the chain of mutual love, and woe be to that state that breaks the compact. Howe is mercifully inviting you to barbarous destruction, and men must be either rogues or fools that will not see it. I dwell not upon the vapors of imagination; I bring reason to your ears, and, in language as plain as A, B, C, hold up truth to your eyes.

I thank God, that I fear not. I see no real cause for fear. I know our situation well, and can see the way out of it. While our army was collected, Howe dared not risk a battle; and it is no credit to him that he decamped from the White Plains, and waited a mean opportunity to ravage the defenseless Jerseys; but it is great credit to us, that, with a handful of men, we sustained an orderly retreat for near an hundred miles, brought off our ammunition, all our field pieces, the greatest part of our stores, and had four rivers to pass. None can say that our retreat was precipitate, for we were near three weeks in performing it, that the country might have time to come in. Twice we marched back to meet the enemy, and remained out till dark. The sign of fear was not seen in our camp, and had not some of the cowardly and disaffected inhabitants spread false alarms through the country, the Jerseys had never been ravaged. Once more we are again collected and collecting; our new army at both ends of the continent is recruiting fast, and we shall be able to open the next campaign with sixty thousand men, well armed and clothed. This is our situation, and who will may know it. By perseverance and fortitude we have the prospect of a glorious issue; by cowardice and submission, the sad choice of a variety of evils—a ravaged country—a depopulated city—habitations without safety, and slavery without hope—our homes turned into barracks and bawdy-houses for Hessians, and a future race to provide for, whose fathers we shall doubt of. Look on this picture and weep over it! and if there yet remains one thoughtless wretch who believes it not, let him suffer it unlamented.

DECEMBER 23, 1776

General George Washington inspects the captured Prussian regimental colors shortly after his victory at Trenton (painting by Edward Percy Moran).

A TRANSCRIPT OF GENERAL GEORGE WASHINGTON'S LETTER TO CONGRESS ON THE VICTORY AT TRENTON

[Author's Note: Spelling is shown as in the original document.]

To THE PRESIDENT OF CONGRESS
Head Quarters, Newton,
December 27, 1776.

Sir: I have the pleasure of Congratulating you upon the success of an enterprize which I had formed against a Detachment of the Enemy lying in Trenton, and which was executed yesterday Morning. The Evening of the 25th I ordered the Troops intended for this Service [which were about 2400] to parade back of McKonkey's Ferry, that they might begin to pass as soon as it grew dark, imagining we should be able to throw them all over, with the necessary Artillery, by 12 O'Clock, and that we might easily arrive at Trenton by five in the Morning, the distance being about nine Miles. But the Quantity of Ice, made that Night, impeded the passage of the Boats so much, that it was three O'Clock before the Artillery could all get over, and near four, before the Troops took up their line of march.

This made me despair of surprising the Town, as I well knew we could not reach it before the day was fairly broke, but as I was certain there was no making a Retreat without being discovered, and harassed on repassing the River, I determined to push on at all Events. I form'd my detachments into two divisions one to March by the lower or River Road, the other by the upper or Pennington Road. As the Divisions had nearly the same distance to March, I ordered each of them, immediately upon forcing the out Guards, to push directly into the Town, that they might charge the Enemy before they had time to form. The upper Division arrived at the Enemys advanced post, exactly at Eight O'Clock, and in three Minutes after, I found, from the fire on the lower Road that, that Division had also got up. The out Guards made but small Opposition, tho' for their Numbers, they behaved very well, keeping up a constant retreating fire from behind Houses. We presently saw their main Body formed, but from their Motions, they seemed undetermined how to act. Being hard pressed by our Troops, who had already got possession of part of their Artillery, they attempted to file off by a road on their right leading to Princetown, but perceiving their Intention, I threw a body of Troops in their Way which immediately checked them. Finding from our disposition that they were surrounded, and that they must inevitably be cut to pieces if they made any further Resistance, they agreed to lay down their Arms. The Number, that submitted in this manner, was 23 Officers and 886 Men. Col Rall. the commanding Officer with seven others were found wounded in the Town. I dont exactly know how many they had killed, but I fancy not above twenty or thirty, as they never made any regular Stand. Our loss is very trifling indeed, only two Officers and one or two privates wounded. I find, that the Detachment of the Enemy consisted of the three Hessian Regiments of Lanspatch, Kniphausen and Rohl amounting to about 1500 Men, and a Troop of British Light Horse, but immediately upon the begining of the Attack, all those who were, not killed or taken, pushed directly down the Road towards Bordentown. These would likewise have fallen into our hands, could my plan have been compleatly carried into Execution. Genl. Ewing was to have crossed before day at Trenton Ferry, and taken possession of the Bridge leading out of Town, but the Quantity of Ice was so great, that tho' he did every thing in his power to effect it, he could not get over.

This difficulty also hindered General Cadwallader from crossing, with the Pennsylvania Militia, from Bristol, he got part of his Foot over, but finding it impossible to embark his Artillery, he was obliged to desist. I am fully confident, that could the Troops under Generals Ewing and Cadwallader have passed the River, I should have been able, with their Assistance, to have driven the Enemy from all their posts below Trenton. But the Numbers I had with me, being inferior to theirs below me, and a strong Battalion of Light Infantry at Princetown above me, I thought it most prudent to return the same Evening, with my prisoners and the Artillery we had taken. We found no Stores of any Consequence in the Town. In justice to the Officers and Men, I must add, that their Behaviour upon this Occasion, reflects the highest honor upon them. The difficulty of passing the River in a very severe Night, and their march thro' a violent Storm of Snow and Hail, did not in the least abate their Ardour. But when they came to the Charge, each seemed to vie with the other in pressing forward, and were I to give a preference to any particular Corps, I should do great injustice to the others. Colonel Baylor, my first Aid de Camp, will have the honor of delivering this to you, and from him you may be made acquainted with many other particulars; his spirited Behaviour upon every Occasion, requires me to recommend him to your particular Notice. I have the honor &ca.

A TRANSCRIPT OF GENERAL GEORGE WASHINGTON'S REPORT TO CONGRESS ON THE VICTORY AT PRINCETON

[Author's note: Spelling is shown as in the original document.]

To THE PRESIDENT OF CONGRESS
Pluckamin, January 5, 1777.

Sir: I have the honor to inform you, that since the date of my last from Trenton I have remov'd with the Army under my Command to this place. The difficulty of crossing the Delaware on Acct. of the Ice made our passage over it tedeous, and gave the Enemy an oppertunity of drawing in their Several Cantonments, and assembling their whole Force at Princeton. Their large Picquets, advanc'd towards Trenton; their great preparations, and some Intelligence I had received, added to their knowledge that the first of Janry. brought on a dissolution of the best part of our Army, gave me the strongest reasons to conclude that an attack upon us was meditating.

Our Situation was most critical and our strength [force] small; to remove immediately, was again destroying every dawn of hope which had begun to revive in the breasts of the Jersey Militia, and to bring those Troops which had first cross'd the Delaware, and were laying at Crosswixs under Genl. Cadwallader, and those under Genl. Mifflin at Bordenton (amounting in the whole to abt. 3600) to Trenton, was [to] bringing of them to an exposed place; one or the other however, was unavoidable; the latter was prefered, and these Troops [they] orderd to join us at Trenton which they did by a Night March on the first Instt.

On the Second, according to my expectation, the Enemy began to advance upon us, and after some skirmishing, the head of their Column reach'd Trenton about 4 O'Clock whilst their rear was as far back as Maidenhead; they attempted to pass Sanpinck [Assunpink] Creek (which runs through

Trenton) at different places, but finding the Fords guarded, halted, and kindled their Fires. We were drawn up on the other Side of the Creek. In this Situation we remaind till dark canonading the Enemy, and receiving the Fire of their Field pieces, which did us but little damage.

Having by this time discoverd that the Enemy were greatly Superior in Numbers, and that their drift [design] was to surround us. I orderd all our Baggage to be removd silently to Burlington soon after dark, and at twelve O'Clock (after renewing our Fires, and leaving Guards at the Bridge in Trenton, and other passes on the same stream above March'd by a round about road to Princeton where I knew they could not have much force left, and might have Stores. One thing I was sure of, that it would avoid the appearance of a Retreat, which (was of Consequence) or to run the hazard of the whole Army's being cut of was unavoidable whilst we might, by a fortunate stroke withdraw Genl. Howe from Trenton, give some reputation to our Arms; happily we succeeded. We found Princeton about Sunrise with only three Regiments of Infantry and three Troops of Light Horse in it, two of which were upon their March for Trenton; these three Regiments (especially the two first) made a gallant resistance and in killed, wounded and Prisoners must have lost near 500 Men upwards of one hundred of them were left dead in the Field, and with what I have with me, and what was taken in the pursuit, and carried across the Delaware, there are near 300 Prisoners, 14 of wch. are Officers, all British.

This piece of good fortune, is counter ballanced by the loss of the brave and worthy Genl. Mercer, [Cols Hazlet and Potter, Captn. Neal of the Artillery, Captn. Fleming, who commanded the 1st Virginia Regiment and four and five] and several other valuable Officers who [with 25 or 30 Privates] were slain in the Field and have since died of their Wounds. Our whole loss cannot be ascertained, as many who were in pursuit of the Enemy (who were chased three or four Miles) are not yet come in. Our Slain in the Field was about 30.

The rear of the Enemy's army laying at Maidenhead (not more than five or Six Miles from Princeton) were up with us before our pursuit was over, but as I had the precaution to destroy the Bridge over Stony Brooke (about half a Mile from the Field of Action) they were so long retarded there, as to give us time to move of in good order for this place. We took two Brass Field pieces from them, but for want of Horses could not bring them of. We also took some Blankets, Shoes, and a few other trifling Articles, Burnt the Hay and destroyed such other things as the Shortness of the time would admit of.

My original plan when I set out from Trenton was to have pushed on to Brunswick, but the harrassed State of our own Troops (many of them having had no rest for two Nights and a day) and the danger of loosing the advantage we had gaind by aiming at too much, Induced me, by the advice of my Officers, to relinquish the attempt but in my judgment Six or Eight hundred fresh Troops upon a forcd March would have destroyed all their Stores, and Magazines; taken (as we have since learnt) their Military Chest containing 70,000 £ and put an end to the War. The Enemy from the best Intelligence I have been able to get, were so much alarmed at the apprehension of this, that they March'd immediately to Brunswick without Halting (except at the Bridges, for I also took up those on Millstone on the different routs to Brunswick) and got there before day.

From the best Information I have received, Genl. Howe has left no Men either at Trenton or Princeton; the truth of this I am endeavouring to ascertain that I may regulate my movements accordingly. The Militia are taking Spirit, and, I am told, are coming in fast from this State; but I fear those from Philadelphia will scarce Submit to the hardships of a Winter Campaign much longer, especially as they very unluckily sent their Blankets with their Baggage to Burlington; I must do them the justice however to add, that they have undergone more fatigue and hardship than I expected Militia (especially Citizens) would have done at this Inclement Season. I am just moving to Morristown where I shall endeavour to put them under the best cover I can, hitherto we have lain without any, many of our poor Soldiers quite bearfoot and ill clad in other respects. I am &c.

Appendix F

General Washington's Speech
to the Officers of the Army
at Newburgh, New York

[Author's note: This document depicts the original spelling and punctuation.]

Head Quarters, Newburgh, March 15, 1783

Gentlemen: By an anonymous summons, an attempt has been made to convene you together; how inconsistent with the rules of propriety! how unmilitary! and how subversive of all order and discipline, let the good sense of the Army decide.

In the moment of this Summons, another anonymous production was sent into circulation, addressed more to the feelings and passions, than to the reason and judgment of the Army. The author of the piece, is entitled to much credit for the goodness of his Pen and I could wish he had as much credit for the rectitude of his Heart, for, as Men see thro' different Optics, and are induced by the reflecting faculties of the Mind, to use different means, to attain the same end, the Author of the Address, should have had more charity, than to mark for Suspicion, the Man who should recommend moderation and longer forbearance, or, in other words, who should not think as he thinks, and act as he advises. But he had another plan in view, in which candor and liberality of Sentiment, regard to justice, and love of Country, have no part; and he was right, to insinuate the darkest suspicion, to effect the blackest designs.

That the Address is drawn with great Art, and is designed to answer the most insidious purposes. That it is calculated to impress the Mind, with an idea of premeditated injustice in the Sovereign power of the United States, and rouse all those resentments which must unavoidably flow from such a belief. That the secret mover of this Scheme (whoever he may be) intended to take advantage of the passions, while they were warmed by the recollection of past distresses, without giving time for cool, deliberative thinking, and that composure of Mind which is so necessary to give dignity and stability to measures is rendered too obvious, by the mode of conducting the business, to need other proof than a reference to the proceeding.

Thus much, Gentlemen, I have thought it incumbent on me to observe to you, to shew upon what principles I opposed the irregular and hasty meeting which was proposed to have been held on Tuesday last: and not because I wanted a disposition to give you every opportunity consistent with your own honor, and the dignity of the army, to make known your grievances. If my conduct heretofore, has not evinced to you, that I have been a faithful friend to the Army, my declaration of it at this moment wd. be equally unavailing and improper. But as I was among the first who embarked in the cause of our common Country. As I have never left your side one moment, but when called from you on public duty. As I have been the constant companion and witness of your Distresses, and not among the last to feel, and acknowledge your Merits. As I have ever considered my own Military reputation as inseperably connected with that of the Army. As my Heart has ever expanded with joy, when I have heard its praises, and my indignation has arisen, when the mouth of detraction has been opened against it, it can scarcely be supposed, at this late stage of the War, that I am indifferent to its interests. But, hoe are they to be promoted? The way is plain, says the anonymous Addresser. If War continues, remove into the unsettled Country; there establish yourselves, and leave an ungrateful Country to defend itself. But how are they to defend? Our Wives, our Children, our Farms, and other property which we leave behind us. Or, in this state of hostile seperation, are we to take the two first (the latter cannot be removed), to perish in a Wilderness, with hunger, cold and nakedness? If Peace takes place, never sheath your Swords Says he until you have obtained full and ample justice; this dreadful alternative, of either deserting our Country in the extremest hour of her distress, or turning our Arms against it, (which is the apparent object, unless Congress can be compelled into instant compliance) has something so shocking in it, that humanity revolts at the idea. My God! What can this writer have in view, by recommending such measures? Can he be a friend to the Army? Can he be a friend to this Country? Rather, is he not an insidious Foe? Some Emissary, perhaps from New York, plotting the ruin of both, by sowing the seeds of discord and seperation between the Civil and Military powers of the Continent? And what a Compliment does he pay to our understandings, when he recommends measures in either alternative, impracticable in their Nature?

But here, Gentlemen, I will drop the curtain, because it wd. be as imprudent in me to assign my reasons for this opinion, as it would be insulting to your conception, to suppose you stood in need of them. A moment's reflection will convince every dispassionate Mind of the physical impossibility of carrying either proposal into execution.

There might, Gentlemen, be an impropriety in my taking notice, in this Address to you, of an anonymous production, but the manner in which that performance has been introduced to the army, the effect it was intended to have, together with some other circumstances, will amply justify my observations on the tendency of that Writing. With respect to the advice given by the Author, to suspect the Man, who shall recommend moderate measures and longer forbearance, I spurn it, as every Man, who regards liberty, and reveres that justice for which we contend, undoubtedly must; for if Men are to be precluded from offering their Sentiments on a matter, which may involve the most serious and alarming consequences, that can invite the consideration of Mankind, reason is of no use to us; the freedom of Speech may be taken away, and dumb and silent we may be led, like sheep, to the Slaughter.

I cannot, in justice to my own belief, and what I have great reason to conceive is the intention of Congress, conclude this Address, without giving it as my decided opinion, that that Honble Body, entertain exalted sentiments of the Services of the Army; and, from a full conviction of its merits and sufferings, will do it compleat justice. That their endeavors, to discover and establish funds for this purpose, have been unwearied, and will not cease, till they have succeed, I have not a doubt. But, like all other large Bodies, where there is a variety of different Interests to reconcile, their deliberations are slow. Why then should we distrust them? and, in consequence of that distrust, adopt measures, which may cast a shade over that glory which, has been so justly acquired; and tarnish the reputation of an Army which is celebrated thro' all Europe, for its fortitude and Patriotism? and for what is this done? to bring the object we seek nearer? No! most certainly, in my opinion, it will cast it at a greater distance.

For myself (and I take no merit in giving the assurance, being induced to it from principles of gratitude, veracity and justice), a grateful sense of the confidence you have ever placed in me, a recollection of the cheerful assistance, and prompt obedience I have experienced from you, under every vicissitude of Fortune, and the sincere affection I feel for an Army, I have so long had the honor to Command, will oblige me to declare, in this public and solemn manner, that, in the attainment of compleat justice for all your toils and dangers, and in the gratification of every wish, so far as may be done consistently with the great duty I owe my Country, and those powers we are bound to respect, you may freely command my Services to the utmost of my abilities.

While I give you these assurances, and pledge myself in the most un-equivocal manner, to exert whatever ability I am possessed of, in your favor, let me entreat you, Gentlemen, on your part, not to take any measures, which viewed in the calm light of reason, will lessen the dignity, and sully the glory you have hitherto maintained; let me request you to rely on the plighted faith of your Country, and place a full confidence in the purity of the intentions of Congress; that, previous to your dissolution as an Army they will cause all your Accts. to be fairly liquidated, as directed in their resolutions, which were published to you two days ago, and that they will adopt the most effec-tual measures in their power, to render ample justice to you, for your faithful and meritorious Services. And let me conjure you, in the name of our com-mon Country, as you value your own sacred honor, as you respect the rights of humanity, and as you regard the Military and National character of Amer-ica, to express your utmost horror and detestation of the Man who wishes, under any specious pretences, to overturn the liberties of our Country, and who wickedly attempts to open the flood Gates of Civil discord, and deluge our rising Empire in Blood. By thus determining, and thus acting, you will pursue the plain and direct road to the attainment of your wishes. You will defeat the insidious designs of our Enemies, who are compelled to resort from open force to secret Artifice. You will give one more distinguished proof of unexampled patriotism and patient virtue, rising superior to the pressure of the most complicated sufferings; And you will, by the dignity of your Conduct, afford occasion of Posterity to say, when speaking of the glorious example you have exhibited to Mankind, "had this day been wanting, the World had never seen the last stage of perfection to which human nature is capable of attaining."

Appendix G
Timeline of the War for Independence

The Timeline below is courtesy of the Library of Congress of the United States of America and is drawn largely from the work of Richard B. Morris, in particular his Encyclopedia of American History.

1768–1769

1768

Massachusetts Circular Letter. Samuel Adams wrote a statement, approved by the Massachusetts House of Representatives, which attacked Parliament's persistence in taxing the colonies without proper representation, and which called for unified resistance by all the colonies. Many colonies issued similar statements. In response, the British governor of Massachusetts dissolved the state's legislature. British Troops Arrive in Boston. Although the Sons of Liberty threatened armed resistance to arriving British troops, none was offered when the troops stationed themselves in Boston.

1769

Virginia's Resolutions. The Virginia House of Burgesses passed resolutions condemning Britain's actions against Massachusetts, and stating that only Virginia's governor and legislature could tax its citizens. The members also drafted a formal letter to the King, completing it just before the legislature was dissolved by Virginia's royal governor.

1770–1772

1770

Townshend Acts Cut Back. Because of the reduced profits resulting from the colonial boycott of imported British goods, Parliament withdrew all of the Townshend Act (1767) taxes except for the tax on tea.

An End to Nonimportation. In response to Parliament's relaxation of its taxation laws, the colonies relaxed their boycott of British imported goods (1767).

Conflict between Citizens and British Troops in New York. After a leading New York Son of Liberty issued a broadside attacking the New York Assembly for complying with the Quartering Act (1765), a riot erupted between citizens and soldiers, resulting in serious wounds but no fatalities.

Boston Massacre. The arrival of troops in Boston provoked conflict between citizens and soldiers. On March 5, a group of soldiers surrounded by an unfriendly crowd opened fire, killing three Americans and fatally wounding two more. A violent uprising was avoided only with the withdrawal of the troops to islands in the harbor. The soldiers were tried for murder, but convicted only of lesser crimes; noted patriot John Adams was their principal lawyer.

1772
Attack on the "Gaspee." After several boatloads of men attacked a grounded British customs schooner near Providence, Rhode Island, the royal governor offered a reward for the discovery of the men, planning to send them to England for trial. The removal of the "Gaspee" trial to England outraged American colonists.

Committees of Correspondence. Samuel Adams called for a Boston town meeting to create committees of correspondence to communicate Boston's position to the other colonies. Similar committees were soon created throughout the colonies.

1773–1774

1773
TEA ACT. By reducing the tax on imported British tea, this act gave British merchants an unfair advantage in selling their tea in America. American colonists condemned the act, and many planned to boycott tea.

BOSTON TEA PARTY. When British tea ships arrived in Boston harbor, many citizens wanted the tea sent back to England without the payment of any taxes. The royal governor insisted on payment of all taxes. On December 16, a group of men disguised as Indians boarded the ships and dumped all the tea in the harbor.

1774

COERCIVE ACTS. In response to the Boston Tea Party, Parliament passed several acts to punish Massachusetts. The Boston Port Bill banned the loading or unloading of any ships in Boston harbor. The Administration of Justice Act offered protection to royal officials in Massachusetts, allowing them to transfer to England all court cases against them involving riot suppression or revenue collection. The Massachusetts Government Act put the election of most government officials under the control of the Crown, essentially eliminating the Massachusetts charter of government.

QUARTERING ACT. Parliament broadened its previous Quartering Act (1765). British troops could now be quartered in any occupied dwelling.

THE COLONIES ORGANIZE PROTEST. To protest Britain's actions, Massachusetts suggested a return to nonimportation, but several states preferred a congress of all the colonies to discuss united resistance. The colonies soon named delegates to a congress—the First Continental Congress—to meet in Philadelphia on September 5.

THE FIRST CONTINENTAL CONGRESS. Twelve of the thirteen colonies sent a total of fifty-six delegates to the First Continental Congress. Only Georgia was not represented. One accomplishment of the Congress was the Association of 1774, which urged all colonists to avoid using British goods, and to form committees to enforce this ban.

NEW ENGLAND PREPARES FOR WAR. British troops began to fortify Boston, and seized ammunition belonging to the colony of Massachusetts. Thousands of American militiamen were ready to resist, but no fighting occurred. Massachusetts created a Provincial Congress, and a special Committee of Safety to decide when the militia should be called into action. Special groups of militia, known as Minute Men, were organized to be ready for instant action.

1775

NEW ENGLAND RESTRAINING ACT. Parliament passed an act banning trade between the New England colonies and any other country besides Great Britain.

NEW ENGLAND RESISTS. British troops continued to attempt to seize colonial ammunition, but were turned back in Massachusetts, without any violence. Royal authorities decided that force should be used to enforce recent acts of Parliament; war seemed unavoidable.

LEXINGTON AND CONCORD. British troops planned to destroy American ammunition at Concord. When the Boston Committee of Safety learned of this plan, it sent Paul Revere and William Dawes to alert the countryside and gather the Minute Men. On April 19, Minute Men and British troops met at Lexington, where a shot from a stray British gun lead to more British firing. The Americans only fired a few shots; several Americans were killed. The British marched on to Concord and destroyed some ammunition, but soon found the countryside swarming with militia. At the end of the day, many were dead on both sides.

THE SECOND CONTINENTAL CONGRESS. The Second Continental Congress convened in Philadelphia on May 10. John Hancock was elected president of Congress.

GEORGE WASHINGTON IS NAMED COMMANDER-IN-CHIEF. On June 10, John Adams proposed that Congress consider the forces in Boston a Continental army, and suggested the need for a general. He recommended George Washington for the position. Congress began to raise men from other colonies to join the army in New England, and named a committee to draft military rules. On June 15, Washington was nominated to lead the army; he accepted the next day. To pay for the army, Congress issued bills of credit, and the twelve colonies represented in the Congress promised to share in repaying the bills.

BUNKER HILL. On June 12, British General Gage put martial law in effect, and stated that any person helping the Americans would be considered a traitor and rebel. When Americans began to fortify a hill against British forces, British ships in the harbor discovered the activity and opened fire. British troops—2,400 in number—arrived shortly after. Although the Americans—1,000 in number—resisted several attacks, eventually they lost the fortification.

OLIVE BRANCH PETITION. Congress issued a petition declaring its loyalty to the king, George III, and stating its hope that he would help arrange a reconciliation and prevent further hostilities against the colonies. Four months later, King George III rejected the petition and declared the colonies in rebellion.

CONGRESS TREATS WITH THE INDIANS. Acting as an independent government, Congress appointed commissioners to create peace treaties with the Indians.

CONGRESS CREATES A NAVY. Congress began to plan for aggressive action against British ships stocked with ammunition. It authorized the building of four armed ships, and began to formulate rules for a navy. On December 22, Congress named Esek Hopkins commodore of the fledgling American navy. Soon after, Congress authorized privateering, and issued rules for dealing with enemy vessels and plunder.

CONGRESS SEARCHES FOR FOREIGN AID. When a congressional committee began to investigate the possibility of foreign aid in the war against Great Britain, France expressed interest.

1776

"COMMON SENSE." Thomas Paine moved many to the cause of independence with his pamphlet titled "Common Sense." In a direct, simple style, he cried out against King George III and the monarchical form of government.

THE BRITISH EVACUATE BOSTON. American Gen. Henry Knox arrived in Boston with cannons he had moved with great difficulty from Fort Ticonderoga, New York. Americans began to entrench themselves around Boston, planning to attack the British. British Gen. William Howe planned an attack, but eventually retreated from Boston.

CONGRESS CALLS FOR THE COLONIES TO ADOPT NEW CONSTITUTIONS. In May, the Second Continental Congress recommended that the colonies establish new governments based on the authority of the people of the respective colonies rather than on the British Crown.

CONGRESS DECLARES INDEPENDENCE. When North Carolina and

Virginia empowered their delegates to vote for American independence, Virginian Richard Henry Lee offered a resolution stating that the colonies "are, and of right ought to be, free and independent States." A committee was appointed to draft a declaration of independence, and Thomas Jefferson was chosen to write it. On July 2, Congress voted in favor of independence, and on July 4, the Declaration of Independence was approved. Copies were sent throughout the colonies to be read publicly.

BATTLE OF LONG ISLAND. After leaving Boston, British General Howe planned to use New York as a base. The British captured Staten Island and began a military build-up on Long Island in preparation for an advance on Brooklyn. Washington succeeded in saving his army by secretly retreating onto Manhattan Island. Washington eventually retreated from Manhattan, fearing the prospect of being trapped on the island, and the British occupied New York City.

CONGRESS NAMES COMMISSIONERS TO TREAT WITH FOREIGN NATIONS. Congress sent a delegation of three men to Europe—Silas Deane, Benjamin Franklin, and Arthur Lee—to prepare treaties of commerce and friendship, and to attempt to secure loans from foreign nations.

THE BATTLE OF WHITE PLAINS. British and American forces met at White Plains, New York, where the British captured an important fortification. Washington once again retreated, still attempting to save his army from the full force of the British army.

RETREAT THROUGH NEW JERSEY. Washington and his army retreated across New Jersey, crossing the Delaware River into Pennsylvania. Congress, fearing a British attack on Philadelphia, fled to Baltimore.

BATTLE OF TRENTON. On December 26, Washington launched a surprise attack against a British fortification at Trenton, New Jersey, that was staffed by Hessian soldiers. After one hour of confused fighting, the Hessians surrendered. Only two American soldiers were killed.

1777–1778
_____

1777

BATTLE OF PRINCETON. British General Howe reacted to the Battle of

Trenton by sending a large force of men to New Jersey. At Princeton, Washington once again launched a surprise attack, and succeeded in defeating the British. His efforts cleared most of New Jersey of enemy forces, and greatly boosted American morale.

AMERICA HAS A FLAG. On June 14, Congress declared that the flag of the United States would consist of thirteen alternating red and white stripes, and a blue field with thirteen white stars.

THE BRITISH ATTACK PHILADELPHIA. British and Americans met at Brandywine Creek, Pennsylvania. The Americans retreated, and the British soon occupied Philadelphia, forcing Congress once again to flee the city. After retreating further during the Battle of Germantown, Washington settled his army for the winter in Valley Forge—a winter of extreme cold and great hunger.

SARATOGA. On October 7, British and American troops engaged in New York. Fatigued from battle and short of supplies, British Gen. John Burgoyne's troops were repulsed by American forces under Gen. Horatio Gates. On October 8, Burgoyne retreated to Saratoga; by October 13th, he asked for terms of surrender. The "Convention of Saratoga" called for Burgoyne's army to be sent back to England, and for each soldier to pledge not to serve again in the war against the colonies.

THE "CONWAY CABAL." Many in Congress were unhappy with Washington's leadership; some murmured the name of Gen. Horatio Gates as a possible replacement. Thomas Conway, the army's inspector general, wrote a critical letter to Gates about Washington, leading many to believe there was an organized effort to replace Washington. Conway resigned from the army, and eventually apologized to Washington.

ARTICLES OF CONFEDERATION. When Richard Henry Lee made a motion for independence (1776), he also proposed a formal plan of union among the states. After a discussion lasting more than a year, the Articles of Confederation were adopted by Congress, although the states did not ratify the Articles until 1781.

1778

FRANCE AND AMERICA BECOME ALLIES. France and America formed an alliance, negotiated by Benjamin Franklin, stating that each would consider the other a "most favored nation" for trade and friendship; France would be obligated to fight for American independence; and America would be obligated to stand by France if war should occur between France and Great Britain. Within four months, France and Great Britain were at war.

THE BRITISH ATTEMPT TO MAKE PEACE. Threatened by the alliance between France and America, Parliament proposed the repeal of the Tea Act (1773) and Coercive Acts (1774), pledged not to tax the colonies, and sent peace commissioners to America. However, most Americans were interested only in British recognition of American independence. When a British commissioner tried to bribe congressmen Joseph Reed, Robert Morris, and Francis Dana, Americans became even less interested in reconciliation. Competing for support from the American people, both Congress and the desperate commissioners appealed directly to them with broadsides, but the British commissioners soon returned to Great Britain, their mission a failure.

JOHN PAUL JONES WINS VICTORIES. Although Esek Hopkins was never very successful with the American navy, Captain John Paul Jones won several victories against the British with his ship, the "Ranger."

THE BATTLE OF MONMOUTH. When the British headed for New York, Washington left Valley Forge to follow. At the Battle of Monmouth, American Gen. Charles Lee gave several confused orders, and then ordered a sudden retreat. Washington's arrival on the scene saved the battle, although the British escaped to New York during the night. Lee was later court-martialed.

1779–1782

1779

THE BRITISH ATTACK IN NORTH AND SOUTH. Fighting continued in both the northern and southern states. In the frontier settlements of Pennsylvania, Loyalists and Indians led by Mohawk Joseph Brant attacked American settlers. The Loyalists soon were defeated, and Americans went on to destroy many Native American villages whose residents were fighting on the side of the British.

SPAIN JOINS THE WAR. Spain asked Britain for Gibraltar as a reward for joining the war on the British side. When Britain refused, Spain joined with France in its war against Britain, although refusing to recognize American independence.

1780
THE BRITISH TAKE CHARLESTON, SOUTH CAROLINA. After a brief fight, the British took Charleston, capturing 5,400 men and four American ships in the harbor. It was the worst American defeat of the war.

A MUTINY IN THE CONTINENTAL ARMY. When the value of Continental currency sank to a new low, Congress had problems supplying the American army. Great shortages of food led to a short-lived mutiny among some Connecticut soldiers at Washington's camp in New Jersey.

THE TREASON OF BENEDICT ARNOLD. American Gen. Benedict Arnold, frustrated and ambitious, began dealing with British Gen. Sir Henry Clinton. After he was promised the command at West Point by General Washington, Arnold told Clinton that he would give the strategic American fortification to the British. But when British Major John André, acting as messenger, was captured, Arnold fled to a British ship, revealing his involvement in the treasonous plan. André was executed as a spy, and Arnold was made a brigadier general in the British army.

1781
CONGRESS CREATES A DEPARTMENT OF FINANCE. American finances were in such dire straits that Congress saw the need for a separate department of finance. Robert Morris was appointed superintendent of finance.

THE ARTICLES OF CONFEDERATION ARE RATIFIED. With the ratification of the Articles of Confederation, under discussion since 1777, Congress assumed a new title, "The United States in Congress Assembled."

THE BATTLE OF YORKTOWN. French and American forces joined at Yorktown, on land and at sea, and attacked British fortifications. Key British points were soon held by the Americans and French, and British General Cornwallis soon surrendered, giving up almost 8,000 men. With this defeat, Britain lost hope of winning the war in America.

1782

PEACE NEGOTIATIONS BEGIN IN PARIS. British, French, and American commissioners met in Paris to discuss peace. The United States sent Benjamin Franklin, John Adams, and John Jay. By November, the commissioners had drafted a peace treaty. Its terms called for Great Britain to recognize American independence and provide for the evacuation of all British troops. Great Britain also gave up its territory between the Mississippi River and the Allegheny Mountains, doubling the size of the new nation.

1783–1784

1783

THE ARMY COMPLAINS. When a delegation of army officers complained to Congress about their unpaid salaries and pensions, Congress had no quick solution. An anonymous letter urged officers to unite and attempt one last appeal to Congress. If its attempt was ignored, the army was prepared to revolt against Congress. Washington, addressing the army in person at its headquarters in Newburgh, New York, convinced them to be patient, and not to dishonor themselves after their glorious victory. Visibly moved, the officers adopted resolutions to present to Congress, and pledged not to threaten violence or rebellion.

CONGRESS RATIFIES THE PRELIMINARY ARTICLES OF PEACE. After Spain, France, and Britain successfully came to terms, the treaty between France, Britain, and America was put into effect, and warfare formally ceased. Congress ratified the Articles of Peace on April 15.

THE LOYALISTS AND BRITISH EVACUATE NEW YORK. New York City was the last Loyalist refuge in America. Starting in April, nearly 30,000 Loyalists, knowing that the British soon would leave New York, packed their belongings and sailed to Canada and England, followed shortly by the British army. In November, when the British sailed away, Washington entered the city and formally bade farewell to his officers. Soon after, he resigned his commission.

THE AMERICAN ARMY DISBANDS. In June, most of Washington's army disbanded and headed for home just before the British evacuated New York. A small force remained until all the British had departed.

BIBLIOGRAPHY

Manuscripts.
Franklin, Benjamin. Papers.

Bibliographies Guides.

Blanco, Richard L. The War of The American Revolution: A Selected Annotated Bibliography of Published Sources. New York: Garland Publishing, 1984.

Baker, Mary Ellen, compiler. "Bibliography of Lists of New England Soldiers." New England Historical and Genealogical Register, 64 (1910), pp. 61–72, 128–135, 228–237, 327–336; 65 (1911), pp. 11–19, 151–159.

Butler, John P. Index to the Papers of the Continental Congress, 1774–1789. 5 vols. Washington: National Archives and Records Service, 1978.

Clark, David Sanders. Index of Maps of the American Revolution in Books and Periodicals: Illustrating the Revolutionary War and Other Events of the Period 1763–1789. Westport, Conn.: Greenwood Press, 1974.

Chernow, Ron. Washington: A Life. New York: Penguin Press, October 5, 2010.

Gephart, Ronald M. Revolutionary America 1763–1789: A Bibliography. 2 vols. Washington: Library of Congress, 1984.

Matthews, William. British Diaries: An Annotated Bibliography of British Diaries Written Between 1442–1942. Berkeley: University of California Press, 1950.

Reference Works.

Babits, Lawrence E. A Devil of a Whipping: The Battle of Cowpens. Chapel Hill: The University of North Carolina Press; New edition edition, December 1, 2000.

Beck, Glenn. Being George Washington: The Indispensable Man, as You've Never Seen Him. New York: Threshold Editions; First Edition edition. November 22, 2011.

Boatner, Mark Mayo, III. Encyclopedia of the American Revolution. New York: David McKay Co., 1966.

Cappon, Lester J., et al., editors. The Atlas of Early American History: The Revolutionary Era, 1760–1790. Princeton University Press, 1976.

Peterson, Harold L. The Book of The Continental Soldier being a complete account of the uniforms, weapons, and equipment with which he lived and fought. Harrisburg: Stackpole Co., 1968.

Sutherland, Stella H. Population Distribution in Colonial America. New York: Columbia University Press, 1936.

Published Primary Sources.

Commager, Henry S., and Richard B. Morris, editors. The Spirit of 'Seventy-Six. New York: Harpers, 1967.

Hamilton, Alexander. The Papers of Alexander Hamilton. Edited by Harold C. Syrett and Jacob E. Cook. 26 vols. New York: Columbia University Press, 1961–1979.

Ryan, Dennis P., editor. A Salute to Courage: The American Revolution as Seen through Wartime Writings of Officers of the Continental Army and Navy. New York: Columbia University Press, 1979.

Published Sources.

Alden, John Richard. The American Revolution, 1775–1783. New York: Harper & Brothers, 1954.

———. The South in the American Revolution, 1763–1789. Baton Rouge: Louisiana State University Press, 1957.

Alderman, Clifford Lindsey. The War We Could Have Lost: The American Revolution. New York: Four Winds Press, 1974.

Archdeacon, Thomas J. "American Historians and the American Revolution: A Bicentennial Overview." Wisconsin Magazine of History, 63 (Summer 1980), pp. 278–298.

Barrow, Thomas C. "The American Revolution as a Colonial War for Independence." William and Mary Quarterly, 3d Ser., 25 (July 1968), pp. 452–464.

Bartky, Eliot M. "War and the American Founding: Volunteerism and the Origins of American Military Policy." Ph.D. Dissertation, Rutgers University, 1983.

Bowers, Roy L., Jr. "The American Revolution: A Study in Insurgency." Military Review, 46 (July 1966), pp. 64–72.

Channing, Edward. The American Revolution, 1761–1789. New York: Macmillan, 1912.

Dupuy, R. Ernest, and Trevor N. Dupuy. The Compact History of the Revolutionary War. New York: Hawthorne Books, 1963.

Fischer, David Hackettt. Washington's Crossing. New York: Oxford University Press, 2004.

Fiske, John. The American Revolution. 2 vols. Boston: Houghton, Mifflin, 1891.

Fuller, J.F.C. Decisive Battles of the U.S.A. 1776–1918. Lincoln: University of Nebraska Press. 2007.

Gingrich, Newt; Forstchen, William R.: Hanser, Albert S. To Try Men's Souls: A Novel of George Washington and the Fight for American Freedom: New York: St. Martin's Press, Thomas Dunne Books; October 20, 2009.

Gottschalk, Louis. "The Attitude of European Officers in the Revolutionary Armies Toward General George Washington." Journal of the Illinois State Historical Society, 32 (December 1939), pp. 20–50.

Harris, Christopher. "Character Portraits of American Military Heroes of the Revolution, 1782–1832." Ph.D. Dissertation, Brown University, 1985.

Higginbotham, Don. The War of American Independence: Military Attitudes, Policies, and Practice, 1763–1789. New York: Macmillan Co., 1971.

Jensen, Merrill. The Founding of a Nation: A History of the American Revolution, 1763–1776. New York: Oxford University Press, 1968.

Lancaster, Bruce. From Lexington to Liberty: The Story of the American Revolution. Garden City: Doubleday, 1955.

Martin, James Kirby, and Mark Edward Lender. A Respectable Army: The Military Origins of the Republic, 1763–1789. Arlington Heights, Ill.: Harlan Davidson, 1982.

McCullough, David. 1776. New York: Simon & Schuster, May 24, 2005.

Middlekauff, Robert. The Glorious Cause: The American Revolution 1763–1789. New York: Oxford University Press, 1982.

Miller, John C. Triumph of Freedom, 1775–1783. Boston: Little, Brown, 1958.

Mitchell, Joseph B. Discipline and Bayonets: The Armies and Leaders in the War of the American Revolution. New York: G. P. Putnam's Sons, 1967.

———. Decisive Battles of the American Revolution. New York: G. P. Putnam's Sons, 1962.

Nisbet, Robert. "The Social Impact of the Revolution." Wilson Quarterly, 1 (Autumn 1976), pp. 93–107.

Palmer, Dave Richard. The Way of the Fox: American Strategy in the War for America 1775–1783. Westport, Conn.: Greenwood Press, 1975.

Paret, Peter. "Colonial Experience and European Military Reform at the End of the Eighteenth Century." Institute for Historical Research Bulletin, 37 (May 1964), pp. 47–59.

Peckham, Howard H. The War for Independence: A Military History. Chicago: University of Chicago Press, 1958.

Rauch, Steven J. Southern Comfort: British Phase IV Operations in South Carolina and Georgia, May–September 1780. Army History, The Professional Bulletin of Army History, PB 20-09-2 (No. 71) Washington, D.C. Spring 2009.

Robson, Eric. The American Revolution in Its Political and Military Aspects, 1763–1783. New York: Oxford University Press, 1955.

Shy, John. A People Numerous and Armed: Reflections on the Military Struggle for

American Independence. New York: Oxford University Press, 1976.

Stoll, Ira. Samuel Adams, A Life. New York: Free Press. 2008.

Wallace, Willard M. Appeal to Arms: A Military History of the American Revolution. New York: Harper and Brothers, 1951.

Weigley, Russell F. History of the United States Army. New York: Macmillan, 1964.

Wood, W. J. Battles of the Revolutionary War, 1775–1781. Chapel Hill: Algonquin, 1990.

About the author

John Antal, Colonel U.S. Army (Ret.)

JOHN ANTAL HAS a passion for history and leadership. He is the executive producer of *Brothers in Arms* video games for Gearbox Software, a military historian, and a leadership expert. He has published ten books about leadership and military science and military history. He is an accomplished public speaker, particularly on the issues of leadership, national security, and military affairs. He has worked with several military history televisions production companies as a historian and military expert for several documentary television shows for the Arts and Entertainment Channel, Military Channel, and the History Channel. His most recent television appearance was on *Patton 360,* the story of Gen. George S. Patton.

John Antal served thirty years of distinguished service in the U.S. Army as a combat arms officer in Armor and Cavalry units, retiring as a full colonel. As a military officer, Colonel Antal has commanded combat units from platoon to regiment and held sensitive key positions on high level U.S. Army, joint, and combined military staffs, including two years in the Pentagon as the special assistant to the Chairman of Joint Chiefs of Staff and as the G3 (operations officer) of the III Armored Corps at Fort Hood, Texas. He has been with American soldiers in Europe, Korea, the Middle East, and Afghanistan. He is an Airborne Ranger and a graduate of the United States Military Academy at West Point, the Army Command and General Staff College, and the Army War College. He has earned a Bachelors of Science degree, a Masters Degree in Military Science, and is working on a Ph.D. in military history. *To contact the author, go to: www.american-leadership.com.*